WOMEN'S WORLDS

WOMEN'S WORLDS

From the New Scholarship

Edited by

Marilyn Safir
Martha T. Mednick
Dafne Israeli
Jessie Bernard

*In Cooperation with the
Society for the Psychological
Study of Social Issues*

PRAEGER

PRAEGER SPECIAL STUDIES • PRAEGER SCIENTIFIC

New York • Philadelphia • Eastbourne, UK
Toronto • Hong Kong • Tokyo • Sydney

Library of Congress Cataloging in Publication Data

Main entry under title:

Women's worlds.

Papers presented at the First International Interdisciplinary Congress on Women held at the University
of Haifa, Haifa, Israel, Dec. 28, 1981-Jan. 1, 1982.
Includes index.
1. Women—Congresses. 2. Feminism—Congresses.
3. Women's studies—Congresses. 4. Feminism—Israel—
Congresses. I. Safir, Marilyn. II. Society for the
Psychological Study of Social Issues. III. International Interdisciplinary Congress on Women (1st:
1982: University of Haifa)
HQ1106.W6658   1985   305.4   84-26327
ISBN 0-03-000539-6 (alk. paper)

Published in 1985 by Praeger Publishers
CBS Educational and Professional Publishing, a Division of CBS Inc.
521 Fifth Avenue, New York, NY 10175 USA

56789 052 987654321

Printed in the United States of America on acid-free paper

INTERNATIONAL OFFICES

Orders from outside the United States should be sent to the appropriate address listed below. Orders from areas not
listed below should be placed through CBS International Publishing, 383 Madison Ave., New York, NY 10175 USA

Australia, New Zealand
Holt Saunders, Pty. Ltd., 9 Waltham St., Artarmon, N.S.W. 2064, Sydney, Australia

Canada
Holt, Rinehart & Winston of Canada, 55 Horner Ave., Toronto, Ontario, Canada M8Z 4X6

Europe, the Middle East, & Africa
Holt Saunders, Ltd., 1 St. Anne's Road, Eastbourne, East Sussex, England BN21 3UN

Japan
Holt Saunders, Ltd., Ichibancho Central Building, 22-1 Ichibancho, 3rd Floor, Chiyodaku, Tokyo, Japan

Hong Kong, Southeast Asia
Holt Saunders Asia, Ltd., 10 Fl, Intercontinental Plaza, 94 Granville Road, Tsim Sha Tsui East, Kowloon,
Hong Kong

**Manuscript submissions should be sent to the Editorial Director, Praeger Publishers, 521 Fifth Avenue,
New York, NY 10175 USA**

FOREWORD

Since its founding in 1936, the Society for the Psychological Study of Social Issues (SPSSI) has had as one of its major goals the encouragement of sound research on important social issues of the times. Through its publication program, SPSSI has a tradition of sponsorship of social science volumes that represent the best of interdisciplinary efforts to address major social concerns from a scholarly point of view. The present volume epitomizes that tradition, both in the significance of the issues that are being raised and in the breadth of perspectives represented in its pages.

The study of women's lives has created a "new scholarship" in ways that go well beyond the establishment of new substantive fields of inquiry. In discipline after discipline, as scholars attempted to apply traditional methods and theoretical frameworks to understanding women's experience various inadequacies were revealed. Hidden assumptions were uncovered, traditional conceptualizations of the distinction between individual and culture were challenged, and boundaries between fields of inquiry were breached. Virtually no discipline relevant to the study of women has been left untouched by this emergent perspective. In this volume, we have an impressive array of contributions from multiple disciplines and multiple cultures, all illustrating the influence of feminist scholarship on social thought and research.

In many ways the history of SPSSI as an organization and the emergence of women's studies and feminist consciousness have been closely intertwined. Thus it seems particularly appropriate that this volume should appear on the eve of SPSSI's fiftieth anniversary. We are proud to sponsor this publication as an exemplar of SPSSI's goals and values.

Marilynn B. Brewer
SPSSI President

PREFACE

The First International Interdisciplinary Congress on Women was held at the University of Haifa, Haifa, Israel, from December 28, 1981 to January 1, 1982. There were 623 scholars from 35 countries around the world who participated in a total of 90 sessions at which 258 papers were presented.

The congress was unique in a number of ways. In historical perspective it was the first international interdisciplinary congress to focus on research on women and to be open to all interested scholars. It was a feminist congress, not only in its scholarship but in its very conception and development. It was a product of the new era of women's intellectual achievement. There was no one organization sponsoring and running the meetings. It was, rather, an informal collection of individuals and professional organizations, joined together for the sole purpose of organizing the event. Open calls for papers appeared in professional and interdisciplinary journals in Europe and North and South America, and over 400 abstracts were submitted to the organizing committee.

A few words are in order about the choice of Israel as the congress site. Much research had been done in Israel on sex roles and sex equality on the kibbutz, a communal society that was designed to free its members from inequities existing in traditional capitalistic societies. For example, Tiger and Shepher (1975) had shown that the kibbutz did not succeed in changing sex roles and offered a biological explanation. This research stimulated much interest. However, the Israeli feminist scholars doing such studies usually worked in isolation, not aware of each other's work, because of the absence of networks. The discipline of women's studies was nonexistent and unknown in academia. The congress seemed to be a way to bring the message of the importance and developing stature of the new scholarship to this isolated place, as well as to create networks.

It is difficult to gauge the impact of the congress on the individual participants; however, the impact on the development of feminist scholarship in Israel is easier to document. In 1982 the Hebrew University started a program on Sex and Gender in Society and in 1983 the University of Haifa inaugurated a Women's Studies program. In 1984 the Israel Sociological Association established a section on Sex and Gender.

The congress organizing process was helped considerably by a large group of organizational cosponsors (see Appendix) of which the Federation of Organizations of Professional Women (FOPW) and the

Division of the Psychology of Women took the lead. FOPW in particular provided a home and served as a funding conduit. Many other individuals and groups provided help with efforts to bring the congress to the attention of a wide range of the scholarly community. While this procedure seemed to work better for the social sciences than for other disciplinary groups, many disciplines were nevertheless represented.

In Israel itself, the cross-discipline effort was most successful. Perhaps the forming of a widely based local committee helped, not to mention the small size of the community (see Appendix for names). The University of Haifa, home base of the congress's organizer, M. Safir, agreed to host the meetings on its campus. The facilities and location proved to be an excellent choice.

The congress organizing committee agreed at the outset to apply feminist principles and hold a nonelitist meeting so as to reach a wide range of scholars. The congress was looked upon as a socializing experience for aspiring and upcoming scholars. Consequently no abstract was rejected outright. Wherever the criteria for acceptance were not met, reviewers asked for improvement or clarification, with an option to resubmit. The committee was rewarded for its efforts. In the majority of cases, the abstracts were resubmitted and integrated into the program. This extra effort had the effect of allowing many students and young scholars to participate.

It was realized quite early in the planning of the book that of the several hundred provocative and enlightening articles, only a handful could be published. We have put together a coordinated sampler of papers whose themes—as described in the introductions—emerged from reading and discussions of the written papers. We assume responsibility for the resulting selection and organization, with all the implications which flow therefrom. We also take blame for the loss, to this volume, of many fine contributions. Most often this was due only to the limits imposed by publishing realities. We hope that all the other worthy articles have found other outlets.

This is the place to thank those who, in addition to the conference organizers and all the participants, made this exploration of women's worlds possible. There were the organizational sponsors, the Ford Foundation, and National Science Foundation, which granted administrative and travel money, respectively, and the Mount Carmel Training Institute, whose government (Israeli) funded workshop enabled participation by women from developing countries.

Local help in Haifa included the Public Relations Department and members of the administration of the University of Haifa and Haifa residents who provided free lodging in their homes to many participants.

The Editors
Washington, D.C.
Haifa and Tel Aviv, Israel

CONTENTS

INTRODUCTION

Now women and men do the same things. Men shouldn't
say any longer that a certain job is for men, another for
women—we now have equality—almost. . . . It's crazy
to say there are occupations which women can not do.
Women can do all the jobs that men can. Personally, I
don't like it when one speaks of the role of women—I think
it's the misogyny of men. Men and women can play the
same role. What I don't like is when one says "men,"
then "women." I don't like this term "the role of women."
Women can do as much as men. . . . (Barthel, 1975,
14-15)

The aim of the [Mozambican] revolution is the ending of
all forms of exploitation and oppression (Resolution of
the Second Mozambican Women's Conference, 1974).

We Corsican women are taking part in this struggle [for
national liberation] but we think that it is as . . . a movement of female liberation that it ought to be led (Canale,
April, 1982, 30).

Echoing and reechoing around the world are words and phrases
like these that alert us to the monumental "earth tremors" currently
shaking societal structures everywhere. Women are becoming vocal
and the world they inhabit, visible. Women have learned the language
of oppression and exploitation from leftist liberation and revolutionary
movements and of role inequality from Western women's liberation
movements. They have learned that they hold up half the sky and that,
in Mao's words, the part they hold up weighs more. They are making
waves. They are researching the reasons for these inequalities. The
chapters in this book are part of this search.

There are great obstacles in such a pursuit including the male
bias in practically all human knowledge. For until now human knowledge has been a creation of the male world. It has dealt with topics
that have challenged men; it has attempted to answer the questions
that have puzzled them, all from a male perspective. That it has been
a great achievement cannot be gainsaid. But it suffers from a serious
lacuna; it does not include an equal corpus of knowledge about the female world. Even when it has concerned itself with women it has dealt

with the position or status of women vis-à-vis the male world, with women as related to men; so it has still been about the male world. More serious is the fact that the paradigms for thinking about the female world have all been created by the male world; the conceptual tool-kit for thinking about themselves and their world has been provided for women by men.

Although the female world has accumulated a great deal of informal wisdom and practical know-how and experience, the systematic formal knowledge that has been transmitted to women has been the male canon. The female world has therefore been, for all intents and purposes, invisible. It is only recently that female scholarship has begun to balance the scale, to fill in some of the lacunae of human knowledge, to encompass the female as well as the male world.

The task is not an easy one, for most scholars—women as well as men—have been trained by men, so that they find it difficult even to conceptualize a female world. Or to recognize the equal validity— not necessarily the priority—of the female perspective on reality. One of the most significant achievements of female scholarship in the past decade and a half has been precisely this challenge to the male hegemony over female thinking that has prevailed for so long.

All over the world there are now women raising feminist issues, raising feminist consciousness, raising feminist sights. Whether or not they are all using a feminist vocabulary is not always clear because so much of what they are saying comes to us by way of translation. But they are surely expressing feminist ideas. A powerful ferment seems to be bubbling throughout the global female world, in Africa, in Latin America, in the Near East, in China. There is an energy here that begins to show what that world is all about.

Another obstacle to overcome in exploring the female world is the parochial bias in our view of it. As a result of the economic and therefore research asymmetry among different parts of the world, much of our knowledge has to do with only the Western world, especially the United States and Europe. These are the areas that have the tradition and the means to support research. Although the chapters in this volume do include data from a variety of countries, the pervading paradigms guiding the research are from the West. Thus the world of women is more visible in the West than elsewhere. There remain great blank spaces on the map of the female world. Much of the research here—though not enough—attempts to overcome this bias.

The tendency, further, of researchers is to become so absorbed in the immediate context of their own research that it is often difficult to look outside the limits of even their particular disciplinary, let alone, national boundaries. Overcoming the many-faceted parochialism of so much of our knowledge is an important task for research on the world of women. This too, is in the process of being addressed.

It is not only ideas that are traveling all over the world. Women themselves are as well.

> For four stimulating days in July, 1983, more than 600 women gathered near Lima, Peru, to attend the II Encuentra Feminista Latinoamericano y del Caribe. The Encuentra was organized by a coalition of feminist groups from Peru, and was the second of its kind, the first one held in Bogota, Colombia, in 1981. Participants came from: Argentina, Bolivia, Chile, Peru, Ecuador, Colombia, Brazil, Dutch Guiana, Mexico, Puerto Rico, Dominican Republic, Costa Rica, Germany, Australia, Canada, Denmark, Spain, United States, France, Holland, England, and Italy (Feminist Forum, 6, #5, 1983, 11).

> On April 23-25, 1983, over 700 women from more than 15 countries, including Australia, the United States, and Japan as well as nearly all those in Western Europe came together at Torino. Eighty-two collectives were represented and many women came on behalf of the women's sections of their trade unions. The conference was organized by three Italian women's groups (Feminist Forum, 6, #3, 1983, vi).

> There is a project in process to consist of eight 30-minute films under the title "As Women See It" by women filmmakers in eight different countries—Senegal, Egypt, Nicaragua, Peru, India, France, West Germany, Italy, and perhaps Poland (Connexions, No. 4, Spring, 1982, 12).

> From May 25 to 31, 1981, the first International Feminist Film and Video Conference was held in Amsterdam. . . . Two hundred women from 32 countries, all involved in film-making and video came to Amsterdam to exchange ideas and information (ibid., 11).

Truly astonishing is the great upsurge in international meetings of women at which they share experiences and engage in discussions, arguments, and debates, all of which vastly expand their own knowledge of their world and moderate their parochialism. The meetings noted above are only a tiny sample of the many kinds taking place of special-interest groups ranging in scope from health to political activism.* Just as the fifteenth century opened an era of voyage and discovery in the male world, so also the second half of the twentieth century has opened an era of voyage and discovery in the female world. More and more of it becomes visible to an increasing number of women as they learn more about it.

The present is an especially auspicious time to try to raise our sights to include this broader perspective. For those of us in the West, Africa until not too long ago, was a "Dark Continent"; the Orient was still "inscrutable." This restricted horizon no longer prevails; still it remains urgent that we extend it further to include women everywhere if we wish to understand the female world anywhere. Such understanding is a major priority. The materials presented in this volume are among the building blocks for the structure of knowledge we have to construct.

Running through many of the chapters is the question of optimum strategy for arriving at the best way for the female world to relate to the male world, separatism or integrationism. It arises in a wide variety of contexts, ranging from—at one end—the modus vivendi of women's groups vis-à-vis leftist liberation or revolutionary groups to—at the other end—the best way to encourage the acceptance of feminist research in academic curricula. Does the female world fare better when it maintains and encourages a separate identity on issues or when it seeks integration with the male world? In 1975 the United Nations came out in favor of integration. Since it is an organization of nations, its recommendations were to governments. In the area of development, the issue is tied up with power relationships. In mixed-group projects, whatever the decision specifies, male members have an advantage because they out-talk women and out-influence decisions. Until women develop their own skills, separate projects may be preferable. Or "affirmative action" in mixed-group projects.

Much of the thinking dealing with change hinges on the nature of the female world. Is it shaped by the nature of women; or is the nature of women shaped by the world they live in? The fact that there are so many commonalities in the relations between female and male worlds in widely different societies might be invoked to support an affirmative reply to the first of these questions. But the great differences among women in, let us say, Senegal and Sweden, are supportive of an affirm-

---

*So numerous have international conferences of women become that the Humphrey Institute of Minneapolis has published a booklet on them. It includes comments on the dynamics of world conferences and the influence women's organizations can have in bringing about change (1984).

ative reply to the second question. Not discussed in the articles here are the demographic differences among women that are biological but not genetic, e.g., longevity. The life expectancy of women in Sweden, for example, is almost twice as long as in many other countries, a telling reflection of the worlds they live in. In general, the emphasis in the chapters here is in the direction of explanations of the nature of women in terms of the nature of the worlds they inhabit.

The image of the female world reflected in this book is suggested by the several parts. Part I specifies three bases for the female world—a sexual division of labor, a sexual specialization of function, and a sexual allocation of space—and illustrates the first and third; it also raises the basic issue of separation and integration. Part II looks at rural women, at urban women, and at some of the differences in the work life of women, as well as at the way income from the outside is channeled within the household. Part III looks at some of the subtler ways women are exploited, put down, harassed, not only by men but also by women. Part IV looks at the way women are challenging the status quo by nonconforming to ancient gender stereotypes and by creating a body of knowledge that calls traditional thinking into question. Part V shows how the waves they are making produce change in the female world.

REFERENCES

Barthel, Diane L. 1975. "The Rise of a Female Professional Elite: The Case of Senegal." African Studies Review, Vol. 18, No. 3, December, 1-17.

Canale, Victoire. 1982. News item, des femmes hebdo, No. 83 (84), March, p. 30.

Feminist Forum. 1983. Vol. 6, No. 3, vi.

James, Diane Belle, 1982. "Celluloid Politics." An interview with Atiat El Aboudi. Connexions, Number 4, Spring.

Second Mozambican Women's Conference, Resolution, 1974. New York: Women's International Resource Exchange, no date.

PART I

THE FEMALE WORLD

There is no attempt in any of the chapters to account for the existence of separate male and female worlds. Almost universally, however, Jessie Bernard notes, in addition to the biological specialization of function in reproduction, several other forces are also at work to differentiate them, namely: the sexual division of labor and the resulting sexual allocation of space. But because of the male bias in practically all human knowledge to date relatively little is known about the female world and the way the two worlds relate to one another. She presents some of the pros and cons of separation and integration gleaned from experience in development, concluding that although in general integrated programs may be the ideal, until the female world achieves greater skill in dealing with the male world, separate programs may be better for women.

The limitation of the concept "labor" to paid work may be useful for economic analysis, but for sociological discussion, "Occupation" might be more appropriate. How do males and females occupy their time? Aili Nenola-Kallio offers a case-in-point from Finland showing how women are occupied in preparing for festivals, looking after the church altar, performing important rituals for the community. These unpaid services are no less important than others in maintaining community stability.

The female world is distinguished not only by the activities, paid or unpaid, which occupy the time of women but also by the site where they take place, by the space allocated to them both in the home and elsewhere. Arza Churchman and Rachel Sebba report interesting differences in territoriality between men and women within the home in Israel. Mária Nordström extends the discussion to the community outside the home in Sweden, and on the basis of her research planners might make better provision for the parts of the community inhabited during the day predominantly by women. (See also paper by Egar, Sarkissian, Brady, and Hartman on planning experience in Australia.)

Florence Denmark brings the discussion full circle, back to the issues of separation-integration discussed in the first article. She assesses the pros and cons, not of physical or spatial separation between the two worlds, but of psychological and sociological separation, from the individual woman's point of view. Is the female world a placebo? A retreat from the male world? Or is it rather a secure base for achieving some part in the important decisions of the day? She warns against using the female world as an escape and urges women to see it as a base for legitimate power. As in the assessment of programs in development, she sees the strength potential in the female world rather than its tempting retreatism.

1 THE FEMALE WORLD: A GLOBAL PERSPECTIVE

Jessie Bernard

The first major theme of this chapter has to do with the conceptualizing of the female world. A second theme deals with the errors in policy in development projects and programs that have resulted from the imposition of Western gender-role conceptions on societies with different gender-role structures. The third looks at the relationship between the female and male worlds in terms of policy options. Before proceeding, however, a semantic comment is in order. The title of this chapter uses the term "global" rather than "international." The term "international" is too restrictive, not encompassing enough to include all of the roughly two-and-a-half billion females in the global female world. Some females, for reasons too complex to explore here, do not live in nations or political units capable of supplying data. They live in tribes, or on reservations, or in actual, if not official, colonies, or in unrelinquished mandates or protectorates or in camps, or in territorial enclaves of one kind or another. Thus any conceptualization of the female world in international terms will be short of the mark. The hundred million tribal women will not be represented. Their problems will not be recognized. They are not included in the discussion here. But if only as a matter of scientific courtesy it seems that their existence be recognized, that our "shared female humanhood" be acknowledged.

CONCEPTUALIZING THE FEMALE WORLD

Ester Boserup (1970) sees the male and female worlds in terms of the gender division of labor. She sketches some of the occupation-related factors that affect the female world in developing countries.

3

She distinguishes male and female rural systems of agriculture, for
example, Africa being par excellence the area of female farming—a
system of "shifting cultivation" in which plots of land are cleared,
cultivated, and, when exhausted, abandoned—and Asia being the area
par excellence of male farming. Differing farming techniques distrib-
ute work differently between the genders. She also distinguishes three
kinds of urban towns or cities on the basis of kinds of work: male
towns (mining, administrative) in Africa and Asia; two-gender towns
in which marketing is run by women, modern industries by men; and
female or semimale towns. Boserup (1970) conceptualizes the almost
wholly rural female world in development as a subsistence economy,
and the male partially urban, world as a cash economy, although
Kenneth Little (1973) refers to the market as "virtually a woman's
world in Africa." But almost everywhere, town or country, the occupational structure is such that it separates the two worlds. Smale (1980)
illustrates this occupational separation among the Bidan of Muritania
and adds a footnote: "One woman, when asked what mutual responsibilities men and women shared, replied 'the work of the night, and
that's it."

The sexual specialization of function in reproduction also distinguishes between the two worlds, child bearing being, of course, universally a function of the female world. But child-rearing as well as
child-bearing tends also to be widely assigned to women, usually though
not always the mother. The result of such division of labor and specialization of function is often a gender allocation of space. To delve into
the causes and consequences of the division of labor and specialization
of the child-rearing function would take us too far afield. But it is
important to note that universally a complex work-related structure
emerges, one characteristic of the male world and one of the female.
We know a great deal about the male world, relatively little as yet in
a systematic way about the female world.

Despite the notable achievements by researchers in many disciplines we are only beginning to explore the female world in all its
complexity. Scholars and scientists in many disciplines—primatology,
anthropology, history, economics, political science, psychology,
sociology, literary criticism, even philosophy and theology—are engaged in this task. The structure and the culture of that world are
becoming more and more clearly limned as a result of their work. A
few examples of their work may illustrate this point.

Cases-in-Point

As long as primatologists were for the most part men, the picture
they drew of life among prehuman primates—and sometimes by implica-

tion extended to human primates—was one of aggression, territoriality, hierarchical order, conflict, the lordly Alpha male. The life of the female world among prehuman primates was almost wholly ignored, invisible. Only when women entered the field did the complex social life of the prehuman primate female world become visible. These women researchers lived among the primates they were studying, came to know them individually, named them, traced their kinship relationships, and revealed an aspect of prehuman primate life quite different from the traditional one. They showed us a busy female world in which females helped one another with infant care and infant protection. If a male was too greedy or if he annoyed an infant, they banded together to chase him away. Other males, even those innocent of wrongdoing, were intimidated enough to run away also (Lancaster, 1973). Sara Hrdy (1981) has summarized a considerable body of recent research describing this female prehuman primate world, revealing a surprising gamut of variability: in relative size, in relationships, in degree of equality or subordination both within the female world and vis-a-vis the male world. The implication is not that we can necessarily interpret the human female world in terms of the prehuman female world but to illustrate how much there is to learn. Both are only now becoming visible.

Women anthropologists, similarly, have been engaged in correcting the male bias in their discipline. They have shown how one-sided field studies of preliterate human societies have often been. Male anthropologists had not had much contact with the females of the societies they studied; their reports were therefore incomplete and even, in some cases, biased (Paulme, 1971; Rosaldo and Lamphere, 1974). Women anthropologists have contributed also a rich cache of data on the female world in preindustrialized societies around the world, again revealing a wide range of variability among them.

So, too, in the case of other disciplines. The male bias in the study of history, as Kropotkin noted many years ago, tended to move it in the direction of war, the rise and fall of empires, of nations, of boundary changes, of government, of industry, and the like, with only occasional glances at what was going on in the female world. Since the economy and the polity have been essentially male turf, it was their history that attracted research. Women historians have been especially skilled in rendering the female world visible. Quarrying archives for documents and records long neglected or ignored as trivial, they have been acquainting us with the history of the female world, giving us new insights with respect to the recent, as well as the remote, past, making visible trends and movements neglected by male-oriented historians, showing how different its history has been from the male's (Schulenburg, 1979). Similarly, women researchers bring into the economic paradigms whole areas of relevant problems hitherto ignored, calling for recognition of the nature of work, of the household's contribution, of defects in such concepts as gross national product and other basic concepts in their conceptual tool-kit. Political science is also being called upon to incorporate the part the female world plays in the polity, to make us aware of what McCormack (1975) calls the "two political cultures," to explain the lack of power in the female world. An enormous body of research by women in psychology has transformed the old stereotyped concept of female psychology which portrayed women as seen from the perspective of the male world. The old approach to the study of sex and gender differences from the male point of view is no longer uncritically accepted. Sociologists have found that generalizations about the male world do not necessarily apply in the same way in the female world; they observe the current scene through increasingly sophisticated research lenses and cull numerous insights from the female world from the miles of computer print-outs that result. Literary criticism, finally, highlights the male bias also in the criteria used in judging literary creations, as does art history, in judging its products. Women students of popular culture sensitize us to the predominance of male taste in television and cinema. Women students of theology and philosophy have shown how the male bias has affected their disciplines. In brief, all the disciplines we profess have been engaged in one of the most significant movements of our time, an effort to correct the male bias in all areas of our thinking and to render visible more and more of the female world.

It is still not easy to think in terms of a sociological entity such as the female world. Women are so accustomed to seeing themselves in the context of a male world, as merely the Other, that no more than men can they think of a female world which is autonomous with a validity in its own right. But the existence of such an entity can hardly be challenged any longer. More and more women now ask themselves vis-a-vis male pronouncements: is this the way it really is for us to go? Is this a reflection of our experience?

Consequences in Development of Western Male Bias

The second theme here has to do with the consequences of the Western male bias in development planning. Only two will be commented on here, one having to do with the importation into developing countries of Western role paradigms and the other with methodological defects in establishing the data bases needed for good planning.

It should be made clear, as Barbara Rogers points out, that the charge is not that the formulators, designers, and implementers of development policies, programs, and projects were deliberately or purposely sexist. The problem was less with their motives than with the adverse consequences for the female world of their thinking. They were men whose thinking about "sex and gender, the division of labor, the role of women and men in child-care and the role of women as domestics" was based on a Western male perspective which viewed it as only "'natural' that a woman's place is in the home and that she has a very specific set of tasks which are thought to be universal because they are based on the biological imperatives of sex." Bearing and rearing children defined a woman's whole life. A man is the natural head of the family; he is, therefore, the person development programs should deal with. "Resources intended for everyone should logically be channeled through [him]."

The result of applying these male concepts of gender roles was to channel many of the most talented Third-World women into Western-defined female gender-related roles even when the women themselves wanted projects in which to learn to be self-sufficient rather than merely "more skillful dependents." In Burkina Faso, for example, "the women wanted help mainly in growing cash crops (in communal fields), making clothes for sale, and in the establishment of a store as an income-producing venture. All these activities were turned down because of the lack of money for 'women's affairs.'" Business was no business of women. Certainly not commercial farming, not the cultivation of cash crops. That was clearly a male occupation.

Boserup had begun to point out the consequences of this particular bias as early as 1970. "Virtually all Europeans shared the opinion that men are superior to women in the art of farming; and it then seemed to follow that for the development of agriculture male farming ought to be promoted to replace female farming." Many Europeans, as settlers, early colonial administrators, as technical advisers and development planners—"did all they could to achieve this." What actually occurred was not a replacement of women farmers by male farmers but a dual economy, one a female subsistence economy and one a male cash economy. The men were taught how to use the new scientific technologies for cash crops while women were left to operate with the traditional old hand tools. The resulting differential between the productivity of the two worlds widened, worsening the relative status of women in development.

Boserup (1970) had not been the first to point to the policy errors resulting from the imposition of Western male gender-role biases in development. She refers to a warning as early as 1952 against limiting modern farming techniques to men; another, in 1960; yet another in 1961. "In spite of these warnings, nearly all technical advisers," even the Taiwanese, made the same mistake. Like their European and U.S. predecessors, they taught only the men, "who took no notice since their wives were the cultivators" while the women continued in the same old way. No wonder "farming improvements are thus concentrated in the male sector, while the female sector continues with traditional low-productivity methods."

It was not only the pattern of discrimination against the female world in technical training that increased the distance in productivity between the two worlds but also male-biased patterns of land ownership. Land reforms were introduced by European male administrators who in some cases objected to the "peculiar position of African women, which was so different from anything the Europeans were accustomed to." Men in missions, as well as those in government, opposed the matrilinear systems they found, which were so counter to the patterns they were familiar with. "Emphasis was laid upon the teachings of the Bible where all authority comes from God through the father." Except in the Congo, where the Belgians had recognized women farmers, African women "were eliminated by European-styled land reforms, and the land was given to their husbands, although before the reforms the women had been independent cultivators." As late as 1975 in the Bikita Reserve in Zimbabwe—then Rhodesia—land was allocated to men and widows only, not to married women. Boserup (1970) cited similar situations in South Africa and South East Asia. The women did not take all these discriminatory measures without protest. They wanted "to restore to women the rights they had to land in the old society." But the inflexible male bureaucracies were indomitable.

Despite Boserup's warnings (1970), Rogers found very much the same situation almost a decade later. "A survey of new books on development reveals that, apart from a handbook of specialized books on women . . . , development studies remain firmly oriented towards men, men being synonymous with all people." Under the stimulus of the Women in Development office (WID) of the U.S. Agency for International Development (AID) there was a diminution of the male bias in thinking about development, and perhaps the organization in 1983 of an Association for Women in Development will eliminate it altogether.

The second comment on consequences of the male bias in thinking in the area of development has to do with the data base on which such thinking rests. Planning for development depends for its success on valid data. The research demanded to produce such data must be as free of bias as possible. Rogers is among those who have been calling attention to the essentially male bias even here, a bias which precludes success on the basis of even male criteria. Especially noteworthy is her critique of the "conventions" used by statisticians. Their categories exclude the unpaid work of women. In a subsistence economy in which the work of women contributes a considerable portion of family income, such exclusion is itself scientifically disqualifying: "Urgent action," she states, "is needed at all levels to change the system for data collection and analysis in order to provide adequate information on women's subsistence work of all kinds, both farm and non-farm.

New measures of the value of this work are also needed in order to include women in the labor force statistics, and in the national accounting systems."

So much, then, for some of the policy and research consequences for the female world in development of the imposition of male-biased policies and the research that supplies the data on which policies rest. Still, the experience with the planning of programs and projects for development in the Third World has by now generated a considerable amount of data useful for learning ways of dealing with the male bias of the past.

POLICY OPTIONS: SOME LESSONS FROM
RECENT EXPERIENCE IN DEVELOPMENT

The third theme of this chapter deals with options for dealing with the relationship between the female and male worlds. These options have been classified on a separatist-integrationist spectrum from: (1) separate women-only projects, in which women are specifically cited as the beneficiaries; to (2) integrated general projects, in which there is an explicit women's component; to (3) overall or general projects whether or not women are specifically integrated into them; to (4) general projects without a specific women's component; to (5) men-only projects (Dixon, 1980). There was a considerable amount of controversy "around the question of whether women benefit more from women-specific projects or from general schemes." Although in general experience had shown that projects in which women played an active part in designing, planning, and implementing, tended to attract more participation and enthusiasm than those in which they were passive "targets" of projects designed, planned, and implemented by men, still the pros and cons added up to sometimes equivocal conclusions.

With respect to the separate women-only projects, the pros took these forms: (1) leadership skills were developed; (2) the women were in a position, and able, to present their point of view; (3) attention was paid to them and their issues; and (4) participation in decision making at both staff and beneficiary levels was higher. These favorable results were, however, not automatic consequences. Participation could not be taken for granted. It had to be encouraged. When encouragement succeeded in attracting participation the results were positive.

But the cons of separate women's projects were also notable. Such projects were likely to receive relatively little funding. In separate organizations, the women could easily become isolated and marginalized (Staudt, 1980). At the same time they would be charged with more responsibilities and greater expectations than it was possible for them to carry out with their limited resources. A major drawback to the separatist strategy resulted from the cross-cutting of loyalties to which it gave rise.

In the United States we have seen many examples of such competing cross-cutting loyalties. One of the most widely discussed is that of black women, who are often conflicted between race and gender loyalties. Equally salient is the cross-cutting of feminist loyalties and loyalty to close male relationships. Although women may share many interests, they face special problems in developing both consciousness of community and practice in organization. So also in the Third World, "numerous complications arise in linking and integrating women's issues into the larger political agenda (Staudt, 1980). Staudt reminds us that "isolated from one another in some social settings, and residing intimately with the dominant [male] group, women's identification [and hence loyalties] tend to be based on the family or on male interests, which cut across (or compete with) female interests. These factors reinforce the difficulty of expressing and acting on sex-based concerns."

The integrationist, as well as the separatist, policy also has its pros and cons. Experience in development programs suggests, as one of its pros, that because separate projects are commonly so poorly funded, "women are likely to benefit more extensively by being fully integrated into general schemes" (Dixon, 1980), even at the cost of female solidarity. Another pro for integrationism is that it sounds so fair. It seems to solve the issue or at least to put it to rest. But there is a negative aspect also. Unless women were "specifically cited as beneficiaries, in whole or in part, planners . . . [were] not likely to seek them out for project participation" (Dixon, 1980). A more clear-cut con was the fact that "women's issues are often accorded a low priority in integrated groups" (Staudt, 1980). Their interests were likely to be watered down. Even if the women were not swamped, the uniqueness of their situation was not recognized or adequately dealt with. "When women's programs are affiliated with larger male-dominated institutions, decision-making on major policy issues tends to be transferred to men in the parent institution" (Dixon, 1980). This experience with integrated projects corroborates findings from experimental research in the United States which shows that in mixed-gender groups males tend to out-talk and out-influence females (Bernard, 1981, Ch. 16; Lockheed et al., 1976). Since so much of our thinking has been based on a male perspective it is the male point of view which tends to pervade mixed-gender groups and prevail—whatever the issue is. Unless women are given space of their own they can be buried in the overall program.

Another con has to do with the potential of male hostility that may arise when the women succeed. Thus, for example, in western Kenya one male-initiated effort to mobilize women "developed into such a successful judicial and political representational system" that the men could not tolerate it (Staudt, 1980). Staudt concludes that this case illustrates the "on-going dilemmas of dependence and seeking power." Any male grant of autonomy to the female world may be withdrawn if it seems to threaten the male world.

But perhaps the most serious con for the integrationist strategy is the hazard of cooption with which it confronts women. An independent women's group coopted into a male-oriented group becomes dependent on it for survival. "Such dependency complicates goal attainment and strains leader-member relations. Indeed, cooption can result in considerable exploitation of members." Such cooption of leaders—in the male as well as in the female world—is a common danger. Coopted female leaders tend to identify with those who hold the power and to neglect the female membership. Thus "it is common for leadership to divorce itself from the membership base and to function as an appendage of the coopting institution." Kenneth Little (1973) illustrates the process from a study of women's organizations in Kenya which found that there was, in effect, a "Government-patron alliance serving to block the [autonomous] militant women's efforts to force the Government's hand." The leaders in the women's organizations were recruited to perform political functions—attending embassy parties, presenting awards, making speeches, officiating at prize-giving days, teas, hand-shaking—which fit in "nicely with the Government's 'do-nothingness' and propensity for ceremony rather than actions." Little was writing in 1973 and he concluded his discussion with the question: would these elite women "fight for women's rights or will they . . . be coopted into the political elite, succumb to the role of patron, and lose any deep commitment to women's goals?" Among the other political uses that can be made of coopted women is as government representatives in national and international meetings of one kind or another where they do, indeed, in Little's 1973 words, "lose any deep commitment to women's goals."

In view of the ambiguities in the relations between the male and female worlds as revealed by development experience, Staudt (1980) concludes that the ideal of integrated programs must be compromised or at least tempered:

> Although sexually integrated organizations are ideal, the need to support a transitional period of sex-separate organizations has been emphasized. First because separateness is a strong tradition in many societies, and second, because such separateness provides women with the opportunity to develop leadership skills and to accumulate

resources for leverage and coalition building with other
groups.

To prevent the hazards of marginalization until women are integrated
into mixed-sex organizations at all levels, "separation permits the
development of organizational capacity, skills, and resources for
leverage in mainstream interaction." Separatism is thus seen by
Staudt as a transitional phase on the way to an ultimate integration,
a time-limited accommodation to a nonsympathetic, at least nonaus-
picious, status quo. Even so, "without a structure and resources,
efforts to integrate women will be unfocussed and dissipated."

Another solution, one which supplies such a structure is a kind
of "affirmative action" policy, suggested by Dixon, who envisions a
form of integration in which the position of women is protected. According to her review of the evaluations of Women-in-Development
projects, "if every general project were to include a women's component commanding half of the resources to be allocated among beneficiaries, the intensive and extensive qualities of both separatist and
integrationist approaches could be maximized." Presumably such integrated groups would not be miscellaneous assemblages of individuals
in which—from what we know from research in the United States about
behavior in mixed-gender groups—men would prevail, but joint councils of members representing women and men, each voting as separate
blocs, sometimes in coalitions. Still we cannot ignore Staudt's point:
such "affirmative action" can be easily withdrawn.

Actually, there can be no universal all-purpose solution to the
separatist-integrationist policy issue. Each situation calls for a policy
tailored to the specific context. But in 1975 the United Nations came
out for integration. A draft resolution, of the Second Committee of
the World Plan of Action for the Decade for Women, included among
its objectives the integration of women in all development activities.
In addition to general statements, it made specific recommendations
that all organs of the U. N. development system:

> (a) give special attention to those development undertak-
> ings which integrate women in the development process;
> (b) incorporate in their . . . plans, programs and sector
> analyses and programme documents, an impact statement
> of how such proposed programmes will affect women as
> participants and beneficiaries . . . (c) establish review
> and appraisal systems, as well as research . . . to pro-
> vide a means of measuring progress in the integrating of
> women in the development process; (d) ensure that women
> are included on an equitable basis with men on all levels
> of decision-making which govern the planning and imple-
> mentation of these programmes (emphasis supplied).

Integration was "in." But what was most notable about this statement was its specification of the terms of this integration. Women were to be integrated into all these plans and programs not as subordinates but on "an equitable basis."

Since there is no alternative to some kind of accommodation between the male and the female worlds either in development or elsewhere—the extinction of neither being likely—both are destined to share the same globe forever. The issue then becomes one having to do with the nature of that accommodation. Until now the commonest one has been one of subordination of the female world to the male world. But for a variety of reasons—economic, political, ecological, technological, sociological, psychological—this accommodation is no longer appropriate in more and more parts of the world. The research, theorizing, experimenting, paradigm-construction which are going on in many parts of the female world today augur well for a suitable successor. Learning what the form a relationship between the two worlds "on an equitable basis" may take—separatist or integrationist—is going to call for all these intellectual activities. I am placing my bets on human intelligence, on the knowledge that it generates. At this particular moment, knowledge about the female world itself.

REFERENCES

Bernard, Jessie. 1971. Women and the Public Interest. Chicago: Aldine.

Bernard, Jessie. 1981. The Female World. New York: Free Press.

Boserup, Ester. 1970. Women's Role in Economic Development. New York: St. Martin's Press.

Boulding, Elise. 1980. Woman: The Fifth World. New York: Foreign Policy Association.

Dixon, Ruth. 1980. Assessing the Impact of Development Projects on Women. A.I.D. Program Evaluation Discussion Paper No. 8. Washington, D.C.: Bureau for Program and Policy Coordination, Agency for International Development.

Glazer, Nona. Sociology of Women and Gender. International Review of Modern Sociology, Vol. II, No. 1-2, 175-200.

Hrdy, Sarah Blaffer. 1981. The Woman That Never Evolved. Cambridge: Harvard University Press.

Lancaster, Jane Backman. 1973. In Praise of the Achieving Female Monkey. In The Female Experience, edited by Carol Tavris. New York: Ziff-Davis.

Little, Kenneth. 1973. African Women in Towns. New York: Cambridge University Press.

Lockheed, Marlaine E. and Katherine Patterson Hall. Conceptualizing Sex as a Status Characteristic; Applications to Leadership Training Strategies. J. of Social Issues, Vol. 32, 33, No. 3, 1976.

McCormack, Thelma. 1975. Toward a Nonsexist Perspective on Social Life and Social Science. In Another Voice, edited by Marcia Millman and Rosabeth Moss Kanter. New York: Anchor Books.

Paulme, Denise, editor. 1971. Women in Tropical Africa. Berkeley: University of California Press.

Rogers, Barbara. 1979. The Domestication of Women. New York: St. Martin's Press.

Rosaldo, Michelle Zimbalist and Louise Lamphere, editors. 1974. Women, Culture, and Society. Stanford, Calif.: Stanford University Press.

Schulenburg, Jane Tibbetts. 1977. Clio's European Daughters: Myopic Modes of Perception. In The Prism of Sex, edited by Julia A. Sherman and Evelyn Torton Beck. Madison, Wis.: University of Wisconsin Press.

Smale, Melinda. 1980. Women in Mauritania. Washington, D.C.: Office of Women in Development.

Staudt, Kathleen A. 1980. Women's Organizations in Rural Development. Washington, D.C.: Office of Women in Development.

2 THE SIGNIFICANCE OF DEATH MOTIFS IN WOMEN'S FOLKLORE

Aili Nenola-Kallio

Anna Caraveli-Chaves recently published a study of laments in the Cretan village of Dzermianthes. Although she analyzed only two dirge texts, her conclusions would appear to apply more generally. Caraveli-Chaves studied the structure of the village community, the position of women and men in it; so her study of laments was based not only on knowledge of the ritual and other contexts of laments but on a broader knowledge of the position of women as the preservers and users of culture. In her (Caraveli-Chaves, 1980, 143-44) words:

> In the context of the tradition segments of the Greek vil-
> lage I have observed, the spheres of activity of men and
> women are strictly separate and, in many ways, parallel
> to, and independent from, rather than subservient to each
> other. Men's power is restricted to the public, visible,
> and official realm. Though it provides them with oppor-
> tunities for social domination, it limits them to a tempo-
> ral sphere of experience. Women dominate the rituals
> connected to the life cycle as well as irregular, secret
> rites such as magic and witchcraft. As midwives, match-
> makers, and singers of bridal songs and, finally, as
> lamenters, they dominate the rites of passage, the per-
> ilous moments of transition from one realm to another.
> Such segregated domains of male and female activities
> render men socially but not culturally dominant and
> establish a complex network of balances within the com-
> munity.

What does cultural dominance mean? Caraveli-Chaves answers

15

the question through the concept of <u>female suffering</u>, which is of central importance to the lament text she analyzes:

> Women's position within the cycle of life is recognised as
> one which affords them an uneven share of suffering as
> well as a privileged understanding. Childbirth and its en-
> suing hardships are at the center of the life cycle. <u>It is a</u>
> <u>woman's capacity for reproduction that also gives her first</u>
> <u>hand access to the realm of death,</u> as she becomes more
> <u>vulnerable to pain and loss than men.</u> (Caraveli-Chaves,
> 1980, 146; emphasis added).

Caraveli-Chaves shows that if we examine laments not as a genderless tradition but specifically as women's folklore, we can use them as material in studying women's outlook on the world and particularly the position of death and suffering in it. In my opinion this does not differ greatly from what we know of the traditional Ingrian or Finnish country village, nevertheless, except that the cultural dominance of women seems to be even stronger in the Greek village.

DEATH AND FEMALE SUFFERING IN THE LAMENTS AND SONGS OF INGRIA

Ingria is a region south of the Gulf of Finland which, until the Second World War, was inhabited mainly by the Baltic-Finnish tribes, Izhors, Votes, and Finns. Finnish folklorists have been greatly interested in Ingria ever since the 1840s, when it was discovered that Ingrian women still sang Kalevala-meter epic and lyrics and used ritual laments in connection with death and marriage rituals.

Starting with the Ingrian folklore material, I have tried to determine in what way female suffering and death are combined in the Ingrian women's tradition. The <u>death of oneself</u> and the <u>death of an-</u><u>other</u> as motifs in Ingrian folklore proved to be interesting tools for examining the position and world view of women.

The Death of Oneself

We can, I suspect, agree with Freud that basically no one believes in his or her own death. Thus the way in which the death of oneself appears in poetry tells more about other matters than about concepts of one's own death. So the <u>death of oneself</u> as a theme in Ingrian poems and laments does not necessarily tell us what Ingrian women already thought about death or how they imagined it would be.

Death is not, according to poetry, something to be feared, and in certain cases it is a preferable alternative to a life full of suffering and humiliation. Paradoxically it most often appears as the longed-for alternative to women's sufferings.

In a lament, a bride sometimes prefers death to being wed. Thus the bride laments to her mother:

> My sweet comber
> my precious bearer
> my dear bringer in-your-womb
> I wish you had dug a grave, my warmer.
> I wish you had laid [me], my luller
> I wish you had streteched [me] on the straws by bringer
> covered me with a linen cloth, my bringer-up.
> You should have moved away the sand with your hands, my
>   rocker
> picked up the shingle with your fingers, my adorner.
> Had you laid me in the warmth of sand, my warmer
> in the shelter of shingle, my adorner
> I would have lain, my bringer-on-earth
> in the warmth of sand, my warmer
> in the shelter of shingle, my adorner.
> You would have been free from worries too, my forsterer
> free from sorrow, my bringer-in-your-womb
> about me, my washer.

(IL 2490)*

The bride in the lament expresses her wish for death, describing how she would rather be placed on a bench, have straw placed under her, and be covered with a cloth: this was how the Ingrians laid out the body at home. But the bride may also express her longing for death in a direct form; the bride laments to her father when the "takers" are coming:

> Dearest, my wide-cloaked one
> gentlest, my beautiful boot.
> Let woodsmoke flame for my lamenting self
> make the smoke of the tar wood flame for my dimmed self
> smother in this agony my agonized self

---

*Contact Dr. Nenola-Kallio for explanation of citations throughout text.

kill in this agony my greatly agonized self
slay in this pain my painful self.

(IL 2411)

Obviously, in a wedding lament, the bride did not really hope
for death. Death represents an alternative to being married; the reluctance demanded of the bride—possibly often close to her real frame
of mind—deriving from the ritual function of the laments, is given as
dramatic expression as possible. The lament and song texts and other
material telling of the hard life of Ingrian wives and daughters-in-law
confirm as highly possible the idea that in comparison with such a life
even death would seem a mild misfortune (Neimi, 1904). So the examples prove not so much what Ingrian women thought about death as
what they thought about the life of a married woman.

The above is also confirmed by the appearance of longing for
death in other laments, dirges, and other occasional nonritual laments:
the hardness of a woman's life is emphasized by the wish-for-death
motif a girl laments to her deceased mother:

My precious bringer-up
my nurse-into-the-world.
You bore me into dark sorrow, on this earth
into great agony, into this world.
You bore me plentiful tears for ever,
you bore me into great bitterness for ever.
I wish you had not born [me] on this earth into a thin lot
I wish you had not brought me into this world, into a short
    fate
since you did not pray God for a better lot
since you did not ask God for a better fate.
I wish you had rather choked [me] in the steam of the
    bathhouse
I wish you had rather smoked me in the smoke of the bathhouse
I wish you had rather covered me with the moss of the
    bathhouse
than borne me on this earth
borne me in the dark of sorrow.
I wish you had rather strangled me with your left heel
I wish you had smothered me, agonized, under the sods
I wish you had rather covered me with the sand of the
    graveyard
I wish you had rather covered me under linen, very worried
I wish you had put me on the bench, lamenting
I wish you had rather stretched me on the straws, unhappy

than born me in plentiful tears, miserable.
You have left me in the dark sorrow for ever
You have left me in bitterness for ever.

(IL 1518)

or:

I wish you had smothered me on my place of birth, agonized
I am truly a sufferer of great mourning, mournful
and bearer of great [sorrow], lost
Alas, my unhappy life
alas, my days, bewailing!
I had a young mind, indeed, depressed
and a child's manners, too much lamenting
when I changed my appearance, sunken [when I got married]
and I changed my life, burned:
to weep forever, ever unhappy.
I changed to the days of a serf, unhappy
to the days of a servant, ill-treated.

(IL 4850)

Lamenting one's birth is extremely common in the Ingrian women's lyrics. When we examine the contexts in which the theme appears, most often in connection with being wed, the state of marriage, with being an orphan, or with the life of want of a girl or women—it is hard to see anything but a rebellion against these conditions of life. It is thus an outburst of revolt against the reality of their life rather than in favor of death.

The conclusion, that the own death motif is used in the laments and songs of the Ingria as a means of reinforcing the suffering that is part of the women's lot, is based on what we call the macrocultural context. We know only too little about the situational contexts of different songs and/or laments or the lives of the singers. But it appears from the fact that both wedding laments and mournful songs were established parts of the wedding festivities, that they must have been very much in harmony with the real world and the outlook on life of their singers. The descriptions in the songs and laments that deal with women's lot, their relationships with others, and death and sufferings, may not constitute those singers' view of the world and concept of life. But, they, however, clearly do indicate the existence of a specific outlook and reality and in their day certainly influenced the formation of a woman's outlook on life.

Death of Another

It becomes evident that <u>female suffering</u>—and here I am concerned with its connections with death—covers the suffering brought
not only by the biology of woman, but also, and above all, by the trials
accompanying her role. The own-death motifs in laments and lyrics
do not prove that women connect the physical suffering associated with
their biological role to their understanding of death; but thoughts of
death do clearly mirror the social and economic position of women.
This becomes all the more obvious when we begin to examine the cases
in which the genre covers the <u>death of another person</u> important to a
woman. Of unusual importance and dimensions in a woman's life is
the loss of a husband, mother, father, son, daughter, or child as
shown by the associated laments and song motifs.

It was women's job to sing the dirges. Even last century the
singers were most often the family's own women. This is why the
dirges noted down in Ingria were usually dedicated to close relatives:
father, mother, husband, son, daughter.

One of the main functions of dirges was to ensure that the deceased would be admitted to the realm of death (cf., Honko, 1978).
The laments ask about the journey of the deceased and his or her re-
ception in the other world; the lamenters likewise pass on the fare-
wells of the deceased and apologies to those left behind. In the present
context it is, however, important to note that even in the last century
concern for the dead in the Ingrian dirges already seems to have taken
second place to the concern of the lamenter for her own and/or her
children's fate. In other words the dirges—like many occasional laments (see Nenola-Kallio, 1982)—clearly reflect the effects of death
on women's everyday life and her position in the community. The
effects can be described indirectly by recalling all that the deceased
was to the lamenter: mother gave birth and cared for, taught, and
instructed, fed, and consoled; father taught and cherished; brought
presents from town, was the "castle-father" to rely on. With her
husband went a woman's economic security and the teacher of her
children; with a son or daughter, the child she had given birth to and
brought up, who was to be her support in old age, and, in the case of
her daughter, who was to lament her death. The widow's and orphan's
lot is described in gloomy terms in the lament: there is no security
at all in the world for them; they are forced to live in eternal want at
the mercy of the richer and more fortunate with no one to say a good
word for them. The only refuge was God in Heaven, to whom they
turned with sighs, as in the following lament. Here an old widow describes her hard life and insecurity; she lives as in a deserted forest,
where dangers threaten from all sides; she lives as in a cold barn,
with the wind blowing in through every crack in the wall. For her,
too, death is the only salvation:

If my golden lord
would only hear my prayers, weeping
and my bowings, miserable.
If he would make my life shorter, my loving Creator
would take me in His shelter, the good Creator
would take me in His protection, my agonized self
from its unhappy life, my unhappy self
from this shelterless life, my shelterless self.

(IL 4544)

Her economic security (the little there was, for people were
extremely poor) and defenders were gone. This situation is described
by both the laments and songs of grief of Ingria. It was particularly
hard to be a widow with many children. Feeding them and raising them
were a constant source of worry:

(from a dirge to a husband)

Where shall I now find shelter, agonized
when I have not got shelter for an hour for my agonized self
and where will my lulled ones find shelter
and where will they look for protection, my good looking
    brought-into-the-world-ones?
For they left you a bevy of bilberries
and a troop of cranberries.
How shall I now bring up my born cranberries
and raise the youngest of my raised ones?
I will start by bringing them up with a bitter mind
I will start to bring [them] in my tears
and shedding rich waters.
I will start separating them from myself.

(IL 1322)

Thus the woman feels she is an object whose position and situation are determined according to whether she has parents or a husband.
On the other hand it is quite obvious that she also sees herself as a
subject who has to bear grief and sorrow. As an object woman is
placed in the role of the ritual lamenter, as a subject she expresses
her own sorrow and her own suffering.

The Death of a Child

The death of a son or daughter, of one's own child in general, is a paradox in Ingrian laments and songs. The laments for a grown or almost fully grown son or daughter often recall how the mother brought her child up to be a support to her in her old age, but now death (or war in the recruit laments, marriage in a wedding lament) had robbed her of this support. The attitude toward the death of a small child, however, is different. We often find in the Ingrian tradition, as elsewhere in the Finnish tradition, lullabies of death directly or indirectly hoping for the child's death. There are many examples of these such as the following:

> I'm rocking my baby under the turf
> I'm swaying him under a tussock of sand
> I'm singing him between the boards.
> Come, Death, along the marsh
> come, Mort, along the well-path.
> I would make Him a pair of socks
> leggings for death's daughter.

(SKVR IV 3918)

Explanations have been sought for these lullabies of death. In my opinion, Chicherov, who studied the Russian "smertnyjebajk," came nearest to the truth in saying that they "reflected the hopelessness that prevailed in the degenerate peasant home of the days of serfdom" (see Kuusi, 1960, p. 129). This explanation should further be amended; they reflect a woman's hopelessness in the face of a heavy, almost insuperable task.

Children were at once a blessing and a curse (Larin Paraske, see Timonen, 1980, p. 84). So the death of a small, often sick, child might be a relief to a mother who had to cope not only with the older children but also the running of the house. Furthermore there was nothing unusual about a child's death. A sick child's suffering undoubtedly helped people to accept, and even wish for, its death.

We find the same attitude in the laments. A lament to a child by the famous singer Larin Paraske begins:

> Thanks to the highest God above
> thanks to the sweet Creator
> for taking my beautiful born one
> from walking here, in this kingdom of hardships.

(IL 1107)

In one of the most touching laments from Soikkola, in West Ingria, an orphan girl weeps on her mother's grave after the death of her youngest sibling for whose care she had been responsible:

Great thanks to my comber
many praises to my bringer-in-her-arms!
She may have spoken sweetly, my comber
she may have spoken dearly, my bringer-on-earth, to the
   great Creators
she may have appeased [them], my rocker
since she came and took away the youngest of her raised ones
the smallest of her washed ones
the tiniest of her cherished ones.
Maybe she could not bear my miserable crying.

(IL 1522)

In cultures and societies where laments are sung in connection with death, the lamenters, who are in most cases women, enjoy great respect because of their skills. It appears, however, that the cultural dominance of women in these affairs is typical; in societies where public authority governs social life, the rites connected with birth, death, and marriage—the special realm of women—have tended to be controlled by legislation. Examples of this are the rules governing funeral rites in ancient Greece, where as Plutarch explains: "All manner of disorder and excess on the part of women in the course of feasts, processions and funerals is prohibited" (Alexiou, 1974, p. 15). The prohibitions of the Byzantine Church in the fourth and fifth centuries A.D. applied not only to the most violent forms of mourning rituals, such as the tearing out of hair, the rending of clothes, and the clawing of cheeks, but also and especially to ritual lamenting, because laments were regarded as self-centered complaints and thus at odds with the Christian faith (Alexiou, 1974, p. 28).

Similar prohibitions were placed on lamenting in medieval Western Europe and the part of Russia covered by the Orthodox Church even as late as the eighteenth century. The justification for prohibiting dirges was most often given as their pagan content and the expression of unchecked grief, which conflicted with the Christian concept of death as a transition to a better life. One is, however, tempted, in the light of these examples, to ask whether this was in fact not a question of a broader tendency that gradually robbed women and female culture of its prestige and influence as society and the Church became more and more male dominated? It is at least easy to see that as the Church took over rites connected with the stages in human life, the so-called rites of passage, the specialist status of women became weaker.

REFERENCES

Alexiou, Margaret. 1974. The Ritual Lament in Greek Tradition.
Cambridge.

Caraveli-Chaves, Anna. 1980. Bridge Between Worlds. The Greek
Women's Lament as Communicative Event. American Journal
of Folklore, 368, 129-57.

Honko, Lauri. 1978. The Ingrian Lamenter as Psychopomp. Temenos
14. Helsinki.

Kuusi, Matti. 1960. Tuuti Lasta Tuonelahan. Kalevalaseuran
vuosikirja 50, 123-32.

Nenola-Kallio, Aili. 1982. Studies in Ingrian Laments. Folklore
Fellows Communications 234. Helsinki.

Neimi, A. R. 1904. Runonkeraajiemme matkakertomuksia 1830-
luvulta 1880-luvulle. Helsinki.

Timonen, Senni, editor. 1980. Nain lauloi Larin Paraske.
Piesksamaki.

3 SEX DIFFERENCES AND THE EXPERIENCE OF THE PHYSICAL ENVIRONMENTS

Måria Nordström

I have interviewed people about their activities in, experiences with, and views of their housing area and its nearby open space as part of a project that evaluated the quality of contemporary areas of multi- and single-family houses in Sweden. I have noted that men and women often emphasize different aspects of the environment. It appears that the environment serves different purposes for men and women. While such differences are related to personality, these seem to be subordinate to sex. When the interview takes place with both husband and wife present, it often turns out that they have divergent views of their environmental conditions. Due to this divergence, one party often tends to dominate the other with his or her views with little protest from the subdued party. During the interview it also becomes clear that in many families one party is regarded as the family's representative and as spokesperson, his or her views tend to gain added importance. The differences between men and women on environmental issues could be well understood by regarding their views in the light of their different family roles and by viewing the environment in the social context of family life. I have reached this conclusion after having analyzed in detail essays written by 15-year-old boys and girls with the title "This is how I would like to live." I shall therefore start by reporting on the results of this analysis.

The boys and girls were given the title "This is how I would like to live" as a theme for an essay to write at school by their teachers. The very theme seems to have stimulated the pupils as the essays are quite long and rich in content, and both boys and girls produced very interesting essays. To start with the boys, their essays are characterized by vivid imagination and some rather fantastic ideas. They imagine themselves as future owners of huge houses full of technically advanced

equipment and luxurious decoration. "Representative" space like ball-
rooms and drawing rooms is also given attention while sleeping rooms,
kitchens, bathrooms, and other everyday activity rooms are either
ignored or given little attention. Some boys declare that they won't be
at home very much as their careers will demand quite a lot of traveling
from them. Generally, it is clear in the boys' essays that the emphasis
is on activities—coming and leaving home often in expensive cars
pausing from their important jobs to have a quick look at their families.
The houses and homes of the boys seem connected with the success and
conditions of their jobs. The house stands as a material symbol of a
successful career.

With the girls the idea of a home is something entirely different.
The home is where the girls will be taking care of their families and
houses adapted to the everyday needs and activities of the family members. Therefore the girls describe in detail the layout, decoration,
and equipment of the sleeping rooms, kitchens, and even the bathrooms
as well as the drawing rooms. While the boys want things in grand
dimensions, the girls emphasize details, describing the colors of walls
and furniture, quality of material, plants, etc. They have a practical
interest which the boys lack for the home as such, but display in connection with their garages and hobby workshops. The girls express
sensitivity to the placement of the various rooms in the house and display spatially detailed orientation—something which is not found with
the boys. In connection with this spatial sensitivity in the girls it should
be mentioned that the immediate environment is of special interest to
the girls. They want their homes situated in the countryside—where
it is healthy to live and raise children—but not too far from shops and
the city—where you meet people. The girls, then, seem anxious to
create homes that will serve social functions while the boys seem
more interested in the material qualities of their future homes. These
different interests in how the girls and boys would like to live do reflect, as far as I understand, the different roles which the teenagers
set for themselves as grown up women and men. My hypothesis is that
their home ideals will stay with them when they are adults and that
these ideals can explain the different environmental emphases which
adult men and women have in the interviews about environmental
quality.

In the interview study with men and women in a newly built single-
family housing area (see Figure 3.1) it turned out that the men generally were very pleased with their new living situation. This could
not be said unconditionally for the women. All the interviewed persons
had previously lived closer to the city in multi-family housing areas.
Some of them had had summer houses, a common Swedish phenomenon,
so they did have some experience with taking care of and managing a
house on their own. The fact is that in Sweden most city dwellers live

FIGURE 3.1: Plan of the single family housing area mentioned in the text. Note the marked cul-de-sac street and the unit which the houses make.

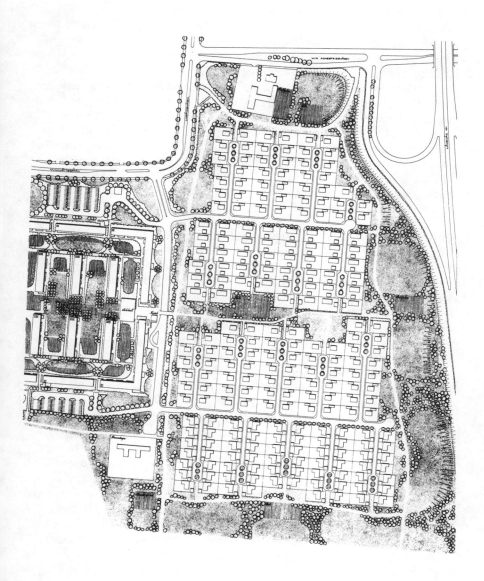

in multi-family houses. During the 1970s many single-family housing
areas were erected outside of the cities. The houses were rather cheap
to buy and not very expensive to maintain because there were profitable
tax deductions tied to the house loans. The consequence of this development was that it became profitable for almost anyone in Sweden to
own a house. This new economic situation made living in single-family
houses more popular than ever, though the reasons for having a house
had not very much to do with the way of living as such. This way of
living also made it important for every family to own at least one car
as transportation had to be arranged privately.

When buying the house the economic situation of the family
changed. In families where the husband still was quite young and had
not as yet reached far in his career the wife took on a job to contribute
economically. The children were taken care of during the day at a
child care center. In many of these families the house was the place
where the members met only at night and during weekends, with nobody at home during the day. In "older" families where the husband's
income was great enough to carry the house expenses alone, the wife
would remain at home if she previously had been a housewife.

This was at least how the family situation was arranged at first.
However, the housewives found it difficult to stay at home all day as
they were very lonely. Since the housing area is situated quite far from
the city center, public transportation is bad, and as these women do
not generally have a driving license of their own or if they have, they
don't have access to the family car, they were bound to stay in the
area during the day.

The housing area has 229 individual houses with common open
space. There are no shops or any other service and social institutions.
There are few places for people to meet and people have little reason
to stay outside of their own ground. People know or know of each other
by being neighbors, seeing each other over the fence, or at the parking
ground belonging to each house and facing the street. Whether intended
or not, the neighborhood unit has turned out to be those houses—about
12 of them—whose entrances and parking grounds face the same cul-
de-sac. The very turning point of the street could be considered the
best socially functioning meeting ground for the houseowners and their
families. It is characteristic of the "car-minded" planning of this
housing area that the turning point is meant to be an extra car parking
space. However, it is mainly used today as a playground for the children of the "neighborhood." Both the children and their parents are
content with this as the children are thus not too far from home. The
expensively equipped playgrounds that are erected in the area have no
such social relation and meaning for the children and are accordingly
not used.

A parallel with the waste of the unused playgrounds is the com-

mon open space in the middle of the area and at its outskirts which
consists of rather large lawns with some shrubs and trees. This open
space—marked out to be a park—is quite expensive to maintain. The
ground is valuable and the cost of erection was considerable, but as
with the playgrounds, this space is unused.

A better planning solution, both economically and socially, would
have been to enrich the cul-de-sac with a square and some benches in
order to functionally make the space meaningfully connected with the
houses and all inhabitants' activities, including those of the children.
Such alternative planning with its emphasis on nearby environmental
assets would correspond to the teenage girls' conception of good living
qualities. As you recall, this conception was characterized as sensitive to immediate environmental arrangements and to easily available
green space. In contrast to this stands the planning principle of the
area. The principle has been to assign a physical space to every individual activity without regard to the character of the activities and
their relatedness to family living and to the neighborhood unit.

The lack of socially well functioning aspects of daily life has
made those inhabitants who have to stay in the area during the day,
mostly elderly housewives, experience it as isolated from city life.
Some of the women have managed to get part-time jobs in the city and
this has been a good solution to the problems of loneliness. Their jobs
provide the social stimulation which they missed at home during the
day and their lives resemble those of their husbands, to whom the
housing area is a place of recreation after having finished work. The
women declare that the housing area as such is no good from the view
of a housewife's work but all right to relax in at night and during weekends. What these women say that they miss the most in the area, and
the women who are still housewives agree, is some place to see and
meet people. In their previous housing areas they had easy access to
shopping centers, the city center areas were populated during the day,
and they regret the loss of this aspect of their social life.

In the very role of being a housewife and taking care of a family,
a well functioning social situation is of utmost importance. Many of
the women interviewed, especially those who have stayed at home for
a number of years to take care of their children, are very dedicated
to their role and regard it as essential to the life of their family. They
believe that they have done the right thing for the well-being of their
children. At the same time they feel that there is no place for a housewife in society today. "As a housewife you are not worth anything,"
one woman says depressed. This seems connected to the lack of support in their housing area for their role. The women who would like
to stay at home while their children are too young to take care of themselves, are in a dilemma. The environment lacks a satisfying daily
quality of life and the social isolation is too great for most of the house-

wives to tolerate. Therefore they long to get a job and to leave the
housing area during the day, a desire which is in conflict with the
obligation they feel toward their children of raising them themselves.

The men on the other hand are very pleased with their living
situation. They have reached an important goal in their lives by being
able to get a house of their own, are pleased with the new leisure
activities which working in the garden and the upkeep of the house
have given them. When living in a flat, they had nothing to do at home
at night. The experience for men (as well as for professional women)
is quite different from that of the housewives. They appreciate being
with their families at night and even the distance from the city and
work. They don't miss the city and city life, of which they get their
fill during the day, and because of their easy access to a car, can get
to quickly, they do not feel isolated. The conditions of those living and
working in the area during the day and of those coming there at night
are certainly very different. Moreover, for men and not for the professional women, the value of buying the house as an investment is
important. This is the reason they bought their houses, not the longing
to live in a house with a garden. The living condition itself is clearly
subordinated to the business success and accepted with delight whether
or not they are keen on working in the house or garden. This is the
grown-up parallel to and realization of the teenage boy's ideal of an
expensive house as an expression of success in professional life.

A housing area such as this of single-family houses functioning
exclusively as a living area with no common daytime activities fits
the male ideal of how to live and not at all the female teenager's ideal.
As noted above, in the interview the men generally speak for the family and their wives remain silent. When asked directly and when being
interviewed on their own, the women criticized the social and environmental poverty of the area. They will modify or abandon their criticism, which the men appear to take personally and which threaten the
contentment which they experience, acting in her role as a social
moderator and promoter of the well-being of her family.

This difficulty of women in asserting their environmental views
also seems to be connected with the character of their views and the
lack of an effective means of communicating these views. As opposed
to the men's views, which concern economic and material realities,
those of the women are quite complex in character and less concrete.
And—perhaps what is most important—concerns are embedded in a
social, cultural, and value context that is invisible, even to themselves.

4 WOMEN'S TERRITORIALITY IN THE HOME

Arza Churchman and Rachel Sebba

We suggest viewing human territoriality as a set of attitudes toward an area and a set of effective and potential behaviors in and toward this physical area. These attitudes and behaviors will be called territorial when they are influenced by the social status of the individual in relation to the area. Since territorial behavior is sociospatial behavior, it is possible to develop a territorial model which matches given areas to given individuals or groups. A model of this type would be characterized by a behavior—attitude repertoire—such that each sociospatial area has a particular set of behavior—attitudes. One's degree of control within each area will be influenced by: (1) the nature of one's relationship to that area within the territorial model; (2) the physical characteristics of the area; (3) one's personal and social characteristics which affect one's status in the social group in question (e.g., role, sex, age, etc.). The resultant degree of control will in turn influence one's behavior within the area and attitude toward it.

The behavioral and attitudinal components, derived mainly from the literature, may be divided into the following groups:

A. Territorial Behavior
   (1) Sociospatial behavior—defined more specifically as one's behavior toward others in the same area when one wants to be alone.
   (2) Behavior within the area of use of the area—where will one perform various optional activities?
   (3) Behavior toward the area—Does one participate in its cleaning and maintenance?
B. Attitudes Toward the Area
   (1) The identification of a place within the apartment as belonging to the individual.

(2) The identification of a place which one sees as expressing
oneself.

(3) A place in which one feels one can do as one pleases without
being disturbed.

The goal of this research was to represent the dwelling unit as
a complete territorial model in which there are both public common
and private areas, each characterized by a different behavioral and
attitudinal set according to the individual's degree of control. In other
words, when one has control over an area one will be more likely to
act in a dominant manner, use it for optional activities, participate
in its cleaning, identify it as a place of one's own, as a place which
expresses oneself and as a place which gives a feeling of freedom of
action.

The research was carried out in a middle-class neighborhood
of Haifa in five high-rise buildings in which all apartments are almost
identical in size and layout. The size of the apartments (65 square
meters) is considered modest by Israeli standards today and, given
the family size of two to four children, somewhat crowded. All families owned their apartments, as is the common practice in Israel.

One hundred and eighty-five structured, individual interviews
were conducted with every member of 45 families (including children
over five years old). Each person was asked to classify each area and
piece of furniture in terms of ownership, and to describe her or his
own behavior and attitude according to the components described before.

The results indicated that the dwelling unit could be represented
as a territorial model. The answers to the question "To whom does
each place in the apartment belong" made clear that:

1. Within each family there was full agreement as to the territorial classification of each area. Each family member was interviewed
separately, and except for three exceptions all answers within each
family were identical. The exceptions occurred in three families where
the mother classified the kitchen as belonging to the whole family,
while the other members of the family classified it as belonging to her.

2. A place was classified as a territorial area only if it had
clear, identifiable physical boundaries. (Despite the fact that they
were asked about corners and parts of the rooms, they defined only
whole rooms or specific pieces of furniture as territorial areas.)

3. There was no territorial classification of an area where
there was no permanence in time. An area that was used by a number
of people at different times was considered to belong to all the users.
An exception was the kitchen in a number of families which was identified as belonging to the mother.

The territorial areas could be classified into three types:

Individual Areas—belonging to one person only. These included all bedrooms; and 56 percent of the kitchens classified by the whole family as belonging to the mother.

Shared Areas—belonging to a subgroup within the family. These included all the parents' bedrooms and the bedrooms where two to three children slept; and 4 percent of the living rooms and 7 percent of the kitchens classified as belonging to the mother and father.

Public Areas—belonging to the entire family. These included 96 percent of the living rooms, 38 percent of the kitchens, and all of the hallways and bathrooms.

We see that the differences between mothers and fathers express themselves in the individual areas that they have in addition to the bedroom area which they share. Three of the fathers have a study of their own in the terrace and for 25 (or 56 percent) of the women the kitchen is classified as their individual area. In other words more mothers have control over individual areas than do fathers. We will explore the implications of this later.

In addition to the territorial areas we found that there were regular places in various rooms. In 98 percent of the families each person had a regular place at the kitchen table with the mother sitting in the place most accessible to sink and stove. In two-thirds of the cases she also sits next to the youngest child even if she or he is presently of school age. Mothers in three-fourths of the families also sleep on the side of the bed closest to the door of the room and continue to do so after the children are already grown. In the living room there were fewer regular places—but fathers significantly more often had one than did mothers (53 vs. 29 percent). The explanation given was that the mother has less time because she is busy preparing the food and washing dishes, etc. There is also a difference in the location and quality of the seat, with fathers sitting in a central area and mothers in a side area or on a couch upon which she can rest. These data illustrate two phenomena: (1) the different responsibilities of mothers and fathers within the home, and (2) the continuation of patterns of behavior long after they are necessary.

Let us look now at the sex differences in territorial behavior and attitudes. Dominant social behavior in the area as defined as the response: "If someone else was in the area and I wanted to be alone I would ask the other to leave." Potentially dominant was that: "It would depend on the circumstances whether I asked them to leave or left myself." Of both mothers and fathers, 96 percent were dominant in their bedroom, and more than 70 percent of both were at least potentially dominant in the living room. However, while 79 percent of the mothers were dominant in the kitchen, fathers were, if at all, only potentially dominant there (27 percent). Children, regardless of sex, were dominant, if at all, only in their bedroom (95 percent of those in single rooms, 35 percent of those in double rooms, and 17 percent of those in triple rooms).

The activity of entertaining guests is thought of as "public" by designers and "placed" in a central open area. However, we found that many of the guests come to visit only one member of the family. In such cases those family members who have areas under their control tend to prefer to entertain there rather than in the living room. Of the mothers, 49 percent used the kitchen to entertain their guests and all three of the fathers who had studies entertained there.

The major sex difference in behavior was in the cleaning and maintenance of the home. The mother is individually or jointly responsible for the cleaning of 93 percent of the rooms. Of the 45 fathers, 5 participate in the cleaning. These are cases where the parents work at different times and the fathers are at home with the children when the mother is at work. The other fathers participate, if at all, only in one-time maintenance activities such as repairs or wallpapering. Children on the whole participate only in cleaning their own room. The only ones who help out elsewhere are girls over 12. Girls participate in cleaning their own rooms more than boys and they also do so at a younger age than the boys. Thus among children, we already find a pattern similar to the adult one, although somewhat less extreme—more boys than fathers do help. However when a boy and girl share a bedroom it is likely to be the younger girl who helps rather than the older boy, which is a discouraging sign.

We asked our respondents: Do you have a place of your own in the apartment? Mothers were more likely to say that some part of the home is theirs and fathers more likely to say they have no place at home. From the places identified as their own, their answers reflect their degree of control over rooms in the home rather than the actual use of them. Thus mothers identify the bedroom or kitchen and fathers the bedroom or study. Whether or not they feel that there is a place in the home that represents them seemed to be related to their involvement in its design and maintenance. Forty percent of the fathers but only 18 percent of the mothers said that nothing in the house represents them. Of those mothers who felt that the whole house represented them 18 of the 24 were exclusively responsible for the cleaning and maintenance of the home. Of the eight fathers who answered that the whole house represents them, three participate in the cleaning and the others participated in its decoration. The other adults referred to specific places that they had designed or built as representing them. Thus mothers exhibit more manifestations of what we have defined as territorial behavior. They have a greater degree of control within the

dwelling and this manifests itself in their behavior within it and attitude toward it.

This research is based upon the assumption that the dwelling
unit's uniqueness does not stem from its functional character but from
its psychological and social role. We therefore asked our respondents
what they felt were the social and psychological needs which the home
fills above and beyond being a place where various activities are performed. There was general agreement among mothers, fathers, and
children as to what needs the home fills, but differences in the relative
importance attached to them, and in the emphasis placed on different
aspects of them. The answers could be divided into five categories:

(1) The home is the sole exclusive area of control of the individual. It answers the need for a space of one's own, a space that others
have no part in. Since it is under the individual's control, the home
permits the individual to act freely, to supervise others within it, to
control everyday routines, etc. (This category was mentioned by 54
percent of mother-homemakers, 79 percent of mothers working outside the home, and 82 percent of fathers).

(2) The home as a physical framework for the institution of the
family. The home is considered the most appropriate setting for
raising children, according to the parents' values as it affords freedom of behavior and enables family members to act naturally and express their emotions to each other (73 percent of mother-homemakers,
79 percent of mothers working outside the home, and 53 percent of
fathers).

(3) The home as a place for self-expression. The home is the
only place that the individual can change, design, and care for. One
organizes the home according to one's needs and tastes, and gives
the home one's personal, unique meaning. One can express oneself
freely in the home and can be oneself. While parents stressed the
self-expression that is afforded by rendering the physical environment meaningful, children stressed that their self-expression is a
consequence of the ability to act freely (27 percent of mother-homemakers, 21 percent of mothers working outside the home, and 40
percent of fathers).

(4) The home gives a feeling of security to its owners. In this
context, it is not a function of physical shelter but of permanency in
the home. One knows the people and customs, the social environment
can be trusted, and one knows what to expect. This feeling of permanency is not connected, according to the respondents, to the length of
time of actual residency but to the knowledge that nobody can force
them to leave (15 percent of mother-homemakers, 5 percent of mothers
working outside the home, and 18 percent of fathers).

(5) The home gives a feeling of belonging. It gives a special feel-

ing of closeness and involvement in what goes on there (31 percent of mother-homemakers, 16 percent of mothers working outside the home, and 7 percent of fathers).

If we look first at the differences among the women, we find that they are agreed on the relative importance of the home as a place for the family and on self-expression and security as less important. On the other hand, mothers not working outside the home are less likely than the others to mention control and more likely than the others to mention belonging.

The most interesting comparison between mothers and fathers is between the first two needs. With regard to control the mothers who work outside the home are similar to the fathers, while with regard to the family they are like the other mothers.

Clearly, the mothers are much more conscious of the family as a major function of the home. The fact that there are no differences between these two groups of women in the other behavioral and attitudinal manifestations that we have examined, indicates that the perceived role of the mother in the home does not change if she works outside the home.

Those who work outside the home, whether mothers or fathers, see control as an important factor. Possibly they become conscious of this aspect because of the comparison with the work situation where they are more under the control of others. This raises an interesting question for further study as to whether people who experience more or less control in their working situation see it as a more or less important function of the home. The fathers view the home as being an area of individual control and yet we have seen that in actuality they enjoy fewer areas of control within it than the mothers. They do perhaps enjoy certain privileges (like a better chair) but they seem more like guests. They are less likely to feel that the home represents them or that they have a place of their own within it.

We have come to the conclusion that the care of the house is an important issue. It is more than a question of an equitable division of labor, but rather that the person who performs the tasks has important consequences for both the behavior and attitudes of the adults toward the home. The fact that there were no differences between the boys and girls suggests that the differences among the adults is a function of the sex-defined roles which they have accepted. However, the differences between boys and girls in responsibility for the care of the home suggest that many of the families are educating their children, either consciously or unconsciously, to continue this pattern.

In conclusion, we have seen that the division of the dwelling unit among the family members is a major factor affecting their behavior within it and their attitude toward it. The fact that this spatial division is related to the sex and role of the adults has a social significance above and beyond its implications for the use of the dwelling unit. It suggests that the spatial division has the possibility of communicating messages either supportive of, or antithetical to, the kinds of relationships desired among family members in particular and between the sexes in general.

5 WOMEN'S WORLDS: GHETTO, REFUGE, OR POWER BASE?

Florence L. Denmark

Women have contributed a great deal to the growth and development of the academic disciplines. They have consistently been productive and innovative, whether working with or independently of men. They have produced, taught, discovered, organized, and been involved in countless activities for the betterment of their field and of life in general. Unfortunately, in all disciplines, women have been unrecognized, undervalued, and invisible (Denmark, 1980).

Women's Studies programs in universities have been developed to counteract this invisibility, to document their contributions, and to study the psychological and social lives of women and of how we interact with the real world. They have been developed in order also to understand what has been happening to women throughout history as a basis for change in the status quo.

In addition, in an effort to break the barriers of male dominance in academia, business, medicine, and the arts, women have developed programs to educate, support, provide networks of communication, and to develop role models for themselves and other women. Women's Studies departments are also places, structural entities, where women can come together for nurturance, information, and support.

Thus, two functions for Women's Studies programs may be delineated. The first is to gain and disseminate knowledge about women. The second is to provide a place for women, a place where women can support one another and learn from each other, in order to further their common goals.

These two functions can be viewed from different perspectives. Some see Women's Studies as a ghetto—a place to keep women "in their place"—and quiet. Others see it as a refuge—a place where women can be themselves—as women—without having to compete with men. Still

38

others view it as a power base—a way to develop methods and launch campaigns by which women <u>can</u> achieve that to which they aspire. The question for us is, "What is the Women's World of Women's Studies? Is it a ghetto, a refuge, or a power base?"

GHETTO

A ghetto is a physical space to which members of minority groups are restricted because of economic pressure or social discrimination. Women have always been economically restricted victims of social discrimination. But women's ghettos are never bounded by walls, are never a definable physical space. We cannot <u>see</u>, cannot identify, the ghettoizing influences upon us. Can it be said that a Women's Studies department is a ghetto? Is it a structural entity that is identifiable and to which women are relegated in order to confine them and continue their economic and social discrimination? We are all familiar with women's clubs and groups whose purposes generally are to exchange child care information, recipes, or to raise money for some worthwhile cause. The women's pages of many newspapers report the activities of these groups in addition to describing the latest fashions and reporting on who is marrying whom. This is the stereotypical view of the areas with which women, all women, are primarily concerned.

It is probable that many view Women's Studies in this way, as a variation on the Women's Club theme and therefore inconsequential and powerless. In fact, Women's Studies departments and activities may be endorsed <u>because</u> Women's Studies is perceived as consisting of innocuous activities on which women's energy may be expended and used up while the "real world" goes on—totally unaffected by what women do.

There is danger in this perception. Courses offered in Women's Studies departments may be viewed as inferior, as having little or no content, and as worthless on a college transcript. The teachers of these courses may be viewed as less qualified and less scholarly than those who teach the traditional curricula, which are seen as more important by the "Establishment." If Women's Studies is viewed as a ghetto, Women's Studies will be viewed as inferior—the curriculum, the students, and the research. Thus, the ghettoizing effect will be total.

An even greater danger than these perceptions from the Outside, is the perception of "ghetto" from the Inside. Those active in Women's Studies may perceive themselves in the same manner. Since women have been socialized to accept themselves as inferior to men, they may feel, since <u>they</u> are comfortable within Women's Studies departments, that the field is <u>inferior</u> to other fields. Women who feel uncomfortable in challenging the status quo, may be comfortable in aligning themselves with Women's Studies.

So Women's Studies may insulate women from the "real world" and perpetuate a parochial view of life and women's place in it. If the "Establishment" view of Women's Studies is that of a ghetto and if a significant number of people within Women's Studies incorporate this view, then the charge becomes true and little or no change will occur in the hierarchical arrangement of men and women.

REFUGE

Berit Aas has stated that "Women live in such a different economic, cultural and social world from men that their reactions cannot be understood from a master model developed in male society."*

Yet that is what women have always been asked to do. Their reactions are most often compared to those of men, they are defined by men, and their perceptions of the world are prescribed by male definitions of the world. Where women are different, they are generally found to be wanting.

The female psychological world is seen as nurturant and submissive, the male world as assertive and dominant. When women are assertive and dominant they are defined as unfeminine; when they are gentle or nurturant they are defined as ineffective. That women concur with the male-defined view of being female is not surprising. There have been no other definitions.

The development of Women's Studies has begun to change this. Women's Studies is a place where women can begin to define themselves. It is a place where they can be assertive, gentle, and/or nurturant, and mold their own definitions of these terms. Women's Studies is a refuge from the male-defined society, a refuge where women can compare and contrast experiences and redefine and reevaluate the terms. It can also be a refuge from the battles, a place to be one's self among friends, a retreat for comfort, and an impetus for continued striving.

As Komarovsky has said: "To be born a woman means to inhabit, from early infancy to the last day of life, a psychological world which differs from the world of the man."* The refuge that Women's Studies is, can offer women freedom and a place to examine that psychological world.

---

*In Safir, M., Program Announcement for the International Interdisciplinary Congress on Women. Haifa, Israel, 1981.

Any change engenders anxiety, and as women aspire and achieve greater visibility in decision-making roles, men and women will become more anxious. Women's Studies can be a place where women can express their anxieties about themselves and their relationships, about new ways of living, develop methods of coping, try new behaviors without fear of recrimination, and to study change in themselves and others.

Of course, the danger of a refuge is that it may become too comfortable and perpetuate parochial views of life in the same manner as previously defined by men. A refuge is a place to feel comfortable, but not complacent. Women's Studies may be a refuge from the male-defined economic, cultural, and social worlds, but it should ultimately be a place to develop and attempt new models for living and learning. A refuge is needed—but is not enough.

POWER BASE

Women's Studies can be a power base for women. As men have had networks—formal and informal linkages for communicating with one another—so women are developing theirs. In addition to giving support, Women's Studies departments provide the means for women to get to know one another, and about their interests and concerns. They provide personal networks and power networks. These networks provide channels for women to use to communicate with other women about research and career goals.

Networking for employment has been found to be very important in a study of the recruitment and placement practices of employers registered at the Eastern Psychological Association (Kessler et al., 1976). It was found that 24 percent of academic employers already had someone in mind for a position for which they were interviewing. Most of the employers who were interviewed said that they filled approximately 30 percent of their positions by means of networking, that is, by personal communications. Thus, qualifications aside, it is necessary to know people, and therefore to be known, in order to get a job.

Since networking is an important facet of recruiting and employment for higher level positions, Wendy McKenna and I wanted to determine if women were systematically being excluded from positions in psychology because of a lack of these informal chains or networks (Denmark and McKenna, 1981). We did this by utilizing Milgram's small-world technique (Travers and Milgram, 1969). We sent 760 persons, both psychologists and nonpsychologists, information about a target person. The targets were all psychologists, male and female, with high or low status. We asked the 760 persons who initially received booklets to forward the booklets describing the target person to a person they knew on a first-name basis who might know the target individual. Three hundred of our chains were completed.

We found that more male- than female-target chains were completed, and that males were more likely than females to use first names. A most interesting finding was that the "gatekeeper," or person immediately preceding the target person tended to be male. When people want to reach a high-status man or woman, they turn to a man, and this is most true in the search for a high-status male. This demonstrates the power of informal networks.

Networks may be formal, operating via newsletters or official communications to an involved population. Networks can also be informal, such as word-of-mouth communications to an interested population. Networks are about employment, but may also be channels of communication about other aspects of life. This congress with its focus on the quality of life for all women everywhere is a place to establish networks that may be used to disseminate information to the women who stayed home. This will also establish networks with people whom we have never met, but with whom we have common interests and goals.

Networking in the male world is often seen as competitive. While helpful and career-enhancing, male networks are frequently used to undermine competitors and to form power coalitions for self-enhancement. This must not happen in the female world of networking. The problems women face are the same, whether they are at the top of their respective professional ladders, or close to the bottom. The issues remain the same. Women must take the model of the male world, but change it to one which is cooperative, thus allowing every person to benefit.

As women become more and more visible in business, politics, the arts, and the professions, they should make a conscious effort to make themselves visible to other younger women who may wish to choose their respective fields. The mentor system has long been operating for men; women need it too. Methods of assisting other women in employment, which are not dependent on hierarchical systems, the time-honored method of the male world, should be developed. While there may be a hierarchy involved, with established women assisting those just beginning in a field, the focus can be more on an interactive or collaborative effort. The more that women, both those who have achieved their goals and those who are attempting to achieve theirs, can understand that achievement can help everybody, the less hierarchical the system will become. If we can view Women's Studies as partly a power base for a change in systems, then we can see the part that we, as role models, have to play. We can change the perceptions of our various fields from that of authoritarian, hierarchical entities to more participatory, interactive ones. Women's Studies can enable us to expand, to learn, and respect differences as well as similarities and to look more closely at how our own discipline affects other disciplines.

Interdisciplinary networks can keep us apprised of growth and development, as well as barriers to growth, to which women in other fields may gain knowledge or give assistance. If we are able to expand our efforts in an interdisciplinary fashion, then Women's Studies can truly be a power base for change in the systems that have been operating in an authoritarian manner for so long.

These interdisciplinary networks can inform women of numbers and/or percentages of women being hired or promoted within individual fields. They can ask for assistance when discrimination seems to be operative. They can also offer suggestions when some method seems to help change some part of a hierarchical system to one which is more collaborative. They can keep women informed as to research completed and research in progress.

Another area in which Women's Studies can act as a power base is in changing what has been called "actuarial prejudice." Actuarial prejudice is a cognitive bias that causes persons to expect inferior performance from all who belong to a designated group (Kiesler, 1975). Thus, if women have always performed in an inferior manner or, in some cases never been allowed to perform, all women will be perceived as being inferior in that field. There are numerous examples of such prejudice in the research literature as well as in real life. Although deeply ingrained, there are ways to change this misperception. One is for the target group to be legitimized by people or institutions who have the power to do so. White males are seen as legitimate because of the power to hire, fire, promote, and demote individuals. These people and institutions can legitimate others. It was found that if holders of legitimate power (generally, white males) supported those with less power, the less powerful persons were legitimized (Fennell, 1978).

Women's Studies can be a legitimizing force, and provide the power base needed for change. Since it is part of an academic institution, and thus viewed, at least in some sense, as important and worthwhile, Women's Studies may help to break the long held patterns of prejudice.

This process of legitimation will affect future interactions with men. Since men, generally, have more power than women, they will be more likely to resist women's aspirations for greater power when they perceive women as powerless. Psychological studies of power have found that a person with high power who is committed to a future interaction with someone with less power, will be more cooperative than a high-power person who is uncommitted. This suggests that powerful men will cooperate more with women if they perceive them to have a power base (Slusher, 1978). It was further found that the expectation of future interaction increases cooperation. If women continue to expect and demand equality and expect to interact with men (and vice versa), men will tend to be more cooperative. The power base developed through Women's Studies, as a legitimized entity, will thus serve to enhance cooperation.

WOMEN'S STUDIES IS GHETTO, REFUGE, AND POWER BASE

In order to understand what Women's Studies really is, we must recognize the interlocking nature of the three labels: ghetto, refuge, and power base. They are not separate entities, but labels attached to different aspects of a single entity. As we ask to be recognized for our diversity, so must we recognize the diversity of those who make up the various aspects of Women's Studies.

Women's Studies should not "ghettoize" itself by insulating itself from a diversity of ideas and people. It should recognize that some sections of the "Establishment" may view Women's Studies as a ghetto, and attempt to discover ways of combatting this view. We should not allow Women's Studies to become a way to reinforce the token status of women.

Women's Studies should be a refuge, but not a "too-comfortable" one. It should offer an opportunity to be free to examine a wide range of ideas, and to study methods of change and growth. It should continue to be a nonjudgmental arena in which to try new methods of interacting with one another.

Women's Studies should become a greater power base in order to change the discipline it encompasses. Jessie Bernard has written, "We all live in single-sex worlds, and most of what we know—from history, the humanities, the social and behavioral sciences—deals with the male world. Even what we do know about the female world from male research is how it impinges upon the male world."

Every discipline must be expanded to reflect women's history, from women's perspective so that through women's own research into each of the disciplines the work becomes truly representative of all people. If we take the view that Women's Studies is a separate entity disconnected from each of our disciplines, we will truly ghettoize ourselves. If we, however, see it as a power base in which we have the power to change the authoritarian nature of the systems, then we will increase opportunities for ourselves as individuals and for populations as well.

REFERENCES

Denmark, F. L. 1980. Psyche: From rocking the cradle to rocking the boat. American Psychologist. 35, 12, 1057-65.

Denmark, F. L., and McKenna, W. 1981. The small world re-visited: Informal communications networks in psychology. Unpublished paper.

Fennell, M., et al. 1978. An alternative perspective on sex differences in organizational settings: the process of legitimation. Sex Roles. 4, 4, 589-603.

Kiesler, S., McKenna, W., Russell, V., Stang, D., and Sweet S. 1976. The job market in psychology: A study in despair. Personality and Social Psychology Bulletin. 2, 22-26.

Kiesler, S. B. 1975. Actuarial prejudice toward women and its implications. Journal of Applied Social Psychology. 5, 3, 201-16.

Slusher, E. A. 1978. Interaction and relative power. Journal of Conflict Resolution. 22, 2.

Travers, J., and Milgram, S. 1969. An experimental study of the small-world problem. Sociometry. 32, 425-43.

PART 2

HOLDING UP THE SKY

One of the most serious charges against early projects in development was that they so seriously ignored the contribution of the female world. They ignored the truth of the old Chinese saying that women hold up half the sky—and Mao's addition, that their half was heavier. The work of the female world was, for all intents and purposes, invisible as a result of the male bias in its research perspective. Ester Boserup (1970) was among the first to call attention to this anomaly, especially with respect to the work of women in agriculture. Although in 1980, 1,300 of the 2,208 billion women on the globe were rural (United Nations Secretariat, 1982), academic research attention to them has been low.

The first article in this Part summarizes the current status of scholarship dealing with women in rural societies. Naomi Nevo finds even today that the subject is still not adequately dealt with. She wonders if there really is "no curiosity concerning the effects of drought or floods, valley or mountain life, isolation or unavoidable gregariousness on the feminine psyche?" Why are rural women less familiar to us than alienated urban women? Than frustrated suburban housewives? The answer reflects the bias in those who ask the research questions and in those who fund the researchers seeking answers.

Bennetta Jules-Rosette reports in her study of Lusaka, Zambia, on rural women who migrate to cities. In contrast to such rural–urban migrants in many other parts of the world, these women do not engage primarily in domestic service but rather in small-scale entrepreneurial self-employment. She suggests a continuum model for the career patterns of these migrant women as they adapt to the urban economy. At the other end of the status scale, Eleanor R. Fapohunda describes the female career ladders in Nigerian academia. There she found, not surprisingly—due to the standardized structure of academia almost everywhere with its built-in power relations—remarkable similarity to the United States.

The next two chapters deal with domestic or household occupations. Martin Meissner, on the basis of historical data in Canada, finds that the total number of hours of work done by women has increased but that this is not reflected in monetary rewards. He asks why has this female contribution remained invisible? And why have even some feminists denigrated domestic work to the status of parasitism? He seeks the answer in a review of the literature from which he concludes that the answer is Marxian but not so much in terms of class as in gender exploitation. Margret Fine-Davis contrasts the quality of the working life of housewives and of employed married women in Ireland and finds it to be related more to socioeconomic status than to employment status per se.

Jan Pahl traces the flow of income derived from outside the home once it reaches the household and finds four patterns. These patterns may be related to life cycle, to household income level, and to the culture—occupational and ethnic—in which the household operates. More knowledge of such flows of income in the household would be useful for policy decisions dealing with poverty, welfare benefits, and contributions made by women's earnings to family living standards.

REFERENCES

Boserup, Ester. 1970. Women's Role in Economic Development. New York: St. Martin's Press.

United Nations Secretariat. 1982. Age and Sex Structure of Urban and Rural Populations 1970-2000. Prepared by the Population Division, Department of International Economic and Social Affairs.

6 WOMEN IN RURAL SOCIETIES: AN OVERVIEW OF THE STATE OF THE SCHOLARSHIP

Naomi Nevo

The identification of developing countries with rural societies is unquestionably valid but it is a fact that there are also rural women in milieux that are not necessarily those of developing countries. Although certainly not a homogeneous category, I would hypothesize that rural women in sophisticated farming systems may display specific characteristics worthy of study, particularly when compared to their urban counterparts. These two contexts of rural women—which I will label as technologically underdeveloped and technologically sophisticated are in general treated quite differently by researchers; I shall review them differently though comparatively. There is far more material on the former than on the latter mainly because, being exotic, it is a more attractive field and there are also more opportunities to study societies where social change is not only rapid but dramatic. Furthermore, official planning bodies and international organizations facilitate applied research in this context. Unfortunately it is precisely in these areas that the data on women are inadequate and/or irrelevant, and the system of collecting and analyzing them is faulty. For instance, there is a blind spot when it comes to defining work. In industrial systems, the spheres of productive labor and service occupations are well defined and well differentiated. In rural systems the answer is almost teleological in character—if women work in it, it must be service work. It is <u>assumed</u> to be unmeasurable. This lack of agreed upon criteria and the assumption that this work cannot be measured are no doubt behind much of the under-estimation of the importance of women in the rural workforce.

Where no measurement tools have been fashioned, tabulated information can only be arbitrary. The shortcomings of data on economically active females (according to country) are remarked upon by the editors of the U. N. publication <u>Rural Women's Participation</u> <u>in Development</u>, (No. 3, 1980). While this problem is also relevant to urban women it is crucial in the case of rural women.

In most official reports submitted to international bodies by governments, descriptions of the work of rural women is conspicuously absent. Indeed, until recently, even the reports of international agencies did not include a breakdown of the rural labor force by gender in contrast to reports about the urban labor force where urban women are described as gainfully employed.

The definition "gainfully employed" is the crux of the matter. Statistical tables deal with formal systems of employment which by definition deprive scholars of valuable raw material concerning the work of rural women. When the agricultural tasks are seen as an extension of the domestic role neither are quantitatively treated, again on the assumption that they cannot be so treated. There have been very few attempts to 'dissect' family labor or subject it to statistical and economic analysis. It is, of course, unpaid and that lets the analysts "off the hook." However, more and more village studies now include time-task tables from which an enormous amount can be learned about the women. Because these are strictly microdata, the statisticians, who are all macroorientated, ignore them and class the woman together with her children as consumers and dependents. Demographers are perhaps the worst sinners in this respect as many demographic forecasts show. Although editors refer to this as a serious omission it has not been rectified.

Many village studies note that women in family farming not only dominate certain branches through their labor but also sell the produce and deploy the profits as they wish. They may thus achieve a certain measure of independence. This type of economic activity occurs in diverse cultures and even where severe cultural constraints on women's behavior operate, such as among purdah women (Simmons, 1976).

Scholars investigating the many segments of social life or the variety of social institutions refer to rural women, if they do so at all, as by-products of their wider findings. Anthropologists and ethnologists are more concerned with women than are sociologists, certainly more than economists, and, surprisingly, more than developmentalists, but even they, with very few exceptions (Nelson, 1979), omit economic data[1] and their treatment is consequently superficial. Boserup's (1970) classic work did not blaze a trail. The economic dimensions of the labor of rural women—whether in subsistence or market economies—are rarely analyzed in case studies. Instead, anthropologists and ethnologists present women as elements in the structure of kinship, as participants in ritual and magic, as objects of social and cultural attitudes. In short, women are generally treated as part of the data on the social order which is under study, an approach which is also very common among the sociologists who write about power, status, and class in terms of 'men only' (Rogers, 1980).

Where a gender-based division of labor is detailed, or specific status for women noted, the explanation offered is all too often solely in terms of cultural values which many researchers and theorists would have us believe are practically immutable. The developmentalists—the planners and implementers working in rural worlds—are only too happy to hide behind the principle of cultural relativism which colors this approach, as an alibi for ignoring women in the development process. But the principle may be mistakenly held (Rogers, 1980) and its restraining influence, exerted mainly on cross-cultural change, may be dangerous. There are, after all, some basic universal conditions necessary for improving the human condition which do not in any way imply ethnocentrism. While not disputing the importance of the cultural variables governing the role of women it would surely be rewarding to examine the economic significance of these variables particularly since there are some indications that cultural codes, if not destroyed, may nevertheless be reformulated when women's economic roles change (Giovanni, 1978).

The assumptions built into research on rural women are numerous. Researchers themselves are frequently unaware of how invidious they are. Many scholars, for instance, praise the family unit as an excellent vehicle for role equality (Olin 1976). But this too, like cultural relativism, may be a mistaken and even dangerous principle to maintain. Some field workers have recorded interviews with women which undermine this assumption (Yishai, 1980). The women interviewed unwittingly show the family—or at least the nuclear family—to be a euphemism for unrewarded female labor and the woman's status as an underprivileged member of the family. The hints in some of the literature that the extended family unit is more favorable in this respect (despite some findings that it permits the exploitation of women by women) should be taken up as research options which could also include the comparison of various family structures, their correlation with different systems of property ownership in agrarian societies—and not only with the type of farming activity.

Many of the assumptions I have mentioned until now characterize the scholarship on women in the technologically sophisticated farming systems. Complementary tasks and traditional duties, family labor—these are the terms in which the gender role differentiation is examined. In this context, too, the economic importance of women's work is either ignored or underestimated. But one great difference is the paucity of material here. I have already referred to the attractions of the Third World for researchers as compared with the industrialized world. The recent renewal of interest in rural society has led to attempts to apply theoretical structures developed in urban settings to

rural areas. This may be due to the conviction of many social scientists that rural society does not differ fundamentally from urban
society. This may well be correct. However, it remains untested.
Ascertaining the state of the scholarship on rural women in the technologically sophisticated context involved a difficult search and meager
rewards. I found no village studies such as we find in other technological contexts[1], and even researchers in Israel have not studied rural
women. Needless to say, I did not cover all possible sources of knowledge on rural women in this context but perused enough to realize that
the great majority of studies rely on figures issued by official bodies
(e.g., the U.S. Department of Agriculture and the Census Bureau).
These data are biased for the same reasons that data on female labor
in other rural studies are unreliable; few attempts are made to estimate women's share in the family labor pool and there are no agreed
upon criteria of productive labor. An interesting exception to the
dearth of empirical data although it, too, relies heavily on official
statistics, is an account of the labor force patterns of mature rural
women comparing those in the labor market with those who "have no
measurable labour market experience" (Maret and Chenoweth, 1979.
See also Sweet, 1972, Pearson, 1979).

European researchers apparently find the subject of rural women
in their own society worthy of study but few research results are accessible. Papers on farm-wives, for example, are tucked away in
anthologies of women in other communities. However there is an
awakened interest in the study of rural women per se and a cross-
cultural empirical study of rural women's work comparing West Germany, France, Austria, Poland, Sweden, and Hungary has been initiated by the European Coordination Centre for Research and Docu-
mentation. Perhaps these data will cover those areas of rural women's
work which are usually assumed to be unquantifiable.

Leaving the scholarship of the continents of North and South
America and Europe, I discovered rural women in Australia. Without
doubt Australia is less urbanized than the other three continents but
it is certainly qualified to be called a technologically sophisticated
society. A series of monographs has emerged from the Roseworthy
Agricultural College in South Australia (Craig, 1979, 1980) dealing
with the entry of women into the rural work force and their increasing
participation in management, the women's role conflicts, and their
place in the class structure. Unfortunately the conclusions are largely
conjectural based on very flimsy data. As the author himself admits
" . . . not a great deal of specific research has been directed to rural
women. Even at the descriptive or empirical level, the number of
studies is very limited and very few writers have addressed themselves to theoretical issues."

The foundations of Israeli society were laid by groups of farming pioneers who were inspired by an ideology of agrarian socialism. Almost from the dawn of the collective and cooperative settlements, researchers—foreign and native—have been studying the innovative rural frameworks. The rural woman, however, is researched only if she is a member of a kibbutz, an area of rich scholarship.[2] Apart from one attempt (Appelbaum and Margulies, 1979)[3] hardly anything has been written about the women on the family farms whether in the cooperative villages (moshav), the private village (moshava), or the traditional Arab villages. From the middle 1950s onward the cooperative villages of Jewish immigrants have been studied intensively by sociologists and anthropologists (Shapiro, 1971).

Nearly all the villages researched have approximated villages in technologically underdeveloped systems undergoing a process of rapid social change. Only one of these has been studied from the point of view of the effects of change on the women (Katzir, 1976). The scholarship on women in veteran villages, the members of which operate sophisticated farming systems that achieve economic prosperity comparable to that of villages in other technologically developed contexts, has received specific attention only in one paper (Nevo and Solomonica, 1981). Although other anthropologists refer to women when analyzing inheritance, labor, and political patterns in the Israeli rural system, the subject is not a principal concern of their research (Nevo, 1979; Baldwin, 1972; Shokeid, 1971).

Some attention has been paid to the Arab woman in Israel in the many anthropological studies on settled rural life as well as on the nomadic system. Only Gillian Lewando-Hundt (1981, 1982) has chosen to concentrate on the subject. Even more surprising is the fact that although the agricultural extension services provided intensive guidance to the neophyte immigrant farmers in the 1950s and 1960s and despite field observations on women farmers, the only follow-up studies on women are in home economics—thus demonstrating that Israel was following developmentalists in accepting ideal norms of women's domestic role as real (Breiman, 1970; Katznelson, no date). Finally, it must be remarked that the one Jewish settlement type (hybrid village with a collective production system and property ownership but a private consumer system based on the nuclear family social unit) which ideologically insists that women fulfill an exclusively normative domestic role has been investigated in only two studies so far (Padan-Eisenstark, 1973; Alfassi, 1975).

The question that exercises the minds of researchers, administrators, and planners is why the women are leaving farm work and retreating to the domestic hearth, a phenomenon also found in kibbutz society. A great deal of empirical material is available and many symptomatic correlations are found—such as specialization, mechanization, and prosperity of the farm. But I would reiterate, this time in the Israeli context, the importance of adequate economic data to the formulation of a satisfactory theory on women's contribution to the labor force.

We have come full circle. From a nonindustrialized society with technologically underdeveloped rural systems to technologically sophisticated rural systems existing within an industrialized society. We find the scholarship on rural women woefully wanting in this respect as in many others.

In this overview—which does not pretend to be exhaustive—assumptions have been discarded and questions changed; some established sociological and anthropological principles have even been challenged. Unless we think in new terms, the subject of rural women will not be tackled. Despite conclusions that revised cultural interpretations reaffirm the subordination of women (Giovanni, 1978; Bourguignon et al., 1980) we should deliberately look for the conditions that indicate the contrary. For instance coercion as a context of social change has been generally neglected by researchers. Cultural restrictions on women have been lifted by governmental edicts, e.g., in Turkey. Other examples of coercive methods used to change cultural codes which subordinate women would provide significant case studies. In short, let us use our own particular bias to guide us in our research. Unfortunately the new scholarship does not display the unorthodox approach which I advocate. I suggest that scholars reformulate their assignments in order to provide planners and politicians with an effective blueprint for reform.

Although I have chosen to criticize mainly sociologists and economists the discipline does not matter. There is appallingly little curiosity about the rural woman. The alienated urban woman and the frustrated suburban housewife have become our intimate friends through research popularizations. Is there really no curiosity concerning the effects of droughts or floods, valley or mountain life, isolation or unavoidable gregariousness on the feminine psyche?

NOTES

1. Edgar Morin's study of Plodomet which, although ignoring economic aspects, at least presents us with a picture of the women as agents of modernization in village France—a phenomenon familiar to field workers in the Third World (Morin, 1970).

2. Papers, articles, books, too numerous to detail. In Hebrew and in English. The one drawback is that too many of them have been written by scholars who are themselves kibbutz members.

3. One attempt to discover the significance of women's work in the moshav is to be found in Appelbaum and Margulies, 1979, pp. 68-

75. The findings appear reasonably convincing when compared to what is observed in the field but nevertheless must be viewed with caution because the interviews were conducted with "the male owners of the farms," in itself a significant expression.

REFERENCES

Alfassi, Shulamit. 1975. La Femme au Moschav Chitoufi. Paris: Ecole des Hautes en Sciences Sociales Centre de Recherches Cooperatives.

Appelbaum, Levia, and Margulies, Julia. 1979. The Moshav—Patterns of Organizational Change. Rehovot, Settlement Study Centre.

Baldwin, Elaine. 1972. Differentiation and Cooperation in an Israeli Veteran Moshav. Manchester: Manchester University Press.

Boserup, Ester. 1970. Women's Role in Economic Development. London: Allen & Unwin.

Bourguignon, Erika, et al. 1980. A World of Women. New York: Praeger.

Breiman, Esther. 1970. "A Survey of Extension Work in Home Economics in the Moshavim." In Agricultural Extension, a Sociological Appraisal, edited by Sara Molho. Jerusalem: Keter.

Craig, R. A. Whither the Women?—Future Prospects for Farm Women in Australia, 1979; Women and the Rural Class Structure, 1979; Social Implications of a Rural Workforce, 1980; Down on the Farm: Role Conflicts of Australian Farm Women, 1979; Women and the Rural Workforce: Perceptions of their Changing Contributions, 1980; Rural Women—An Annotated Bibliography, 1980. Roseworthy Agricultural College, Roseworthy, S. Australia.

Galbraith, J. K. 1975. Economics and the Public Purpose. Great Britain: Pelican Books.

Giovanni, Maureen. 1978. "Comments," Current Anthropology, June.

Katzir, Yael. 1976. The Effects of Resettlement on the Status Role of Yemeni Jewish Women: The Case of Ramat Oranim Israel. University Microfilms International.

Katznelson, Yehiela. No date. Analysis of Activities Performed by the Rural Homemaker: Research Findings Based on Population of Cooperative Farms in Israel. Ministry of Agriculture, Extension Service, Home Economics Department, Tel Aviv.

Lewando-Hundt, Gillian. 1981-82. "From Tents to Huts and Houses—the Effect of the Process of Settlement on Negev Bedouin Women's Status." Unpublished paper presented at the International Interdisciplinary Congress on Women, Haifa, December, Symposium No. 68 Rural Women in Israel.

Maret, Elizabeth, and Chenoweth, Lilian. 1979. "The Labour Force Patterns of Mature Rural Women." Rural Sociology, Vol. 44, Winter, No. 4.

Morin, Edgar. 1970. Plodomet, Report from a French Village. New York: Pantheon Books, Random House.

Nelson, Nici. 1979. Why Has Development Neglected Rural Women? London: Pergamon International Library, Pergamon Press.

Nevo, Naomi and Solomonica, David. 1981. Ideological Change of the Rural Woman's Role and Status in Settlements and Movements Based on the Family as a Social and Economic Unit. Rehovot Settlement Study Centre, Working Paper.

Nevo, Naomi. 1979. Social Change in a Veteran Moshav Ovdim. U.S.A.: University Microfilms International.

Olin, Ulla. 1976. "A Case for Women as Co-Managers: The Family as a General Model of Human Social Organization." In Women and World Development, edited by Irene Tinker and Michele Bo Bramsen. Washington, D.C.: Overseas Development Council.

Padan-Eisenstark, Dorit. 1973. Women in the Moshav Shitufi: A Situation of an Ideological Catch. Tel Aviv University mimeograph.

Pearson, Jessica. 1979. "Note on Female Farmers." In Notes and Comment, Rural Sociology, Spring, No. 1.

Rogers, Barbara. 1980. The Domestication of Women. New York: Tavistock Publications.

Rural Women's Participation in Development, Evaluation Study, No. 3, 1980. U.N. Development Programme.

Shapiro, Ovadia, editor. 1971. Rural Settlements of New Immigrants in Israel, Rehovot Settlement Study Centre.

Shokeid, Moshe. 1971. The Dual Heritage: Immigrants from the Atlas Mountains in Israel. Manchester: Manchester University Press.

Simmons, Emmy B. 1976. Economic Research on Women in Rural Development in N. Nigeria. Washington, D.C.: Overseas Liaison Committee, September (OLC Paper 10).

Sweet, James A. 1972. "Employment of Rural Farm Wives." Rural Sociology, Vol. 37, December, No. 4.

Yishai, Yael: "Summing Up and Conclusions of Interviews with Past Students at Carmel International Training Centre 1980." Unpublished.

7 WOMEN AND TECHNOLOGICAL CHANGE IN THE INFORMAL URBAN ECONOMY: A ZAMBIAN CASE STUDY

Bennetta Jules-Rosette

The socioeconomic situation of urban women in Africa is narrowly represented by existing national and international statistics that concentrate mainly on wage employment in the formal sector. This paper analyzes the role of informal sector employment as a survival strategy for women living in the townships surrounding Zambia's capital. Further, it considers the types of technological specialization that women bring to the informal economy as part of their career patterns.

My observations are drawn from interviews with women working in four of Lusaka's townships: Marrapodi, Mandevu, Chawama, and Mtendele.[1] Underequipped by virtue of education and opportunity for the technological sophistication of urban society, many women in these townships have turned to self-employment as an option. This situation, however, is by no means peculiar to urban Zambia. Informal sector employment that requires little or no training is an outlet for new urbanites throughout the Third World, in particular women who have had few opportunities for education.

Zambia is currently the most urbanized country in sub-Saharan Africa with the exception of South Africa (cf., Little, 1974). Census data indicate that over 40 percent of Zambia's population now lives in cities and towns.[2] A preponderance of adult males living in culturally rootless but highly supervised urban settings was characteristic of the period from World War I to the 1960s in Zambia despite the rising migration of entire families and lone females in the decades directly preceding independence in 1964. Contract migrants usually sent cash back to their villages and oriented their lives toward the kin who stayed home. Meanwhile, the women who remained in the rural areas assumed the responsibilities for agricultural production and marketing (although the fruits of their labor were often turned over to the men). Women constituted an important category of potential migrants. Historical data indicate that by the mid-1950s, two-fifths of the male population of the Copperbelt had at least ten years of urban living experience, and nearly two-fifths of them brought their wives to the city (Little, 1973). These migrant populations had become stabilized in the city and had established a record of urban living experience.

In addition to the women who migrated with spouses, many came to town initially as widows and divorcees who could no longer function effectively in the village context or as single girls in search of alternative life options. They migrated to the city to earn a living just as the men had. Currently, women migrating to Lusaka outnumber male migrants. Yet, these women face significant barriers to full participation in the Zambian wage labor sector. As of 1975, Zambian Labor Exchange figures listed 45 percent of Lusaka's adult female population as unemployed and seeking formal sector jobs (Annual Report, 1969-75). Census figures compiled for Zambian rural and urban areas as of 1970 show a labor force participation rate of 71.2 percent for African men and 28.8 percent for women of all ethnic backgrounds. Labor force projections from Lusaka's Central Statistical Office (1976) record 20 percent of Zambia's population as working within the informal sector, a total of approximately 135,000 people (cf., Todd and Shaw, 1979). Of these individuals, about half are women concentrated primarily in petty trades. There is, however, a critical need to update these estimates.

These figures call into question the long-term economic benefits of development and modernity for Zambian women. It may actually be argued that certain types of technoeconomic development destroy rather than improve the living conditions of the masses of African women who have limited access to educational opportunities. Recently, the relative decline of the position of women and their increasing marginalization as a result of national economic development in Africa has been well documented (Boserup, 1970; Remy, 1975; and Mullings, 1976).

Urban Zambia offers no exception to this trend, which stems from the history of migration patterns and legal policies under colonialism. The restriction of women's physical movements and legal migration was typical of central and southern Africa generally (cf., Pons, 1956; Minon, 1960). Colonial mining and industrial concerns required the labor of men, not women (cf., Van Allen, 1974). Self-employment has emerged as a means of urban economic adjustment and survival among women. Margaret Peil's (1972) study of Ghanaian factory workers found that many postindependence factories hired only a few women in basic hand-assembly jobs. In Zambia, marketing, small business enterprises, and cottage industries are the principal outlets for urban marginals. In particular, migrant women have played

a significant role in developing informal employment networks and
strategies in Lusaka's squatter areas.

Informal sector activities in Zambia may be divided into four
basic categories: (1) informal petty trading, (2) licensed marketeering,
(3) small craft circles, and (4) cottage industries. Women participate
primarily in the first category of activities and more sporadically in
the others. Petty trading without a license is both illegal and dangerous. Women engaging in this sort of trading are not able to provide a
steady and unencumbered income for their families. Nevertheless,
because of their lack of access to educational and apprenticeship opportunities, it is difficult for these women to break the vicious cycle
of illegal, low-income trading and enter into more lucrative and stable
informal sector enterprises. Overall, women in the townships tend to
engage in home trades and petty market vending. Although I observed
some women in Marrapodi and Mandevu townships engaged in brick-
making enterprises with their husbands, they were employed as silent
assistants rather than business partners.[3]

A MODEL FOR STUDYING ZAMBIAN WOMEN
WORKING IN THE URBAN INFORMAL SECTOR

Technological change within the informal sector may be analyzed
in terms of two basic criteria: (1) the level of complexity of the task
and (2) the personnel used to complete the work at hand. Petty trading
can be conducted alone and requires no formal training if vegetable
produce or second-hand items are marketed locally. However, petty
trading introduces another set of variables in assessing informal sector activities—the legal status of the operation. The most lucrative
enterprises are those that are legal, involve high output, and service
a broad consumer audience that extends beyond the immediate local
community.

Corner stores and small businesses are also enterprises that
involve more than a minimal level of technological training. The owner
must have some familiarity with licensing requirements, quality control, formal distribution outlets, and bookkeeping. In the city, most
of these activities require some degree of literacy and familiarity with
urban economic exchange networks. It takes time for a first-generation
urban migrant to build up the experience and the capital to establish a
corner store in one of Lusaka's townships. Women can seldom do this
alone unless they are able to make urban contacts quickly and save
enough money from petty or middle-level trading to break into this
type of entrepreneurship.

On the contrary, most Zambian women in the petty trades have
difficulty obtaining sales licenses. These licenses are limited in num-

ber, and official preference is given to male household heads. Although some vegetable vendors set up mats in front of neighborhood markets, these market sales are regulated and require a health check. Consequently, those women who are squeezed out of the local markets resort to selling goods from their homes. The illegal and clandestine nature of these sales means that they must be intermittent, limiting both the regular clientele of the home traders and the profits that can be realized from sales. Home stalls are periodically raided by the police, and their owners are arrested and fined. Hence, the situation of the home traders in Lusaka contrasts markedly with that of the more lucrative West African market women who have been able to develop independent marketeers' unions and accumulate capital through credit associations (cf., Faladé, 1971; Lewis, 1976).

Women's isolation inhibits their entrepreneurship in the informal sector. Most of the activities for which women are socialized in the rural areas, including food preparation and home crafts, are based upon isolated domestic activities. In this context, they are not trained to work together in cooperative craft or marketing enterprises that have growth potential. They must learn to use these cooperative networks in the process of redirecting their skills.

The sale of homecrafts is not subject to intensive legal monitoring. While these crafts provide a valuable contribution to the household economy, individual craft enterprises hold little promise for increased autonomy among women. Quite to the contrary, my interview findings suggest that the home trades reflect women's increasing dependence on marginally employed men to make household ends meet.

As one of the most common home enterprises among township women in Lusaka, the beer trade can involve some group cooperation. It is an integral part of the transitional economy of the townships and has the added cultural significance of perpetuating home and regional ties through the beer-drinking circle or mikotokoto (cf., Epstein, 1961). Although some beer trading is legal, most township brewers have not been licensed to trade. Most of the women brewing chibuku (local grain beer) have been under government surveillance at some point, and they frequently have to close on short notice. Thus, although the beer trade meets the structural requirements of a cottage industry in terms of manpower and possible returns, the market is often limited to the local community. Furthermore, its illicit character makes production sporadic.

Other cottage industries and craft collectives rarely include women. Indigenous church women with polygynous families in Marrapodi township have profit-making home sewing circles that are labor intensive, but these are exceptional. Young men become apprentices while women remain the silent assistants in cottage enterprises with no formal possibilities for advancement.

Conversely, some women who are successful in obtaining the coveted marketeers' licenses enabling them to work outside of the home have developed community reputations and have been instrumental in organizing marketeers' unions. A few prosperous home and street traders are able to accrue enough expertise and financial backing to move into large market stalls, tea cart vending, and small restaurants or grocery stores. This sort of career pattern, however, is more typical of official market vegetable vendors, fishmongers, and home charcoal traders than it is of women individually producing and selling home crafts. The increased profits in craft sales come from a combination of potting with beer brewing. Although such a combination may be economically beneficial to migrant women, it effectively bars them from extensive public trade and confines their activities exclusively to a township area.

HOME TRADES AS URBAN ENTREPRENEURSHIP: THE CASE OF THE WOMEN BREWERS

Zambian society unofficially fosters the brewing of home beverages by placing a positive social valuation on the beer drinking circle. During the colonial period, Zambian urban migrants were denied access to imported alcoholic beverages. Moreover, the drinking circle was a significant part of village social life for men, and it was readily adapted to the urban industrial centers. In the late 1970s, the Lusaka city council legalized the controlled brewing of higher grades of chibuku for sale in taverns to increase its revenue. "Legalized" chibuku is supposedly made according to specific health regulations and is sold at fixed prices. Nevertheless, the sale of illicit chibuku and stronger beverages continues. It is punishable by a nine-month jail sentence or a fine of up to 600 Kwacha (United States $650). The association of the home beer trade with prostitution persists among Zambian law enforcement agencies. A recent survey (Mwanamwabwa, 1977) claims that 70 percent of the home-brewed beer produced in Zambia is connected with some form of prostitution.

The shebeen queens or women who brew beer for community gatherings and trade are careful to cultivate good relationships with local officials. Like the home vegetable vendors, they must be circumspect about their activities. It is not, however, possible to hide the brewing process completely, as it entails long hours of outdoor cooking before the beer can be brought inside to settle. Despite the potential official harassment, the shebeen queens do not appear to have developed collective resources for their own legal and economic protection. They cooperate in small brewing groups, but their produce and marketing are coordinated on a large scale only by the new middlemen or shebeen kings who have established networks that cross township barriers and intersect with the public bar trade.

As sporadic vegetable vending proved less lucrative, some married women in the squatter townships moved into permanent and temporary beer trading in competition with the established shebeen queens. These women, however, tend to confine their activities to the production and brewing of beer. Permanent brewers commissioned to make legal chibuku can operate openly and plan their business activities on a long-term basis. Temporary traders strictly engaged in illegal brewing rely on connections with an underground network and brew on a sporadic basis. None of the brewers whom I interviewed in Marrapodi was licensed to trade officially.

Potting and Beer Brewing as Combined Home Trades

The beer trade emerges in a fuller perspective when we consider the mixed career patterns of many women brewers. Women who pursue combined trades that incorporate brewing generally do so on a permanent basis and shift from an emphasis on one or the other depending upon economic and seasonal variations. Combining trades requires considerable familiarity with the urban scene and intersecting social networks. The women potters of Lusaka provide an excellent example of the combination of the shebeen trade with craft enterprises. As a contemporary adaptation of traditional skill, potting may be relied upon to bring in a steady although small source of revenue. The shebeen traders make the pots to be used for their weekly beer parties. Moreover, these pots and other ceramic figures are sold independently as craft articles during peak tourist seasons. In this case, the potter develops some notion of the craft articles that appeal to an outside audience while continuing to produce a basic set of pots for home use and the chibuku trade.

Generally, the more experienced master potters are able to adapt to the external tourist trade while the younger women who learn ceramic skills as part of the urban shebeen activities have difficulty diversifying their products because of lack of skill and experience. These limitations stem chiefly from their lack of knowledge of traditional potting skills. This range of adaptation is a key feature of urban potting that may be characteristic of other women's trades as well.

LEGAL AND POLICY IMPLICATIONS OF THE DATA

Employment in the formal sector depends upon educational and technical qualifications. In preindependence Zambia, mission educa-

tional efforts were focused upon men. A 1970 report of the Central
Statistical Office lists only 21 percent of Zambia's female population
as literate. It might be argued that town-born women now have increased opportunities for schooling and formal wage employment.
However, the fourth grade (formerly known as Standard II in Zambia)
constitutes the terminal educational level of many of the urban poor,
both males and females. By the time Zambian school children reach
the seventh grade (Standard VI), young women constitute only 37 percent of the school-aged population nationwide.[4] At this point, the students must pass a comprehensive examination to enter Forms I and
II of lower secondary school. The women who have not been excluded
at the lower primary levels usually drop out at this point.[5] By the
time of high school education, males outnumber females in the Zambian public schools by a ratio of almost three to one. Needless to say,
migrant women and many of their first generation daughters are excluded from reaping the benefits of higher education and the economic
opportunities that accompany it.

Some of the town-born second generation women have obtained
secondary education and specialized postsecondary training. In increasing numbers, these women are entering the formal economic
sector in clerical, secretarial, and managerial positions. As a result, they are able to develop independent lifestyles and maintain
moderately high standards of living. These subelite or white collar
women are still, however, in a relatively precarious socioeconomic
situation (Schuster, 1979).

The informal sector absorbs both school dropouts and jobless
graduates of secondary and technical schools. The transient white
collar "drifter" may well, at some point in her occupational career,
engage in informal sector employment. Official statistics indicate
that all Zambian urban women are overwhelmingly underemployed.
Similarly, the ethnographic data suggest that the employment experiences of urban Zambian women of every stratum reflect transiency,
instability, and marginal access to the benefits of modern urban life.

From the perspective of relative educational opportunities, the
informal sector appears to be a socioeconomic repository for school
dropouts, the sporadically unemployed, and the underemployed. Accordingly, those who cannot find work attempt to "make" work. A
prevalent argument to account for the economic adjustment of poor
and undereducated urban women revolves around kinship and ethnicity.
It is presumed that ethnic networks are transplanted from villages and
socially enlarged with the rural-urban migration process (cf., Gutkind,
1965). Through using these networks as resources for self-employment and mutual aid, migrant women can facilitate their socioeconomic adaptation to the city.

Lusaka's townships including the squatter areas, however, are

characterized by a high ethnic mix, with a city government policy prohibiting numerical domination by a single ethnic group. My data demonstrate that women working in the informal sector come from many
different regional and ethnic backgrounds and live in a wide variety
of family situations ranging from single parent homes to polygynous
units. Strategies of familial adaptation to town life certainly vary
based upon ethnicity. Nevertheless, the cooperative associations and
apprenticeship circles established among women marketeers and craft
workers in Zambia are not directly tied to ethnicity and appear to be
more limited than those of men from the same cultural backgrounds.

The most viable community networks are based upon local residence and the exchange of goods, ideas, and services. Some experienced women traders are able to exploit these immediate community
networks and move beyond them to consumer markets that transect
social class and regional background. Descriptive data suggest that
women's collectives and voluntary associations are far more important than ethnicity as factors in urban adjustment (cf., Little, 1978).

Isolated women in illicit home trades, however, seldom operate
on a collective basis either in terms of production or marketing. They
must retain a low community profile. In their case, extensive kin and
ethnic ties are often a liability because they result in added home responsibilities. Many squatter women attempt to maintain anonymity
and social distance from their neighbors by reason of their tenuous
legal status, transient residence in the townships, and conflicts between domestic and commercial relationships.

The innovative nature of shebeen trading coupled with crafts
derives from the structure as well as the substance of this type of
trading. Women in the shebeen trades offer a key example of "layered"
entrepreneurial career patterns in the informal sector as opposed to
sporadic single-item trading. This pattern suggests the importance
of reexamining successful informal sector entrepreneurship with respect to the combination of trading options employed rather than
merely assessing the viability of a single type of trade (for example,
vegetable sales versus fishmongering). Although it is difficult for
individual women to generate much cash, capital could be saved
through rotating credit associations of the type found among West
African market women (cf., Lewis, 1976) and through urban marketing and craft cooperatives. Similarly, women engaged in home craft
enterprises involving tailoring, knitting, or crocheting could benefit
from a collective system of generating working capital for material
and machines. Through a cooperative effort, basic working capital
and a labor supply large enough to lead to increased profits could be
developed. The domestic association of these activities, however,
discourages women from combining their technical abilities, talents,
and resources.

As formal education and employment opportunities increase for town-born women, marketeering and home entrepreneurship may decline in importance as urban socioeconomic options. The hopes and aspirations of many women in the transitional generation may be realized as their daughters gain greater access to formal educational opportunities that will allow them to reap the benefits of urban social and economic life. The Zambian case suggests that it is important to develop a model that links the career patterns of rural and urban women in development. To this end, the following methodological suggestions emerge:

(1) There is a need to structure an innovative approach to the study of African women in development that uses criteria that are both subjectively and objectively relevant to the topic by avoiding premature abstraction about the role of women in development prior to requisite field inquiries.

(2) The assembly of an adequate primary data base requires longitudinal case study materials on women's rural and urban career patterns in combination with quantitative data on migration and socioeconomic adjustment.

(3) In this regard, subject feedback is critical to collecting case study profiles that fill important information gaps concerning the life options and career choices of particular strata of urban women (e.g., informal versus formal sector workers and the urban poor versus the elite and subelite women).

(4) The present research serves as a point of departure for devising a model that integrates data on women of diverse strata in rural and urban areas as part of a comprehensive overview of women in development. Such a model may eventually be used to facilitate the inclusion of women of rural and urban backgrounds in overall strategies of national development.[6]

(5) In order for these research data to have an impact on policy, the legal implications of women's home trades and crafts need further examination. Social visibility is detrimental to women who are not licensed to trade from their homes. Yet, acquiring the expanded marketing possibilities that lead to a higher standard of living requires the visible integration of marginal urban women into projected development plans and policies.

CONCLUSIONS

Urban women in Zambia's informal sector are only part of a larger social and economic picture. The technological level of informal sector entreprises relies on community networks and resources for training new participants. Women's enterprises begin at a disadvantage because most of them are based upon an isolated, home-trade model. Collective resources and middlemen are seldom employed in purchasing basic goods, production, or marketing. Formal education is not the only solution to women's employment problems in this area. The type of apprenticeship relationships developed in men's cottage enterprises could be explored as a means of practical training for women.

The skills for successful urban survival require a breakdown of the sexually segregated and isolated activities that characterize the lives of many women who resort to informal sector employment. This discussion is intended as a resource for comparisons with similar cases in which a substantial gap persists between the technoeconomic goals of development and women's access to formal employment. There is a critical need for further investigation of the home crafts and trades with regard to the gender, technological preparation, and relative urban experience of the participants. Understanding how women of various strata adapt technologically to the expanding commercial markets of the African city is an important prerequisite for the thorough reassessment of policy issues related to the role of women in development on an international scale.

NOTES

1. My research was conducted under National Science Foundation grants nos. Soc. 76-20861 and Soc. 78-20861 from 1974 through 1979. The data from the Marrapodi and Mandevu townships of Lusaka were derived from my four-year longitudinal study of the area. The materials on Chawama township to which I refer were collected by Catherine Mwanamwabwa and assembled in her 1977 report on women's income-generating activities. Karen Hansen (1973 and 1975) has analyzed similar data on the work experiences of women in the Mtendele township of Lusaka. I have also drawn on these materials for comparison.

2. This information is based on data from the Census of Population and Housing. Central Statistical Office: Lusaka, Zambia, August 1970.

3. This problem raises questions about the relationship between marriage and informal sector employment. Hansen (1975) found that older women married for longer periods tended to engage in informal sector employment. In Marrapodi, I observed that women in polygynous households also tended to work in the informal sector (Jules-Rosette, 1979).

4. These figures are taken from Educational Statistics for 1973,

Zambian Ministry of Education, Lusaka, Zambia, 1975. Official statistics indicate a large number of dropouts after the fourth grade (from 127,390 students in grade Four to 95,350 total students in grade Five for 1973). The largest percentage of young women drop out after the sixth grade and do not continue for presecondary training.

5. While the percentage of female students in Grade 7 and Form I remained the same in 1973, total student enrollment figures dropped from 85,213 for Grade 7 to 17,570 for Form I secondary preparation.

6. In Africa, Asia, and Latin America, women among the urban poor are doubly marginal (cf., Perlman, 1976). They are physically and culturally isolated in many ways, and they tend to be excluded from both economic development plans and the central political processes.

REFERENCES

Annual Report of the Department of Labor: Zambian Population Census, 1969-1975. Lusaka, Zambia: Government Printing Office.

Boserup, Ester. 1970. Woman's Role in Economic Development. New York: St. Martin's Press.

Central Statistical Office, Government of the Republic of Zambia. 1970. Census of Population and Housing: First Report. Lusaka, Zambia: Central Statistical Office.

Central Statistical Office, Government of the Republic of Zambia. 1975. Educational Statistics for 1973. Lusaka, Zambia: Ministry of Education, September.

Central Statistical Office, Government of the Republic of Zambia. 1976. "Projection of the Labour Force 1969-84." Population Monograph No. 3. Lusaka, Zambia: Government Printing Office.

Epstein, A. L. 1961. "The Network and Urban Social Organization." The Rhodes Livingstone Journal, 29, 4: 29-62.

Faladé, Solange. 1971. "Women of Dakar and the Surrounding Urban Area." In Women of Tropical Africa, edited by Denise Paulme, pp. 217-29. Berkeley: University of California Press.

Gutkind, Peter C. W. 1965. "African Urbanism, Mobility and the Social Network." International Journal of Comparative Sociology, 6, 6: 48-60.

Hansen, Karen T. 1973. "The Work Opportunities of Women in a Periurban Township: An Exploratory Study." Unpublished doctoral dissertation, Arhus, Norway: Arhus University.

Hansen, Karen T. 1975. "Married Women and Work: Expectations from an Urban Case Study." African Social Research, 20:777-99.

Jules-Rosette, Bennetta. 1979. "Alternative Urban Adaptations: Zambian Cottage Industries as Sources of Social and Economic Innovation." Human Organization, 8, 2, Fall: 225-38.

Jules-Rosette, Bennetta. 1981. Symbols of Change: Urban Transition in a Zambian Community. Norwood, N.J.: Ablex Publishing Corporation.

Lewis, Barbara C. 1976. "The Limitations of Group Action Among Entrepreneurs: The Market Women of Abidjan, Ivory Coast." In Women in Africa, edited by Nancy J. Hafkin and Edna G. Buys, pp. 135-56. Stanford, Calif.: Stanford University Press.

Little, Kenneth. 1973. African Women in Towns. Cambridge, England: Cambridge University Press.

Little, Kenneth. 1974. Urbanization as a Social Process. London: Routledge and Kegan Paul.

Little, Kenneth. 1974. Ministry of Rural Development Extension Services Report. Lusaka, Zambia: Government Printing Office.

Little, Kenneth. 1978. "Countervailing Influences in African Ethnicity: A Less Apparent Factor." In Ethnicity in Modern Africa, edited by Brian Du Toit. Boulder, Colo.: Westview Press.

Minon, Paul. 1960. "Katuba: Étude Quantitative d'une Communauté Urbaine Africaine." Lubumbashi: CEPSI, Collection de Memoires, 10: 2-90.

Mullings, Leith. 1976. "Women and Economic Change in Africa." In Women in Africa, edited by Nancy J. Hafkin and Edna G. Bays. Stanford, Calif.: Stanford University Press.

Mwanamwabwa, Catherine. 1977. "Suggested Income Generating Activities for Women: Proposal for a Pilot Project." Lusaka, Zambia: Unpublished manuscript. August.

Peil, Margaret. 1972. The Ghanaian Factory Worker: Industrial Man in Africa. Cambridge, England: Cambridge University Press.

Perlman, Janice E. 1976. The Myth of Marginality: Urban Poverty and Politics in Rio de Janeiro. Berkeley: University of California Press.

Pons, V. G. 1956. "The Growth of Stanleyville and Composition of its African Population." In Social Implications of Industrialization and Urbanization South of the Sahara, edited by Daryll Forde. Paris: UNESCO.

Remy, Dorothy. 1975. "Underdevelopment and the Experience of Women: A Nigerian Case Study." In Toward an Anthropology of Women, edited by Rayna R. Reiter. New York: Monthly Review Press.

Schuster, Ilsa M. Glazer. 1979. New Women of Lusaka. Palo Alto, Calif.: Mayfield Publishing Co.

Todd, Dave, and Shaw, Christopher. 1979. "Education, Employment and the Informal Sector in Zambia." Urban Community Reports Series, 2, Lusaka, Zambia: Institute for African Studies.

Van Allen, Judith. 1974. "Women in Africa: Modernization Means More Dependency." The Center Magazine. Santa Barbara: Center for the Study of Democratic Institutions, May/June: 60-67.

8 THE DOMESTIC ECONOMY— HALF OF CANADA'S WORK: NOW YOU SEE IT, NOW YOU DON'T

Martin Meissner

THE CASE OF MRS. GRIFFITHS

Not far from Hope, British Columbia, in 1973, a Canadian Pacific locomotive collided with an automobile at a level crossing. Mrs. Griffiths, a passenger in the car, died a week later. Nellie Griffiths and her husband had left their home in Edmonton, for what may have been the first real vacation of their married life. After a rough time, with Mr. Griffiths in and out of work, and a Family Aid Service worker coming to the house to help "with budgeting and with cooking low-cost nutritional meals" (Mackoff, 1974:6), David Griffiths had begun to manage.

David Griffiths sued Canadian Pacific Railways. However, that matter was in the hands of the professionals. At home in Edmonton, things were going from bad to worse. It became hard to keep a job, to keep the children out of trouble, and to keep up the payments on the house. The mortgage company repossessed the house and rented it back to Mr. Griffiths. The plumbing was not working. The social workers were back.

The lawyer asked me to be an expert witness at the trial in the Supreme Court of British Columbia and to prepare an estimate of the number of housework hours that a woman in Mrs. Griffiths' circumstances would do for the remainder of her life with Mr. Griffiths; an actuary was asked to translate these hours into a monetary claim. At age 30, with a husband aged 35, and five children between 4 and 11 years old at the time of her death, Mrs. Griffiths would have done over 84,000 hours of housework until her husband reached the life expectancy for men of his age.

In his decision, Justice Mackoff reduced the amount claimed

under the Families Compensation Act for "the loss of household services accustomed to be performed by the wife, which will have to be replaced by hired services" (Mackoff, 1974:11) from $157,410 to $40,000. His reasons went as follows:

> The actuarial evidence . . . only places a dollar value on services but it does not subtract therefrom . . . the dollar cost to obtain those services. It fails to take into consideration the cost to the husband in providing for the wife's food, clothing, shelter, etc., for the period of time for which damages for the loss of her services is claimed. It also fails to take into account the contingencies of life.
> The prospects of remarriage of the husband require consideration. At the present time, realistically, the prospects are poor indeed. The plaintiff stated, "I don't think I would want to remarry." But even if he had affirmatively expressed his wish to remarry, it is most unlikely that any reasonable woman would marry this man and assume the burden of raising five children in the circumstances herein described. However, with the passage of time, as the children grow up and leave home, his prospects for remarriage, should he wish to remarry, will brighten. He is 39 years of age and his youngest child is 7. Ten years from now he will still be a relatively young man, the children will have grown up and the prospects of his remarriage will be totally changed from what they are at present. As well to be taken into consideration in such cases was the possibility of the loss of the wife's services by reason of her being incapacitated, either temporarily or permanently, because of illness or accident. Nor can it be assumed in today's society that a marriage will not terminate by separation or divorce. None of the foregoing were taken into account by the actuary and that being so, the figure arrived at is obviously not the answer to the question before me (Mackoff, 1974:12-13).

A double irony seemed at work. A man received money for the missed personal services of his dead wife, while she was paid nothing for it when alive. (Note the exclusion of conceivable money transfers to the wife from the judge's list of the costs of household services.) The improbable future wife was also not worth the money from Canadian Pacific that would have been meant for that part of Nellie Griffiths' unlived housekeeping life which she, the unlikely second Mrs. Griffiths, would perform.

The case was a "first." It introduced into Canadian courts the recognition of the full value (in hours at least, though not in money) of a woman's lifetime of domestic labor. At the same time it confirmed its worthlessness for a living wife, while granting its value for the benefit of the husband.

In one breath, almost, housework is first noticed and valued and then disappears again. It suffers that peculiar fate—now you see it, now you don't—from all sides. The magazine for women, Ms., put the phrase 'working women' prominently on its cover of May 1980, and specified inside (p. 2) who they are: decidedly not housewives. Over the full spectrum of opinion, the pervasive usage of "working," "productive," and "active" (as in "the active population") turns the domestic work of women into nonwork, the daily, year-long and life-time effort into inactivity.

ECONOMIC ACCOUNTS

Housework has not figured much in economic work, in theory or in economic accounting. On the accounting side, seven U.S. estimates from 1919 to 1970, and a British and a Swedish estimate were reviewed and made comparable by Hawrylyshyn (1976:108–11). These estimates were expressed as a ratio of the value of housework relative to the value of the GNP exclusive of housework, and averaged 34 percent. Hawrylyshyn also made three assessments for Canada with the census of 1971. The opportunity cost, the cost of replacing individual functions, and the cost of replacement by a housekeeper came to a dollar value of housework "equivalent to 39, 40, and 33 percent of GNP" respectively (Hawrylyshyn, 1978:29).

When I take my estimate of labor-force hours as the time equivalent of the GNP, and domestic work hours as equivalent to the dollar value of housework, the result is a figure of 95.7 percent, a ratio of domestic to market activity two-and-a-half times that of the average money estimates. Each of the three methods of estimating the money value of housework has built into it the social prejudices that make for different incomes of women and men. At the same time that this rare instance of economic accounting seems to give housework its proper place, it takes much of it away again in the undervaluation of women's work which underlies the wage rates used for these calculations. A similar "now you see it, now you don't" has occurred in the Marxist-feminist debate (summarized in Fox, 1980; Kaluzynska, 1980; and Molyneux, 1979), on the question of whether housework is "productive labor."

How Much Housework Does a Woman Do?

How much housework has there been, relative to other work, and how has that relation changed in the 65 years from 1911 to 1976 in Canada? In answer to the question of how much, I start with hours of work in three different ways. One of these tells of average hours spent in a week, for samples of people with different characteristics. I then go back to the court case, in order to estimate the life-time hours that one (artificially constructed) married woman would devote to domestic work. The third answer is an assembly of contemporary averages applied to the population figures for an estimate of the collective magnitude of domestic work, in comparison to nondomestic work hours, in the entire economy, and changes in that relation in past decades. These factual accounts signify that much is omitted in the "nonwork," "unproductive," "inactive" accounts of domestic work.

The first kind of account, the contemporary averages, is shown in Table 8.1. It shows a breakdown of housework into component activities, and lists the average hours spent in each by women with and without paid employment and with or without at least one child under ten years old. It also shows hours of domestic work for employed men. The table reports research results from data gathered in 1971, for 340 married couples in Vancouver. It tells us the difference that employment and young children make, and how much less husbands contribute. When excluding necessary transportation, a full-time housewife works a full-time working week of over 40 hours. In comparison, the domestic work week of employed women drops drastically, while their workload goes up, combining job and domestic work.

A Lifetime of Housework

For an account of how much time a woman might spend doing housework during her life as a wife, I have put together the life of a 'typical' woman, Molly, and her family, as a repository of population distributions. The account takes Molly through the 50 years of her married life, from the average age of first-time brides and bridegrooms (Canada, 1977:209-10) to the time when her husband reaches the age of his life expectancy (Canada, 1979:14 and 16). These 50 years contain 19 of the 22 years in the labor force which correspond proportionately to the labor-force participation rate of married women. She will have two children, for the average family size, and return to a job in the labor force after the youngest has started going to school.

Molly can expect in her married life 106,032 hours of domestic work, an average of 2,121 hours a year, a quantity similar to the 2,000 hours that a man's 50 40-hour weeks would come to. Making

TABLE 8.1: Domestic Work Hours, by Employment Status and Children Under Ten (Estimated Weekly Hours, 340 Married Couples In Vancouver, B.C., in 1971)

Activities	Housewives		Employed wives		Employed husbands
	No child under 10	Child under 10	No child under 10	Child under 10	
Cooking and meal preparation	8.5	9.7	5.3	7.2	0.7
Dish washing and kitchen	1.9	2.1	0.9	1.3	0.3
House cleaning	9.1	8.6	5.1	6.9	1.1
Laundry	3.4	3.9	1.3	1.9	0.1
Shopping	4.9	5.1	2.8	3.0	1.2
Care of children	0.7	8.7	0.2	4.2	0.7
Gardening and animals	3.5	2.6	0.8	0.0	2.5
Irregular food preparation and clothes	5.0	2.4	1.6	2.0	0.1
Repairs and sundry services	3.3	1.6	0.7	1.5	3.8
Total domestic work per week	40.3	44.7	18.7	28.0	10.5
Necessary transportation	6.4	6.4	8.7	6.9	8.8
Total including transportation					
per week	46.7	51.1	27.4	34.9	19.3
per day	6.7	7.3	3.9	5.0	2.8
(Number of cases)	(131)	(106)	(85)	(18)	(340)

these calculations with the U.S. data from Walker and Woods (1976: 52-53), the total comes to 102,382 and the annual average to 2,048 hours.

We can build up a comparison of Molly's and her husband's life-time workloads which include their estimated housework hours during the marriage and the job hours in the labor force for the years from 15 to 65, reduced according to the proportion of women and men in the labor force. I take the job week of men to be 40 hours, and of married women 35 hours. (The Vancouver time budgets have about one hour a weekday of job time less for women than for men, the result of a greater proportion of married women in part-time jobs, and in office jobs where the hours are shorter). With two weeks vacation, the job year comes to 50 weeks. Molly's job year would be 1,750 hours and her husband's 2,000. The labor-force participation rate of men 15 years and older in 1976 was 75.5 percent. Applying that percentage to the 50 years from 15 to 65 makes for a 38-year job life of Molly's husband, or 76,000 life-time job hours. A married man's domestic workday in the Vancouver study is 2.8 hours, including 1.3 hours necessary transportation (mostly journey to and from work), or 1,022 hours a year. For 50 married years, that comes to 51,100 hours. The life-time workload of Molly's husband adds up to 127,100 hours.

Molly's 22 years employment in the labor force amount to 38,500 hours, and her 50 years of housework are 106,032 hours. Her total life-time workload is 144,532 hours, or 114 percent of her husband's. (I have ignored housework that Molly and her husband might have done before marriage, and that Molly would do for herself after her husband's death, for lack of comparable data.)

We have so far the daily domestic work hours derived from contemporary time-budget studies, and the life-time working hours of one typical woman compared with her husband's. Both accounts tell us that housework is substantial in relation to labor-force job time, and that married women's share in overall working hours is large. We now turn to the working hours of the population and a history of working hours at home and on the job.

THE CONTEXT OF LABOR AND LEISURE IN CANADA 1911-76

The context of changes in working hours is defined critically by three developments in men's contribution to work. (1) The labor-force participation rate of men has dropped by 14 points from 89.6 percent in 1911 to 75.5 percent in 1976. (2) The percent of the male labor force in agriculture has declined 45 points from 51.3 percent to 6.5 percent from 1911 to 1971. (3) Weekly job hours in the nonagricultural labor force have gone down nearly 14 hours from 49.6 hours in 1926 to 35.8

hours in 1976. (These and subsequent labor-force participation data are from the Labour Force (Industries) sections of successive censuses of Canada; nonagricultural labor-force hours from Ostry and Zaidi, 1979:80; and the agricultural hours from Urquhart and Buckley, 1965:105.) All these tendencies add up to a decline in men's contribution to work. There have been proportionately fewer men at work. The agricultural labor force has shrunk (with its longer work hours of about one-third more than the nonagricultural labor force). Job hours themselves have been reduced. These facts correspond with the rosy picture of "the leisure society," characterized by fewer and fewer men (meant literally) spending fewer and fewer hours "at work," the result of automation. However, these facts are countered by other facts.

The labor-force participation rate of married women has risen dramatically from 4.5 to 43.7 percent between 1941 and 1976. According to several comparisons of earlier and more recent time budgets, the hours of housework have remained stable for wives with and without labor-force employment (Robinson, 1980). When taking housework hours to have been nearly stable, the labor-force participation of married women to have increased, and the housework contribution of husbands to remain small and unchanged regardless of different household demands, we would expect a collective increase in the overall workload of women, compared to a decline in that of men: the leisure society to be carried on the backs of women.

THE COLLECTIVE WORKLOAD OF CANADIANS

In order to estimate labor-force job hours and the hours of domestic work for each census year 1911-71, and the mid-census of 1976, we need the number of men, and of married and not married women, in the agricultural and nonagricultural labor force, that is, six categories of persons. These numbers have to be reduced by those not at work in the labor force and multiplied by the estimated weekly work hours in labor-force jobs.

No Canadian time-budget studies were made before 1965. Results of comparisons of older and more recent time budgets in the United States (Robinson, 1980:54) suggest generally unchanged average housework hours. A long series of eight time-budget studies in the Soviet Union allows an assessment of changes in housework time between 1923 and 1968. Housework hours have remained more or less the same (Zuzanek, 1979:208-09). The seemingly best approach to estimating collective hours of domestic work for the 1911-76 period was to multiply the same time-budget averages each census year by the number of married women in and out of the labor force, not married women, and married and not married men. ("Not married" in-

cludes single, divorced, and widowed, while "married" includes
separated.)

The data sources and composition of the time-budget averages
for domestic work hours are described in Table 8.2. (The Vancouver
figures for married women are weighted averages of the two categories, with or without children under ten, of Table 8.1. Necessary
transportation was excluded from these estimates, in order to avoid
distortions in the comparison of job and domestic hours.) The average
weekly hours were multiplied by the number of persons in each of the
five categories. Similarly, the weekly labor-force job hours were
multiplied by the number of persons in the six categories developed
for that purpose. For each census year, I calculated the sum of all
work hours, including domestic work hours and labor-force job hours
of women and men, calling it the "collective workload."

The contribution made to this workload by domestic work and
labor-force work, and by women and men, married and not married,
is expressed as a percentage of the collective workload in Table 8.3.
It shows that the proportionate contribution of men's job hours has
been shrinking during the period 1911-76. The major interruption to
the trend was introduced through the depression represented in the
1931 figures, and the war-time experience indicated in 1941. The collective domestic work hours of men, and all work hours of not married
women, have remained the same as a proportion of the collective workload. The proportionate contribution of married women has risen
steadily, except for wartime 1941. Since then the increase has been
produced by the greater contribution of job hours and domestic growth

TABLE 8.2: Domestic Work Hours Per Week: Port Alberni,
Vancouver, Halifax

Sex, work type, and marital status	Port Alberni 1965	Vancouver 1971	Halifax 1971-72	Average
Married women				
not in labor force	No data	42.3	48.8	45.5
in labor force	22.0	20.3	24.5	22.3
Married men	13.0	10.5	9.8	11.1
Nonmarried women	13.1	No data	16.1	14.6
Nonmarried men	9.0	No data	7.7	8.3

Sources: Port Alberni time budgets (Meissner, 1971, pp. 255
and 257); Vancouver time budgets (Meissner et al., 1975, pp. 434-
35); Halifax time budgets (Harvey and Clarke, 1975, pp. 12 and 15).

TABLE 8.3: The Composition of Working Hours in Housework and Jobs in the Labor Force of Married and Not Married Women and Men, 1911–76

Work hour category, sex, marriage and work type	1911 %	1921 %	1931 %	1941 %	1951 %	1961 %	1971 %	1976 %
Married women								
Work at home full time: domestic work hours	22.6	25.6	28.3	26.0	29.4	29.0	24.4	22.8
At work in labor force: domestic work hours	0.3	0.4	0.5	0.5	1.8	3.7	5.7	7.1
At work in labor force: job hours	0.7	0.8	0.9	1.0	3.1	6.4	9.7	11.1
Married women's workload	23.6	26.8	29.7	27.5	34.3	39.1	39.8	41.0
Not married women								
Domestic work hours	5.6	5.9	7.0	6.2	5.8	5.8	6.5	6.9
Job hours	6.4	7.2	7.8	8.3	7.2	6.3	6.9	6.9
Not married women's workload	12.0	13.1	14.8	14.5	13.0	12.1	13.4	13.8
Men								
Married: domestic work hours	6.1	6.7	7.5	6.7	8.1	9.0	8.8	9.0
Not married: domestic work hours	4.3	3.8	4.6	4.0	3.4	3.4	3.5	3.7
All men: job hours	54.0	49.5	43.4	47.3	41.2	36.4	34.5	32.5
Men's workload	64.4	60.0	55.5	58.0	52.7	48.8	46.8	45.2
Women's and men's collective workload	100.0	99.9	100.0	100.0	100.0	100.0	100.0	100.0
Domestic work hours as percent of total	38.9	42.4	47.9	43.4	48.5	50.9	48.9	49.4
Women's work hours as percent of total	35.6	39.9	44.5	42.0	47.3	51.2	53.2	54.8

in married women's labor-force participation, the housework hours (in percent) of married women working at home full time has shown a noticeable decline since 1961.

As shown at the bottom of Table 8.3, domestic work hours as a percent of the collective workload have increased throughout the period (always with the 1931-41 dip), by 12 percentage points from 1911 to 1961. They had reached 50 percent in 1961 and leveled off to within one or two percentage points since then. If one were to assess the value of economic activity in working hours (as, for example, Marx suggested one should) the domestic economy <u>equals</u> the value of the nondomestic economy.

The last row of Table 8.3 illuminates the long-term increase in women's share of economic activity, a rise by 19 percentage points from 1911 to 1976 in women's proportion of the collective workload. The increase passed the 50 percent mark between 1951 and 1961, and reached 55 percent in 1976. When expressing the relation in proportions, the spare-time gain of men <u>had</u> to be women's loss. To what extent the shift in burden was "real" can be seen in Figure 8.1, for which the collective workload hours were divided by the population 15 years and older. The central, broken line describes the experience of women and men combined, and it suggests that the working popula-

FIGURE 8.1: Weekly workload hours per person 15 years and over, by sex, 1911-76.

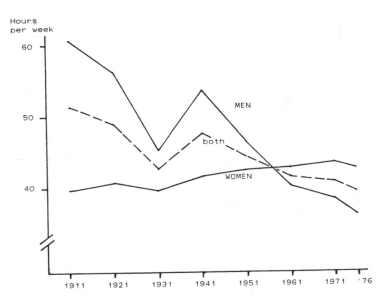

tion has profited from an 11.9-hour drop in workload hours per person from 1911 to 1976. When such a per capita workload is separated for women and men, it becomes apparent that it was only men who gained (34.7 hours less work), while women's workload increased slightly by 2.6 hours per person. Between 1951 and 1961 the workload of women began to exceed men's, and the gap has been widening ever since.

CONCLUSIONS

The estimates of working hours developed in this chapter draw attention to some important facets of the relation of housework and labor-force work, and of the work of women and the work of men. Since 1961 Canadians have been putting half of their collective working hours into the unpaid labor of the domestic economy, and half into the monied labor force. In 1971, Canada's domestic work hours were 49 percent of all working hours. In the life-time economic contributions of a typical wife and husband, a married woman's workload comes to 53 percent of the life-time work hours of both combined. From 1911 to 1976 the contributions of men in their job hours have declined, and the contributions of married women in their overall working hours have increased. Domestic working time as a proportion of all work hours has increased to 1961 and then leveled off. The working time of women as a proportion of all work hours had increased to 55 percent by 1976. Women carry more than "half of the sky," and half of the work of Canadians is not in the market economy, but in the household.

At the core of the varieties of economic activity is the domestic work of women, estimated for 1971 as 37 percent of all working hours of Canadians. This effort is being made at once visible and invisible, valued and devalued, in such critical contexts as a judgment in litigation for the value of a dead housewife; in economic accounting of the money value of housework in relation to the gross national product; and the application of Marxian value theory to housework.

REFERENCES

Canada, Statistics Canada. 1977. Canada Year Book 1976-77. Ottawa: Publications Distribution, Statistics Canada.

Canada, Statistics Canada. 1979. Life Tables, Canada and Provinces 1975-1977. Ottawa: Minister of Supply and Services.

Fox, Bonnie. 1980. "Introduction." In Hidden in the Household: Domestic Labour Under Capitalism, edited by B. Fox, pp. 9–23. Toronto: Women's Educational Press.

Harvey, Andrew S., and Susan Clarke. 1975. Descriptive Analysis of Halifax Time-Budget Data. Halifax: Institute of Public Affairs, Dalhousie University.

Hawrylyshyn, Oli. 1976. "The Value of Household Services: A Survey of Empirical Estimates." Review of Income and Wealth, No. 2 (June): 101–31.

Hawrylyshyn, Oli. 1978. Estimating the Value of Household Work in Canada 1971. Ottawa: Statistics Canada.

Kaluzynska, Eva. 1980. "Wiping the Floor with Theory: A Survey of Writings on Housework." Feminist Review, 6:27–54.

Mackoff, A. A. 1974. Griffiths et al Versus Canadian Pacific et al: Reasons for Judgment. Vancouver: Supreme Court of British Columbia. No. 29830/74.

Meissner, Martin. 1971. "The Long Arm of the Job: A Study of Work and Leisure." Industrial Relations, 10:239–60.

Meissner, Martin, E. W. Humphreys, S. M. Meis and W. J. Scheu. 1975. "No Exit for Wives: Sexual Division of Labour and the Cumulation of Household Demands." Canadian Review of Sociology & Anthropology, 12:424–439.

Molyneux, Maxine. 1979. "Beyond the Domestic Labour Debate." New Left Review, 116:3–27.

Ostry, Sylvia and Mahmood A. Zaidi. 1979. Labour Economics in Canada. 3rd ed. Toronto: Macmillan.

Robinson, John. 1980. "Housework Technology and Household Work." In Women and Household Labor, edited by Sarah Fenstermaker Berk, pp. 53–68. Beverly Hills: Sage.

Urquhart, M. C. and K. A. H. Buckley, editors. 1965. Historical Statistics of Canada. Toronto: Macmillan.

Walker, Kathryn E. and Margaret E. Woods. 1976. Time Use: A Measure of Household Production of Family Goods and Services. Washington: American Home Economics Association.

Zuzanek, Jiri. 1979. "Time-Budget Trends in the USSR: 1922-1970." Soviet Studies, 31:188-213.

9 MALE AND FEMALE CAREER LADDERS IN NIGERIAN ACADEMIA

Eleanor R. Fapohunda

INTRODUCTION

For the last 15 years, social scientists in western industrial economies, perhaps under the impetus of the Women's Movement, have been concerned with the nature and consequences of sex discrimination and occupational segregation. In this context, university scholars have focused considerable attention on the sex-linked characteristics of their own profession. Generally, in countries such as Great Britain and the United States, female university scholars are relatively few in number, are concentrated in a limited number of departments, and are, on the average, at a significantly lower rank than their male counterparts. In addition, they secure significantly lower average salaries (Williams et al., 1974; Rossi and Calderwood, 1973). In an ongoing debate, social scientists, analyzing a variety of cross-sectional and cohort data sources, attribute rank and salary differentials primarily either to objective differences in male/female characteristics or to employers' discriminatory practices (Johnson and Stafford, 1974; Regan, 1975; Loeb and Ferber, 1973).

Within Nigeria and other West African countries, social scientists, partly because of data limitations, have done little empirical work on the nature and consequences of sex discrimination in the modern public sector, which includes the universities. Similarities exist, however, between the work experiences of Nigerian female-scholars and those in other countries. For example, in 1977 women were only 6 percent of the Nigerian Academic staff and were concentrated in a few faculties, primarily Education and Arts. Further, in these two faculties, women constituted more than 10 percent of the academic staff (National Manpower Board, Federal Ministry of National Planning, 1980).

As no national data are available on Nigerian academic salary and rank differentials by gender, the purpose of this chapter is to investigate the extent of wage disparity by sex at a particular Nigerian University. Regression analysis is used to examine whether the pattern of sexual wage disparity is due primarily to overt discrimination on the part of university authorities or is rather a reflection of productivity differentials by gender. To supplement the quantitative data, this chapter draws on in-depth interviews with women scholars at the university to investigate how the role of women and the structure of families in an African society at a particular stage of economic development affect the relative productivity of female academics. The University of Lagos, one of Nigeria's older universities, was selected as the case study since the proportion of women among its staff (over 13 percent) was much higher than the national experience. [1]

In 1980, information concerning economic and rank characteristics of the University of Lagos academic staff was collected for the four faculties which employed 81 percent of all nonmedical women teachers in the university: the Faculties of Science, Social Science, Arts, and Education. [2] The sample of 36 women and 82 men included all females and a random sample of every third male in these faculties as recorded by the Faculty Welfare Office of the Registry. [3] The average salary for women (N 5, 971) was significantly lower than that for men (N 7, 158). Salary differences by sex increase with age and are greatest for those aged 40 to 49 years. These differences reflect sex differences in academic rank. Women tend to be clustered in the lower academic status ranks. Only 14 percent of the women were Senior Lecturers or above compared to 42 percent of the men. Women comprised in declining order of rank, 0 percent of the Associate Professors, 13.9 percent of the Senior Lecturers, 36 percent of the Lecturer I, and 42.8 percent of the Lecturer II categories.

Thus at the University of Lagos, as in universities of industrialized countries, the average salary of female academics is significantly lower than that of their male colleagues. The lower average female salary has important implications not only for reasons of equity, but because within a Southern Nigerian context, women and men are usually jointly responsible for family finances (Fapohunda, 1978). Items of expenditure such as furniture or children's clothes tend to be gender specific.

ANALYSIS OF AVERAGE WAGE DISPARITY BY SEX AT THE UNIVERSITY OF LAGOS

A Nigerian university's staff is paid according to the unified salary structure of the Nigerian Civil Service. [4] The salary structure consists of a ladder of fixed salary grades with corresponding salary scales. Each of the academic ranks from Graduate Assistant to Professor is assigned a given salary grade. Each grade has a varying number of step increments which are awarded yearly based on satisfactory service. For example, Associate Professor, grade level 15, has a base salary of N 9,168 and three-step increments of N 320. An individual can proceed from salary grade 08 (Graduate Assistant) to 13 (Senior Lecturer) either by promotion from within or appointment from without the university. An individual in the university can advance to grade level 15 (Associate Professor) or to level 16 (Professor) by appointment only if there are vacancies. Appointment involves an advertised open competition for the post. The candidates' academic papers are sent for evaluation by outside experts and they must present themselves for an interview.

A candidate's suitability for promotion or appointment is determined by the University's Appointment and Promotions Committee upon the advice of the concerned faculty's dean. Each candidate is assessed according to an explicit weighting scheme totaling 100 points. The major factors evaluated in the weighting scheme are a candidate's recognized publications, his teaching responsibilities, and academic qualifications. To be promoted or appointed to a post, a candidate must achieve the minimum aggregate number of points associated with the position. For high ranking posts, a minimum score under the category "recognized publication" is required by university regulations. (University of Lagos Regulations Governing Service Senior Staff No. 5, March 1978:14.)

The salary for Nigerian University academic personnel is determined by rank. Men and women are paid the same salaries for the same rank. The average salary disparity occurs because women are clustered in relatively lower academic ranks than men. The question arises whether clustering occurs because of discrimination or as a result of productivity differences between the sexes. Are women being denied opportunities for promotion by male administrators and male-dominated committees who interpret and apply the criteria for promotion and appointment?

In trying to explore this issue, it will be first hypothesized that men's and women's academic rank can be predicted by the same structural equation including as independent variables years of experience, the number of recognized publications, and highest academic degree held. These three variables account for 55 percent of the total maximum points used in promotion decisions. Data for other promotion criteria such as information on current research and contributions to the university community are not readily available. Moreover, it was not possible to consider quality dimensions of publications. The regression equation is of the form below: (Malkiel and Malkiel, 1973:703).

$$S = a_0 + a_1 \, Ex + a_2 \, Ex^2 + a_3 \, Pu + a_4 \, Qu + E,$$

where S = academic rank (range: 1 to 7); Ex = years of work experience (at a university or recognized equivalent institution); Qu = qualifications (dummy variable: has Ph. D. degree or not); Pu = number of recognized publications (a weighted dummy variable: it takes the value 1 if the individual has no recognized publications. Each journal article is weighted 2 points; each book 3 points); and E = error term.

According to the regression results, 66 percent of the variance in male academic rank can be explained by three productivity variables: experience, publications, and qualifications (Table 9.1). Similarly, the equation for women explains 60 percent of the variance.[5] In addition, for men the experience and publication variables are significant at the 99 percent confidence level; the qualification variable is significant at the 95 percent confidence level. However, for the women staff only the publication variable is significant at the 99 percent confidence level. Therefore, the hypothesis that the equations to predict academic rank by gender are the same can be rejected as they do not have the same coefficients for all variables. Structural differences in the rank predicting equations may be regarded as a priori evidence of discrimination.

As the rank predicting equations for men and women are different, they can be used to estimate an upper limit for the extent of discrimination. The strategy is to calculate the actual male and female average status from their respective equations. The gross difference in the average rank by gender can be then broken down into two components: (1) the difference in average rank attributable to differences in average characteristics, and (2) the residual difference not ac-

TABLE 9.1: Estimates of Equations to Predict Academic Status by Sex

Status	a	Ex	Ex^2	Pu	Qu	R^2
Males	1.3206	0.2818[b] (3.1113)	-0.0067 (-1.3029)	0.0300[b] (3.3097)	0.4247[a] (2.3870)	0.66
Females	1,4666	0.2245 (1.8051)	-0.0093 (-1.2326)	0.0636[b] (3.9584)	0.4787 (1.9389)	0.60

[a], significant at 95 percent confidence level.
[b], significant at 99 percent confidence level.
( ), t value.

counted for by variation in average characteristics and consequently attributed to discrimination (Malkiel and Malkiel, 1973, p. 700).

Since status discrimination exists only if women with the same characteristics as men receive lower salaries, the estimated female status is calculated by applying the vector of the mean female productivity characteristics to the male status predicting equation (Table 9.2). Thus, the gross difference in average rank (Male Actual-Female Actual) can be broken down into:

(1) Male actual-female estimate/the difference in average rank attributed to differences in average productivity characteristics; and

(2) Female estimate-female actual/the residual not accounted for by characteristics, thereby indicating discrimination.

TABLE 9.2: Mean Values of Independent Variables in Academic Status Prediction Functions by Sex

	Male average	Female average
Qualifications	1.65	1.39
Experience	8.13	6.69
Publications	10.30	6.42

The statistical analysis of rank differentials shows that 89 percent of the gross difference in rank by gender can be attributed to a difference in mean productivity characteristics.[6] The unexplained residual, 11 percent of the gross difference, can be attributed to discrimination. However, as some of the productivity variables were omitted or their quality dimensions unaccounted for, the adjusted residual would be smaller. The analysis, therefore, shows that when productivity variables are considered, discrimination plays a small part in explaining rank differentials by gender at the University of Lagos.

NIGERIAN WOMEN'S ROLES, FAMILY STRUCTURE, AND ACADEMIC PRODUCTIVITY

The results of the statistical analysis were corroborated by in-depth interviews with 15 female lecturers drawn from the original sample.[7] Only four of these women felt that they had experienced sexual discrimination during an employment interview or a promotion review.

Underlying the previous statistical results was the fact that on the average women publish less than men. In a fundamental sense, women's academic productivity is influenced by the social definition of women's roles in a particular country and by the structure of families at a given stage of economic development. Within a Nigerian context, the importance of these factors in explaining academic productivity differentials is highlighted by the 15 women interviewed. To understand their responses, however, it is first necessary to briefly describe traditional family organization in Southern Nigeria.

In the subsistence agricultural economy of Southern Nigeria, the main institution for economic security was the extended family. The extended family communally owned the land, provided agricultural assistance, and guaranteed aid in time of adversity. Within the family, power and access to economic resources, including leisure time, varied by gender and age. The males of the family, particularly the aged, held respected and privileged positions. The male elders arranged marriages to provide for the continuity of the family. Marriage was seen as a union of two extended families for the primary purpose of producing children.

In theory, upon marriage a woman became part of the husband's extended family. In reality, she was viewed as a member of a different family. Moreover, she actively maintained her ties to her own lineage by exchanging gifts and by attending ceremonial occasions. In times of marital dispute, disruption, or death, a woman would look to her own lineage for solace. Under this system, the emotional bond between spouses was deliberately depreciated in order to promote the solidarity of the larger family.

Spouses provided socially defined goods and services for each other. The division of labor within the conjugal unit was strictly defined by gender. A woman was expected to engage in remunerative activities as well as domestic tasks. She had the independence to undertake her work activities without hindrance and to use her gains freely at her own discretion. Women often engaged in trading activities that, at times, required long distance travel. Women were expected to provide for some of their own and their children's expenses. To support a woman's work effort, members of the extended family provided child care services. At times, children would be sent to live in the homes of relatives. Traditionally, women were encouraged to have and also desired many children. Children provide a woman with a social position, care in old age or sickness, and emotional happiness often missing in the marital relationship.

Nigerian female academics have been exposed to Western ideas about marriage and the family during their education and training, often at foreign institutions. Their expectations and behavior, however, are best understood as a continuation of traditional norms and roles with some modification. Generally, the Nigerian female lecturers in the sample said they had expected to work outside the home from early childhood. As one lecturer succinctly stated, "You go to school to prepare for work. You are expected to work. Nigerian men do not earn enough to support the family." Nine of the fifteen interviewed women stated that they work for economic reasons including the desire for economic independence.

The great majority of Nigerian female scholars are married with children. Of the total sample of 36 University of Lagos female lecturers, 34 women were married. Two were divorced. The interviewed 15 women had an average of 3.6 children and wanted an average of 4 children. Many of these women had their children and reared them during their academic training and work experiences. Eleven women had been married while undertaking a master's program; seven of these had children. Six of the fifteen had been married with children while completing their Ph.D. degrees. Only two women ever took time off from their academic work to have or rear children. Both women left the academic labor force for a period of less than one year and, significantly, both were foreigners married to Nigerians.

Within traditional society, motherhood is the main culturally valued role for women. A woman without children to care for and train was considered to be a cursed individual and in many ways a social outcast. The women in the sample were asked to rank their occupational, maternal, and marital roles in order of their importance to themselves. Eight of the 13 women with children ranked the maternal role first. No one ranked the occupational role first. The majority listed maternal, marital, occupational roles in descending order of importance. Subsequently, the women were asked to rank these same roles in terms of their ability to fulfill their respective responsibilities. The majority (62 percent) said that they were best able to fulfill their maternal responsibilities as compared to the requirements of their marital or occupational roles.

Although the majority of the interviewed women ranked the maternal role as being most important to them, they expressed high motivation in terms of their academic careers. Sixty percent of the women expected to achieve the rank of professor within a specified period of time; 27 percent had no goal orientation in their academic career; and 13 percent expressed an accommodated goal orientation. The accommodated group could not see themselves rising above the grade of Senior Lecturer because of family responsibilities. As one lecturer stated, "Originally I defined myself as a lecturer and I saw this as the most important thing. Now my image has changed, lecturing is only part."

As maternal activities are of great importance to Nigerian female lecturers, they are forced to try to integrate these activities with their occupational activities. A traditional family division of labor in which the wife is primarily responsible for the home and children persists in the homes of female lecturers. Of the 13 married women interviewed, 9 claimed that their husbands did not help them at home.

In the past, Nigerian working women did not experience problems of role conflict; given the nature of their work, they could bring their children with them to the fields or markets. At times, a member of the extended family acted as a mother surrogate. The child care support of the extended family system, however, has been deteriorating with urbanization and economic development. Aged parents are unwilling to remain in cramped and lonely Lagos for long periods of time to take care of their grandchildren. In the past, poorer rural relatives' children were sent to live and work in the homes of their Lagos kin. These working children helped with the care of their relatives' children while perhaps receiving some educational or vocational training. Since the federal government initiated the Free Primary Education scheme in 1976, rural parents see new opportunities for their children and are reluctant to follow old practices (Fapohunda, 1982:279-80). At the same time, economic growth has generated better paying jobs that offer more freedom to youths who otherwise would have sought employment as household helpers. Women lecturers are, therefore, finding it increasingly difficult and more expensive to hire dependable female household help to care for preschool children on a permanent basis. One lecturer, unable to find household help for a substantial period of time, explained, "I have a set of twins, twelve months of age. I carry them to work and ask one of the cleaners or messengers to stay with them in my office or in the common room while I teach."

Sick children pose additional problems for female lecturers as the vast majority claimed that it was their responsibility to take a sick child to the university health center. A visit to the health center is a time-consuming activity as the center is understaffed in relation to the size of the population it serves, a condition not unique to the university. Nine of the female lecturers claimed that they spent more than two hours each time they visited the health center. As the female lecturers have several children, they can make many trips to the health center in a three-month period.

Moreover, the lack of a dependable technological infrastructure limits the women's household productivity. For example, a poor electric power supply forces the women to go often to the food markets. Further, they spend much time getting to the markets because of poor traffic control. The women, in addition, have to spend a great deal of time in the markets because they are poorly organized. As one woman explained, ". . . shopping takes a lot of time and tires me out."

At Nigeria's level of economic development, personal relations and connections through the extended family or friends are important in solving the problems of daily emergencies. Academic women must invest time in solidifying social relationships by helping with and attending the social ceremonies of family and friends. Ten of the interviewed women attended at least one social ceremony during the three months prior to the interview. Of these women, three attended three or more ceremonies. Eight of these ceremonies involved traveling outside of Lagos. In addition, the academic women are involved in other activities to help members of the extended family. One female lecturer commented, "When relatives come to stay, I am involved in seeing that they are taken care of. Also, I ran around trying to get his brother (a member of the extended family) admitted into the university several hours a day for a couple of weeks."

Many of the interviewed said that their status as married women adversely affected their research activities. Nine explained that their family responsibilities limited their ability to travel to conferences or for research purposes. Nine women also stated that such duties limited the time they had to devote to the professional literature.

The majority of the interviewed women felt that their male colleagues were more productive principally because they had more time and fewer responsibilities.[8] In highly industrialized societies, urbanization with its network of economic, social, and personal services and modern technology has greatly reduced the number of instrumental tasks performed by women in the home. In Nigeria, academic women have taken on an additional time-consuming role while still expected and often required to meet all the responsibilities of women's domestic roles in a largely traditional society. Perhaps then the emphasis should not be on how much more productive Nigerian male scholars are compared to the females, but rather on how productive the academic women are, considering the problems of role incompatibility and severe time constraints which they face.

NOTES

1. According to the <u>University of Lagos Calender 1979-81</u>, 62 of the permanent nonmedical teaching staff of 462 were women.

2. These data were gathered by Adesikeola Olateru-Olagbegi under supervision of the author as part of her senior essay in the Department of Economics, University of Lagos, from the Welfare Office and Bursary of the University.

3. The sample included only permanent, noncontract staff of teaching departments.

4. In 1982, a separate new salary structure for the universities was implemented by the Nigerian government.

5. Adesikeola Olateru-Olagbegi programed the calculations.

6. ANALYSIS OF SOURCES OF SEX DIFFERENCES IN STATUS

Status	Percent of Gross Difference
M actual = 4.1785	
F estimate = 3.6888	
F actual = 3.6259	
Gross difference = 0.5526	
Difference due to characteristics	
M actual - F estimate = 0.4905	88.76
F estimate - F actual = 0.0629	11.38

7. These women were asked open-ended questions by the author in September 1981 concerning their occupational motivations and expectations, work experiences, family arrangements, and use of time.

8. Of the 15 interviewed women 11 thought men were more productive. Of the 11 women, 8 attributed this to the fact that men had more time and fewer responsibilities.

REFERENCES

Fapohunda, E. R. 1978. "Characteristics of Women Workers in Lagos: Data for Reconsideration by Labour Market Theorists." Labour and Society, 3(2):157-71.

Fapohunda, E. R. 1982. "The Child-Care Dilemma of Working Mothers in African Cities: The Case of Lagos, Nigerian." In Women and Work in Africa, edited by Edna G. Bay, pp. 277-88.

Federal Republic of Nigeria, National Manpower Board. 1980. Study of Nigeria's Manpower Requirements, 1977. Lagos: Federal Ministry of National Planning.

Johnson, G. E. and F. P. Stafford. 1974. "The Earning and Promotion of Women Faculty." American Economic Review, 64(6): 888-902.

Loeb, June W. and Marianne A. Ferber. 1973. "Representation, Performance and Status of Women on the Faculty at the Urbana-Champaign Campus of the University of Illinois." In Academic Women on the Move, edited by Alice S. Rossi and Ann Calderwood. New York: Russell Sage Foundation.

Malkiel, B. G. and J. A. Malkiel. 1973. "Male-Female Pay Differentials in Professional Employment." American Economic Review, 63(4):693-705.

Regan, Barbara B. 1975. "Two Supply Curves for Economists? Implications of Mobility and Career Attachment of Women." American Economic Review, 65(2):100-7.

Rossi, Alice S. and Ann Calderwood, editors. 1973. Academic Women on the Move. New York: Russell Sage Foundation.

University of Lagos. 1978. Regulations Governing Service Senior Staff No. 5. March. Lagos: University of Lagos.

Williams, Gareth Tessa Blackstone and David Metcalf. 1974. The Academic Labour Market: Economic and Social Aspects of a Profession. New York: Elsevier.

10 THE ALLOCATION OF MONEY WITHIN THE FAMILY

Jan Pahl

Clap hands, clap hands for Daddy to come,
Daddy's got money and Mummy's got none.

Traditional British nursery rhyme

Traditionally the family has been construed as a sort of black box, within which the resources acquired by individuals are assumed to be shared with members of the same family living within the same household. One aim of this chapter is to open up the black box, in order to investigate some of the social processes involved in the flows of money within households. Money enters the household in a number of different forms, for example, as wages and salaries, as social security payments, as gifts, interest on savings, or rent from property owned. It leaves as payment for a whole range of household expenditure, in the form of cash and checks, hire purchase, and credit card payments, and so on. Thus both at the point when it enters and at the point when it leaves the household it is effectively in the hands of individuals. What happens between these two points? What form do flows of money within the household take? And what do we mean by control and power in this context? This chapter represents an attempt to answer these questions.

FINANCIAL ARRANGEMENTS WITHIN HOUSEHOLDS

There is an infinite variety of different allocative systems within the great variety of types of households. This chapter will focus on that particular household type which is composed of two parents and their

dependent children. The word "family" will be used to describe the
group of people living in such a household, though of course households
can take many forms other than this one type. The chapter will also
differentiate four different types of allocative systems. I shall draw
on my own and other research to indicate the differences between the
four systems and to discuss the implications of each system for individual members of the household. [1]

At the onset it is important to make a distinction between control, management, and budgeting. [2] Control is concerned with decisions such as which allocative system should be adopted within the
household, which spouse should have final say on major financial decisions, and with the extent to which spouses have control over personal spending money of their own and access to joint money. Management is concerned with putting into operation the particular allocative
system which the couple has adopted. Household expenditure takes
place within a number of different categories, such as food, fuel,
clothes, rent or mortgage, insurance, transport, leisure activities,
and so on. The management function can extend over all of these categories, or it may be confined to just one or two. Budgeting is concerned with spending within expenditure categories. In the four-part
typology outlined in this chapter, the criteria that distinguish one
allocative system from another are essentially related to management.
Two other criteria are central in distinguishing one allocative system
from another: these are, first, each individual's responsibility for
expenditure between and within expenditure categories, and second,
each individual's access to household funds, other than those for
which he or she is responsible.

The Whole Wage System

In this system one partner, usually the wife, is responsible for
managing all of the finances of the household and is also responsible
for all expenditures, except for the personal spending money of the
other partner. The personal spending money of the other partner is
either taken out by him before the pay packet is handed over, or is
returned to him from collective funds. If both partners earn, both pay
packets are received and administered by the partner who manages
the money. Where a whole wage system is managed by a husband, his
wife may have no personal spending money of her own and no access
to household funds. The whole system is also known as the "tipping up
system" (Barrett and McIntosh, 1982).

The Allowance System

In the most common form of this system the husband gives his wife a set amount and she is responsible for paying specific items of household expenditures. The rest of the money remains in the control of the husband and he pays for other specific items. Thus each partner has a sphere of responsibility in terms of household expenditures. If a wife does not earn she has access only to the 'housekeeping' allowance and, since this is allocated for household expenditures, she may feel that she has no personal spending money of her own; the same phenomenon can also be seen in the case of the whole wage system where the wife is responsible for all family expenditures but has no personal spending money. The allowance system has many variations, mainly because of the varying patterns of responsibility. At one extreme a wife may be responsible only for expenditures of food; at the other extreme she may be responsible for everything except the running of the car, and the system may come close to resembling the whole wage system. The allowance system is also known as the "wife's wage" and the "spheres of responsibility" system (Barrett and McIntosh, 1982).

The Shared Management System

The essential characteristic of this system is that both partners have access to all the household money and both have responsibility for expenditures out of that pool. The partners may take their personal spending money out of the pool. On the other hand one or both of them may retain a sum for personal spending; when this sum becomes substantial the system begins to acquire some characteristics of the independent management system, which is described below. Usually there is some division of responsibility in management such as she does the shopping and he pays the bills.

The Independent Management System

The essential characteristic of this system is that both partners have an income and neither has access to all the household funds. Each partner is responsible for specific items of expenditure, and though these responsibilities may change over time, the principle of keeping flows of money separate within the household is retained. Expenditure responsibilities may change over time while the principle of the separation of flows of money is retained.

THE POLITICS OF DOMESTIC BUDGETING

What are the variables that determine the allocative system adopted by any one couple at any one time? What are the implications for the couple as a whole, and for individuals, of adopting one system rather than another? The rest of this chapter considers these issues, particularly in the context of the relationship between the distribution of power and the distribution of money within the marriage.

Previous work done in Britain and Australia suggests that there are three main variables in determining the allocative systems adopted by couples. These are the income level of the couple, the sources of their income, and the normative expectations of the culture within which the household is located.

The Income Level of the Couple

Most commonly, couples whose income is low, by comparison with average incomes in their society, are most apt to be using the whole wage system, managed by the wife. An increase in household income, however, is related to a change in the allowance system and a greater involvement of the husband in management of the family finances. This finding suggests that a couple's position in the socioeconomic structure is central in patterning relations within the domestic sphere: if middle income levels are associated with a change to the allowance system, this may mean that greater affluence for the couple leads to greater inequality between the husband and the wife. Stearns (1972) has documented the changing patterns of working-class life in Britain between 1890 and 1914. His work suggests that "As wages advanced men took the bulk of the gain for themselves and abandoned the traditional pattern of turning most of their income over to their wives for family use."

Middle income levels, however, are also the point at which pooling systems become common. It is likely that a couple's choice of allocative system at the middle income levels reflects normative assumptions, especially on the part of the husband, about the nature of marriage. Higher income levels, on the other hand, are associated with the independent management of financial resources, especially when both partners are earning. Researchers from different parts of the world have confirmed these associations between income levels and allocative systems (Edwards, 1981a & b; Gray, 1979; Hunt, 1978; Pahl, 1980; Rubin, 1976; Sharma, 1980; Stebbing, 1982; Whitehead, 1981). However, income level is just one of the variables with which we must be concerned.

The Sources of Income for the Couple

This heading covers both whether the income is drawn from un-employment or from social security, and the question of whether it is earned by one or both spouses. There is some evidence to suggest that when a household income is drawn from social security it is more likely that financial management will be in the hands of the wife; how-ever, it is possible that this is a product of low income level rather than income source (Land, 1969).

One clear conclusion is that when wives earn in their own right they are more likely to have a measure of power over the spending of the money. However, this power is still shaped by ideologies about the nature of marriage, as held by both the husband and by the social worlds in which they live (Evason, 1982).

Normative Expectations about the Allocation of Money

These expectations may be embedded in the socialization of hus-band or wife or both; they may be held to by the couple's social net-work or the local community, ortthey may arise out of the occupational structure of the local labor market. Edwards (1981a or b) suggested that many wives perceived their husbands as being 'rightfully' in con-trol of family finances, and there is a substantial body of evidence testifying to the deferential dialectic in which wives are seen as sub-ordinate to their husbands, largely because of their financial depend-ence (Bell and Newby, 1976; Hunt, 1978). Cass (1978, p. 30) has noted that while paid employment and a measure of economic power may constitute a base for confidence and independence:

the wife's inclination towards deference may not be
affected by her work experience, particularly if she
is involved in a relationship of authority and deference
in the work place.

Work in the United States has shown that 'contemporary' atti-tudes toward the female role are associated with a greater involve-ment by the wife in the management of family finances (Green and Cunningham, 1975). British communities studied have documented the ways in which the expectations of occupational cultures can be translated into patterns of allocation of money within the household; thus a strongly male occupational culture may express itself in heavy drinking after work which necessitates male control of finances, while in areas of traditional female employment, women are more likely to control financial affairs. Thus normative expectations can structure the power of individuals within marriage; it is to the question of power and its relevance to this issue that we now turn.

POWER AND MONEY AND THE STRUCTURING OF INEQUITY WITHIN MARRIAGE

Work on inequity, and on the distribution of power and advantage, has pointed to money as a key element. I shall argue that in societies in which money is a source of power, and income and wealth are central expressions of advantage, the relative economic positions of husband and wife must be reflected in their relationship. Conversely, it is likely that the balance of power between husband and wife will be reflected in their control over economic resources.

Most studies agree in finding a positive correlation between level of income and responsibility for decision making. Typically the greater the proportion of the household income which a spouse brings to the household, the greater part will that partner play in decision making. The husband's marital power increases as his income increases, and it is highest at that stage in the life cycle when the wife is at her most dependent; when she is engaged in looking after young children and is not earning. The wife's power relative to that of her husband increases when she is earning (Blood and Wolfe, 1960; Lupri, 1969, Kendel and Lesser, 1972; Bahr, 1974; Oppong, 1981). Other studies have demonstrated the importance of capital or land in strengthening women's power within the household (Salamon and Keim, 1979; Gasson, 1980). Advances in the understanding of marital power have been built on both resource theory and social exchange theory, and both lines of thought have pointed to economic resources as the single most important source of power. It must not be forgotten that other resources, such as prestige, force, and likeableness, are also very significant, and that many other qualities, such as respect, fear, and love influence what goes on within families and within marriages (Scanzoni, 1979; Cromwell and Olsen, 1975).

It is clear that it is impossible to make a straight connection between making decisions and holding power, between handling money and gaining in power by so doing. Indeed, being able to off-load certain decisions and certain money-handling chores onto the other spouse can itself be a sign of power. For this reason it is important that we cease to regard the household as a unit through which resources flow unimpededly; instead we need to look at particular points in the flow and at the social and economic relationships which structure the control that different members of the household have over the flow at each point.

A problem is posed by those wives who appear to have great power in financial matters and within the household, but who also appear to lack power by comparison with their husbands and in the world outside the domestic setting. As an example of this we might consider the Japanese marriages documented by Morsbach (1978) in

Corbin's The Couple. Morsbach describes the typical pattern as one in which the husband hands over his entire salary to his wife and expects her to administer the financial affairs of the household. This pattern is said to have its origins in the samurai traditions: since men in that class seldom bothered themselves with money matters, it was up to their wives to balance the income and the expenditure. As it was below a man's dignity to involve himself in the woman's sphere, her authority inside the home was rarely challenged. The powerfulness of women within the home was in sharp contrast to their powerlessness, outside it. A married woman was expected to subordinate her interests to those of her husband, even to the extent of accepting his concubine's children as his heirs if she were unable to bear children herself. The Japanese example is only one of the many which could have been taken to make the point about the crucial difference between power that is confined to intra-household issues and power that can be wielded in broader areas of social life (Rosaldo and Lamphere, 1974; Pahl, 1983).

It seems that a high degree of separation between control and management is associated with a rigid separation of spheres in terms of the sexual division of labor. In the traditional whole wage system the husband earned the money and delegated to his wife the chore of managing it; when money is short, managing and budgeting become chores rather than a source of power within the household. In the Japanese household described by Morsbach a similar pattern prevailed. The wife had the appearance of holding power through management of all the family finances, but in broader terms this power was largely illusionary. The illusion, in both these examples is based on the fact that the household within which the wife exercises power is ultimately not important, not a powerful location. Either power is located elsewhere, in the public as opposed to the private sphere, or, as in the case of the whole wage system, it is not located in those particular households because of their disadvantaged position in the overall class system.

CONCLUSIONS

Finally, it is important to see the relationship between patterns of allocation and patterns of inequality within marriage in terms of social processes which may change over time. Much social and economic policy at the present time is based on the assumption that the "normal" family is composed of the breadwinner husband and a dependent wife—what Poster (1978) called the "bourgeois family." Similarly, much popular thinking about the allocation of money within the household appears to regard the "housekeeping allowance" as the normal form for money transfer to take. It may be that one particular historical configuration, at its most powerful among the middle classes in the first half of the twentieth century, has molded thinking on the topic. This configuration was characterized by the dominance of the bourgeois family form, by a high degree of segregation between husband and wife, limited opportunities for women to earn in their own right, a rising standard of living which gave rise to the existence of financial "surpluses" in family budgets, and the predominance of the allowance system.

Thus, it is perhaps significant that we are now seeing both a new surge of interest in the allocation of money within a household, and a demand for disaggregation of financial arrangements within families, both an increase in the contribution married women make to the family budgets and a decrease in the predominance of the allowance system.

NOTES

1. The research on which this paper is based was funded by the Social Science Research Council and the Joseph Rowntree Memorial Trust. For further details about the research and about the findings, contact Jan Pahl, George Allen Wing, University of Kent, Canterbury, Kent, CT2 7NF, England.

2. For this distinction, and for much else, I am very grateful to Meredith Edwards, of the Canberra College of Advanced Education. Her generosity in sharing ideas and information makes her the best of colleagues.

REFERENCES

Bahr, J. 1974. Effects on power and division of labour within the family. In Working Mothers, edited by L. W. Hoffman and F. I. Nye. San Francisco: Jossey-Bass.

Barrett, M., and McIntosh, M. 1982. The Anti-Social Family. London: Verso Editions.

Bell, C., and Newby, H. 1976. Husbands and wives: the dynamics of the deferential dialectic. In Dependence and Exploitation in Work and Marriage, edited by D. Leonard Barker and S. Allen. London: Tavistock Publications.

Blood, R. O., and Wolfe, D. M. 1960. Husbands and Wives. New York: The Free Press.

Cass, B. 1978. Women's place in the class structure. In Essays in the Political Economy of Capitalism, edited by E. L. Wheelwright and K. Buckley, Vol. 3. Sydney Book Company.

Cromwell, R. E., and Olsen, D. 1975. Power in Families. New York: Wiley.

Edwards, M. 1981a. Financial Arrangements within Families. National Women's Advisory Council, Canberra, Australia.

Edwards, M. 1981b. Financial arrangements within families. Social Security Journal, 1-16.

Gasson, R. 1980. The Role of Women in British Agriculture. London: The Women's Farm and Garden Association.

Gray, A. 1979. The Working class family as an economic unit. In The Sociology of the Family, edited by C. Harris. University of Keele. Sociological Review Monograph.

Green, R. T., and Cunningham, I. C. 1975. Feminine role perception and family purchasing decisions. Journal of Marketing Research.

Hunt, P. 1978. Cash transactions and household tasks. Sociological Review Monograph, Vol. 26, August.

Kendel, D., and Lesser, G. 1972. Marital decision making in American and Danish urban families. Journal of Marriage and the Family, 34, 134-38.

Land, H. 1969. Large Families in London. London: Bell.

Lupri, E. 1969. Contemporary authority patterns in the West German family. Journal of Marriage and the Family, 31, 134-44.

Morsbach, H. 1978. Aspects of Japanese marriage. In The Couple, edited by M. Corbin. Harmondsworth: Penguin.

Oppong, C. 1981. Middle Class African Marriage. London: George Allen and Unwin.

Pahl, J. 1980. Patterns of money management within marriage. Journal of Social Policy, 9, 3, 313-35.

Pahl, J. 1983. Police response to battered women. Journal of Social Welfare Law.

Poster, M. 1978. Critical Theory of the Family. London: Pluto Press.

Rosaldo, M. Z., and Lamphere, L. 1974. Woman, Culture and Society. Stanford, Calif.: Stanford University Press.

Rubin, L. B. 1976. Worlds of Pain: Life in the Working Class Family. New York: Basic Books.

Salamon, S., and Keim, A. 1979. Land ownership and women's power in a Midwestern farming community. Journal of Marriage and the Family, February, 109-19.

Scanzoni, J. 1979. Social processes and power in families. In Contemporary Theories about the Family, edited by W. Burr, R. Hill, I. Nye, and I. Reiss. New York: The Free Press.

Sharma, U. 1980. Women, Work and Property in North-West India. London: Tavistock.

Stearns, P. M. 1972. Working class women in Britain 1890-1914. In Suffer and Be Still, edited by M. Vicinus. London: Methuen.

Stebbing, S. Personal communication. See also Stebbing, S. 1982. Some aspects of the relationship between rural social structure and the female sex role. Thesis for University of London Ph.D. degree.

Whitehead, A. 1981. "I'm hungry, mum." The politics of domestic budgeting. In Of Marriage and the Market, edited by K. Young, C. Walkowitz, and R. McCullagh. London: CSE Books.

11 HOUSEWORK VERSUS EMPLOYMENT: QUALITY OF WORKING LIFE AND PSYCHOLOGICAL WELL-BEING AMONG IRISH MARRIED WOMEN

Margret Fine-Davis

During the 1970s several studies were carried out, both by psychologists and sociologists, which examined the differential satisfaction of housewives and employed married women. Some of these studies also examined the effect of social class on satisfaction with one's role. These studies addressed the basic questions: Does housework or paid employment outside the home lead to greater satisfaction? Is the housewife role more gratifying for certain groups of women (i.e., those less well educated or of lower socioeconomic status) or is the converse true? Although some of these studies revealed no difference between employed married women and housewives on measures of life satisfaction (Spreitzer et al., 1975; Shaver and Freedman, 1976) and work satisfaction (Weaver and Holmes, 1975), others, using smaller, more homogeneous samples, have revealed differences. In a study of U.S. women living in a working-class neighborhood, Ferree (1976) found that full-time housewives were more dissatisfied than women who were employed. Their dissatisfaction with housework was found to be related to a sense of isolation, powerlessness, and low self-esteem. Ferree's

*Support for this research was provided by the Statistical Office of the European Communities, Luxembourg, and the Committee for Social Science Research in Ireland; both of these bodies are gratefully acknowledged. The author also wishes to thank Professor Earl E. Davis, Professor Martha T. S. Mednick, and Dr. Myra Marx Ferree for their very helpful comments on an earlier draft of the paper; and Mr. Niall Bolger and Ms. Anne Mills for their valuable assistance during the course of the study.

findings corroborated earlier findings obtained by Komarovsky (1962) to the effect that less educated women were somewhat happier (or less unhappy) at home than better educated women; however, Ferree found that these less educated women were even happier if they were employed. The importance of employment status, rather than class, would appear to have been reinforced in a study of British housewives by Oakley (1974) in which no class differences in satisfaction were obtained. Both working-class and middle-class housewives were equally likely to express dissatisfaction.

In addition to looking at satisfaction, some investigators have looked at the relationship of employment status to physical and psychological symptoms and, indeed, significant differences have been found. Shaver and Freedman (1976), in a large-scale study in the United States, found that while housewives said they were as happy as employed wives, they nevertheless were more likely to report psychological symptoms such as anxiety, worry, loneliness, and feelings of worthlessness. Powell's (1977) study of "empty nest" U.S. women in their fifties also found a higher level of psychiatric symptoms among full-time housewives than employed women; women employed part-time occupied an intermediate position.

Further findings, consistent with the above, which are perhaps even more noteworthy, since they are based on an actual behavioral measure, were reported by Cumming et al. (1975), who analyzed nation-wide suicide statistics from British Columbia. These authors found that housewives were significantly more likely than employed married women to commit suicide. These findings were even stronger in an analysis of 1971, as compared with 1961 data, which the authors interpreted as indicative of the greater normative support for employment in 1971, resulting in its offering even greater protection from suicide than it did 10 years previously. Like several other investigators, Cumming et al. (1975) interpreted their findings as suggesting that housewives may be more likely to experience isolation, loneliness, and lack of social integration, and that the main benefit of employment may be affiliative rather than economic.

The present study was carried out in Ireland, where employment on the part of married women is far less common than in the United States, Great Britain, or most of Western Europe. Although the labor force participation rate of Irish married women was only 16.4 percent in 1979, this represented a threefold increase since 1961, when the rate was only 5.4 percent. Several factors were responsible for this. While women have traditionally had good access to education in Ireland, many barriers to equal employment opportunity, particularly for married women, remained until relatively recently. These included the "marriage bar" (in which women had to resign from their jobs upon marriage), differential salary scales, lack of access to contraceptives, and tax laws which acted as a strong deterrent (treating the wife's income as that of her husband and taxing it at his highest marginal rate). The period from 1973 to 1981 saw most of these deterrents removed and strong antidiscrimination legislation passed. Nevertheless, attitudes, although having undergone change, have tended to remain relatively traditional in the area of women's role and the family. They have, furthermore, been underpinned by a strong religious ethos and enshrined in the Constitution of the Irish State.

The purpose of the present study was to examine the cross-cultural generalizability of the previous findings concerning the psychological effects of employment for married women, as well as to see whether these effects occurred in both working-class and middle-class women. A second major purpose was to explore a variety of measures relating to the quality of women's working lives, both inside and outside the home, which might help to explain any obtained differences in reported well-being.

METHODS

The Irish data presented here were collected in the context of a survey of the quality of working life which was carried out in eight member countries of the European Community. A nation-wide representative sample of 1,862 respondents aged 18 and over was selected using the Electoral Register as the sampling frame. The data were collected in the fall of 1978 by means of individual interviews in the respondents' homes. The present analysis compares 539 nonemployed married women (i.e., housewives) and 76 employed married women, aged 18 to 65, who emerged in the nation-wide sample. To the extent possible, the same questions were asked of both of these groups and it is these common questions that are focused upon here. Specifically, the two groups were asked about: their satisfaction with eight different aspects of their work, the qualities required by their work, the demands made by their work, and their degree of coping with work demands. Both groups were also compared on several measures of phsysical and psychological well-being: (1) two measures of health (number of sick days in the last 12 months and overall satisfaction with health); (2) overall satisfaction with work; and (3) two measures of life satisfaction—one a single item 4-point satisfaction measure and the second a composite score of four factorially pure Likert items, rated on 7-point scales of agreement versus disagreement (e.g., "Taking all things together, I would say I am very happy these days," "In general, I find that the way I am spending my life these days is not very satisfying," etc.). In the case of all of the comparisons, three-way analysis variance was used with a 2 x 2 x 2 factorial design, varying two levels each of employment status, socioeconomic status, and age.

TABLE 11.1: Summary of analysis of variance results: source level means for main effects of three independent variables on satisfaction with various aspects of work (n = 578 married women)[a]

Satisfaction with:[b]	Employment status		Age		SES		Significant interaction effects
	Employed (n = 70)	Nonemployed (n = 508)	18-39 years (n = 261)	40-65 years (n = 317)	Low (n = 285)	High (n = 293)	
Work environment	3.45	3.48	3.47	3.49	F = 22.8*** 3.33	3.63	Age x employment status F = 4.6*
Importance of respondents work in the eyes of the public	F = 21.5*** 3.52	2.97	F = 11.9*** 2.89	3.16	3.02	3.06	None
Content and type of work	F = 5.9* 3.58	3.38	F = 7.6* 3.32	3.47	F = 15.0*** 3.29	3.50	Age x SES x employment status F = 9.3**
Stress due to nature of work	3.37	3.17	3.14	3.23	3.14	3.24	None
Opportunities for further training/vocational qualifications	3.03	2.87	2.81	2.94	F = 15.7*** 2.71	3.06	None
Earnings/housekeeping money	3.19	3.23	3.30	3.17	F = 26.6*** 3.03	3.45	Age x employment status F = 7.9**
Provision of enough material, equipment, and staff to complete work	3.33	3.33	F = 4.0* 3.40	3.26	F = 13.4*** 3.19	3.48	Age x employment status F = 5.1*
Autonomy	3.51	3.59	3.59	3.57	F = 14.0*** 3.48	3.69	None

[a] In some cases the n drops to a lower figure due to nonapplicable responses; however, in no case do such variations change the basic trends or alter the interpretations made.

[b] Satisfaction measured on 4-point scale: 1 = very dissatisfied; 4 = very satisfied.

*** = p < .001.

** = p < .01.

* = p < .05.

108

RESULTS

Satisfaction with Aspects of Work

Table 11.1 presents analysis of variance results for eight dependent measures of satisfaction with various aspects of work. In the case of the employed women, these questions referred to their employment; in the case of the housewives, they referred to their work in the home. Employed married women were found to be significantly more likely than housewives to be satisfied with the perceived importance of their work in the eyes of the general public ($F = 21.5$; $p < .001$). Employed married women were also significantly more likely than housewives to report satisfaction with the content and type of work they were doing ($F = 5.9$; $p < .05$). However, a significant three-way interaction between employment status, age, and socioeconomic status (SES) indicated that, whereas satisfaction with work content was greater for young, high SES employed women, this was not the case for young low SES employed women ($F = 9.3$; $p < .01$). Among the latter group, there was little difference between housewives and those in paid employment. These results suggest that the work available to young lower SES women is slightly less desirable or roughly equivalent to housework, whereas the work available to high SES women in this age group (18 to 39) would appear to be more stimulating than housework.

In this context, it is interesting to consider that previous research conducted in Ireland showed that employment was related to higher self-esteem on the part of high SES young women, whereas it was related to lower self-esteem on the part of low SES employed women, which may reflect different social class norms concerning the sex-role appropriateness of employment on the part of married women of child-bearing age (Fine-Davis, 1979a). Consistent with this interpretation, the present results showed that older low SES employed women (i.e., those 40 to 65) expressed much higher levels of satisfaction with their work content than did their younger counterparts. This may reflect a greater attachment to the work situation during the phase of the life cycle when family responsibilities have diminished, as well as the possibility of having attained more responsible or interesting jobs. However, other findings offer further insights into the discrepancy between older and younger low SES women. First, lower SES women were less satisfied generally with the amount of money they received, whether in employment or as housekeeping money ($F = 26.6$; $p < .001$). Second, younger employed women were less satisfied with their earnings than older employed women ($F = 7.9$; $p < .01$). Since the younger low SES employed woman is less satisfied with her earnings than her older counterpart, a perception which probably reflects her lower wages, employment may thus be less attractive to her.

Work Requirements and Demands

In addition to assessing levels of satisfaction with various aspects of work, the study compared the skills and qualities employed married women and housewives perceived as required in their work. As may be seen in Table 11.2, there were no differences between the two groups on any of the indices (i.e., (1) psychomotor, (2) manual/technical, or (3) conceptual/verbal and interpersonal). However, a significant interaction effect occurred for the index of conceptual/verbal and interpersonal skills. This index (reliability = .82) included such qualities as leadership, decision making, creativity, planning, negotiating, expressing, etc. The interaction effect demonstrated that high SES employed women were most likely to use such skills in their work, next most likely to use these skills were housewives of both social classes, and least likely to use them were low SES employed women (F = 12.3; p < .001).

There were no differences between employed married women and housewives in the extent to which they perceived their work as "demanding," nor in their ability to cope with the demands of their work. Younger women (both housewives and employed), however, were more likely to perceive greater demands (F = 4.0; p < .05). Women in this age group (18 to 39) are most likely to have increased family responsibilities, which constitute additional demands upon the basic workload, be it inside or outside the home. However, in spite of their greater work demands, younger women were not less able to cope; they were in fact more likely to report that they were able to cope than older women (F = 11.3; p < .001).

Subjective Measures of Well-Being

To what extent is a married woman's employment status related to her feelings of well-being? The employed married women and housewives were compared on five different measures of physical and psychological well-being. These included a relatively "objective" measure of health (i.e., the number of sick days in the previous year), a subjective measure of health status, as well as measures of satisfaction with one's work and one's life in general. Table 11.3 presents analyses of variance for the two groups (employed vs. housewives) while simultaneously exploring the effects of age and socioeconomic status. The results indicate that employment status is associated with

TABLE 11.2: Summary of analysis of variance results: source level means for main effects of three independent variables on various characteristics of work (n = 613 married women)

Work characteristics	Employment status		Age		SES		Significant interaction effects
	Employed (n = 76)	Nonemployed (n = 537)	18–39 years (n = 278)	40–65 years (n = 335)	(Low) (n = 303)	(High) (n = 310)	
Index of psychomotor skills	3.09	2.95	3.19	2.79	2.96	2.98	None
			$F = 15.5***$				
Index of conceptual/ verbal/interpersonal skills	4.28	4.20	4.32	4.12	4.00	4.41	SES x employment status $F = 12.3***$
					$F = 9.0**$		
Index of manual/ technical skills[a]	1.45	1.61	1.60	1.59	1.56	1.62	SES x age x employment status $F = 12.1***$
Assessment of demands made by daily work[a]	3.64	3.64	3.74	3.56	3.58	3.70	None
			$F = 4.0*$				
Degree of coping with work requirements[b]	2.90	2.76	2.88	2.70	2.77	2.79	None
			$F = 11.3***$				
Length of work week (hours)	36.13	66.23	62.43	62.46	62.36	62.54	None
	$F = 150.9***$						

[a] Five-point scale: 1 = demands very small; 5 = demands very great.

[b] Four-point scale: 1 = "often requires too much"; 2 = "sometimes requires too much"; 3 = "generally able to cope"; 4 = "underemployed, could do more."

*** = p < .001.

** = p < .01.

* = p < .05.

TABLE 11.3: Summary of analysis of variance results: source level means for main effects of three independent variables for various aspects of health, work, and life in general (n = 615 married women)

	Employment status		Age		SES		Significant interaction effects
	Employed (n = 76)	Nonemployed (n = 539)	18–39 years (n = 278)	40–65 years (n = 337)	Low (n = 304)	High (n = 311)	
Number of sick days[a]	1.87	2.09	$F = 6.0$* 1.91	2.19	$F = 7.3$** 2.21	1.91	None
Satisfaction with health[b]	$F = 4.3$* 3.66	3.48	$F = 23.1$*** 3.65	3.37	$F = 9.1$** 3.41	3.59	None
Satisfaction with present work[b]	$F = 13.3$*** 3.77	3.52	3.53	3.56	$F = 14.8$*** 3.46	3.64	None
Life satisfaction I[b]	3.62	3.55	3.61	3.52	$F = 11.0$*** 3.48	3.64	None
Life satisfaction II[c]	$F = 4.8$* 5.77	5.44	$F = 10.0$** 5.65	5.34	$F = 13.0$*** 5.30	5.66	None

[a]Five-point scale: 1 = "no sick days"; 5 = "more than 28 sick days."
[b]Four-point scale: 1 = very dissatisfied; 4 = very satisfied.
[c]Composite score ranging from 1 to 7, based on level of agreement (1 = strongly disagree; 7 = strongly agree) with 4 factorially pure Likert items measuring life satisfaction.

*** = $p < .001$.
** = $p < .01$.
* = $p < .05$.

greater perceived well-being on three measures: satisfaction with one's health (F = 4.3; p < .05), satisfaction with one's work (F =13.3; p < .001), and life satisfaction (F = 4.8; p < .05). It is interesting to note that the lesser satisfaction with health on the part of housewives was not associated with a significantly greater number of sick days, suggesting that the phenomenon we are seeing is primarily psychological in nature.

Far more significant than employment status, however, was socioeconomic status. Lower SES respondents were worse off on all measures and all differences were highly significant. The lower SES group was more likely to report a greater number of sick days, greater dissatisfaction with their health, and greater dissatisfaction with their work as well as with life in general. Older respondents were also worse off in terms of three of the five measures. They reported a greater number of sick days, greater dissatisfaction with their health, and a lesser degree of life satisfaction than younger women.

DISCUSSION AND IMPLICATIONS

In summary, the findings have shown that employed married women in Ireland are significantly more likely than housewives to express overall satisfaction with their work and with two major aspects of it: its content and its perceived value in the community. One exception to this was the finding that younger low SES employed women were not more likely than housewives of similar age and SES, to express satisfaction with their work content. Several possible interpretations of this were put forth, including (1) that the work available to young, low SES women may be less interesting than housework; and (2) that social pressures and norms may be exerted on younger women from working-class backgrounds to exercise a more traditional role. Lower SES women, regardless of age or employment status, reported less satisfaction with their work in several respects, i.e., it did not offer as much autonomy, opportunities for further training, income, etc. as did the work of higher SES women. It was also found that among lower income women, paid employment drew upon fewer of their conceptual/verbal and interpersonal skills than did housework. Such findings clearly suggest that the skills of lower SES women are not being fully utilized in the workplace, a factor which may in part be responsible for the lower work satisfaction of these women. However, in spite of this, the overall scores of employed women—regardless of social class—indicated that they were more satisfied generally with their work, their health, and their life in general than were housewives. Thus, the data show that employment is related to greater satisfaction and sense of well-being among married women of both social classes, but it is related to even greater satisfaction for high SES women.

The increased workload of a job outside the home, together with that of a housewife after working hours, did not seem to lead to such work overload that health problems ensued. No differences in sick days were reported and, as noted above, employed women reported significantly greater satisfaction with their health. One cannot impute causality here: we do not know if healthier women join the workforce or if holding a job outside the home in some way contributes to health. However, a plausible interpretation, based on the data, is that the satisfaction gained from the work itself may contribute in part to a feeling of health and well-being.

The fact that the single item 4-point scale measure of life satisfaction did not pick up differences based on employment status and age, but that the 4-item factor analytically derived measure using 7-point agree-disagree scales did, provides further support for the usefulness of more robust measures which are capable of picking up greater subtlety of response. The single item measure of life satisfaction may indeed be eliciting a social desirability response (Robinson and Shaver, 1973). As Shaver and Freedman (1976) also found, more specific measures, such as psychological symptoms of anxiety, feelings of worthlessness, etc. did yield significant differences between the employed and nonemployed women in their sample.

While employment status significantly predicted three of the five measures of well-being, socioeconomic status predicted all five and at a highly significant level in each case (p < .001). These findings clearly show that the quality of life of lower income women is inferior, regardless of whether they work inside or outside of the home. These findings were underpinned by many specific results documenting the ways in which the quality of their working life was inferior.

In view of previous research findings in Ireland concerning the attitudes and other characteristics of employed and nonemployed married women, the relative dissatisfaction of housewives is somewhat surprising. For example, housewives were found to hold more traditional sex-role attitudes, to be less supportive of maternal employment, and to be less likely to perceive limitations in the housewife role (Fine-Davis, 1979a). Thus, their own behavior (i.e., being housewives) is quite congruent with their attitudes about appropriate sex-role behavior. Furthermore, they were found to be more religious (Fine-Davis, 1979a)—and religiosity was found to be significantly related to traditional sex-role attitudes (Fine-Davis, 1979b). Housewives were also found to have a larger expected family size and to be less likely to use contraceptives than employed married women (Fine-Davis, 1979a). They also reported that their important others (i.e., husband, mother, and father) would be disapproving if they took up employment (Fine-Davis, 1979a). Thus, their entire lifestyle, values, and attitudes are supportive of their current behavior. Why then, are they less satisfied than employed women with their health, their work, and their life in general? It may be that they are not fully aware that they are relatively dissatisfied, or if so, why they are. If they were, it would generate a state of cognitive dissonance which would exert pressure toward a shift in either attitudes or behavior. Apparently, precisely this must be happening to sizable numbers of Irish married women, since their rate of labor force participation has trebled in the last 20 years (Sexton, 1981) and all evidence points to its continuing.

REFERENCES

Cumming, E., Lazer, C., and Chisholm, L. 1975. Suicide as an index of role strain among employed and not employed married women in British Columbia. Canadian Review of Sociology and Anthropology, 12(4), 462-70.

Ferree, M. M. 1976. Working class jobs: Housework and paid work as sources of satisfaction. Social Problems, 23(4), 431-41.

Fine-Davis, M. 1979a. Social-psychological predictors of employment status of married women in Ireland. Journal of Marriage and the Family, 41(1), 145-58.

Fine-Davis, M. 1979b. Personality correlates of attitudes toward the role and status of women in Ireland. Journal of Personality, 47 (3), 379-96.

Komarovsky, M. 1962. Blue collar marriage. New York: Vintage Books.

Oakley, A. 1974. The sociology of housework. London: Martin Robertson & Co. Ltd.

Robinson, J. P., and Shaver, P. R. 1973. Measures of social-psychological attitudes (rev. ed.). Ann Arbor: Institute for Social Research, University of Michigan.

Sexton, J. J. 1981. The changing labour force. Paper presented at Conference on "The Irish Economy and Society in the Eighties," The Economic and Social Research Institute, Dublin, 6 October.

Shaver, P., and Freedman, J. 1976. Your pursuit of happiness. Psychology Today, 10(3), 26-33.

Spreitzer, E., Snyder, E. E., and Larson, D. 1975. Age, marital status, and labor force participation as related to life satisfaction. Sex Roles, 1(3), 235-247.

Weaver, C. N., and Holmes, S. L. 1975. A comparative study of the work satisfaction of females with full-time employment and full-time housekeeping. Journal of Applied Psychology, 60(1), 117-18.

PART 3

THE DARKER SIDE

The chapters in this section deal with social constraints and violence. Violence takes many forms, according to Webster's Third New International Unabridged Dictionary 1971, including a common definition: "Erection of any physical force so as to injure or abuse"; or a less obvious and more insidious form: "Injury in the form of revoking, repudiation, distortion, infringement or irreverence to a thing, a notion, or quality fitly valued or observed."

The more subtle aspects of violence, those which are often unidentified, are reflected in cultural prescriptions, for example, that lead to sex differences in intellectual functioning. Lieblich presents her findings for Israel where, contrary to those reported in Western societies, boys begin out-pacing girls on verbal abilities at age 9, and by age 12 are significantly superior. These results, which have been replicated with different tests and different age groups (Nevo et al., 1982; Cais, 1981), contrast with the findings in Western studies (Maccoby and Jacklin, 1974) and lend credence to a cultural hypothesis of sex-related differences in intelligence.

A subtle kind of violence takes the form of derisive humor. Nevo (Chapter 14) finds great similarity between the humor responses generally found to differentiate Jews and Arabs in Israel and those generally found to differentiate men and women. She suggests that it is the lower social status of Arabs and women that underlies the similarity. One of the patterns identified is that the higher status group tends to take a more aggressive stance toward the lower status group. An even more subtle form of violence occurs when the lower status group identifies with the aggressor, internalizes the stereotype of the dominant group, and shows aggression toward itself. Nevo further argues that change in a group's status is related to change in the humor about and within this group.

117

Unger deals with another subtle aspect of social control: attitudes about physical appearance. She demonstrates that stereotypes about attractiveness are more prevalent about women than about men and that like humor, they operate as mechanisms to keep women in their place. Such forms of social control, in which the victim unconsciously accepts and incorporates the damaging stereotypes, are especially pernicious since this dynamic makes them highly resistant to change.

A similar dynamic occurs in the case of sexual harassment. Tangri et al., in their study of civil servants show that victims become more aware of harassment at work when there is a gap in the status of the harasser and the harassed. Power differences and lack of power to combat harassment are the important issues—to object or complain could cost one's job. They report also that harassment violates the emotional and physical functioning of the victim.

Powerlessness is an issue for both white and black women in South Africa. Stracker clearly shows the violent nature of the constraints for black women in that society; they suffer from race and class exploitation as well as sexual oppression. Racial laws divide women, and at the same time, bind them to the social system. The daily experience of white women who are freed from household chores by the labor of their black servants, blinds them to their own subjugation and powerlessness and gives them a vested interest in maintaining the system.

Court presents evidence to demonstrate that a loosening of controls on pornography is accompanied by an increase in rape, whether in sexually liberal Denmark or in more conservative Hawaii. He accuses scientists themselves of violence in misreporting available data which clearly show this connection between pornography and sexual violence toward women.

The last chapter deals with acts that most societies define as the most extreme form of personal violence—taking the life of another. Jones makes the case that most women who kill are battered women who kill their batterers. The situation for these women is kill or be killed—a matter of self-defense. She explains, however, that the original legal rules governing self-defense are based on the assumption of two individuals of equal strength and of lack of premeditation. The fact that most men are physically stronger than women, and that women must resort to a weapon to "equalize" the situation, is not taken into account. These conditions and the inability of the woman to get help may compel her to "premeditate" defense. When this premeditated self-defense results in her killing her batterer, she herself becomes a victim of society's violence toward her by being convicted of murder and jailed.

The chapters in this section deal with the darker side of social life. They make an impressive plea for recognition that violence

against women takes many forms—violation of her intellectual potential through cultural constraints, humor, her humiliation and subordination through prejudicing and harassment, and the final irony—the
legal systems which, in failing to recognize women who kill as victims
themselves, victimize women in the name of justice.

REFERENCES

Cais, J. 1982. Teach Thy Daughter the Torah: The Verbal Behavior
of Israeli Boys and Girls, paper presented at the First International Interdisciplinary Congress on Women, Haifa, Israel,
December–January.

Maccoby, E. E., and Jacklin, C. N. 1974. The Psychology of Sex
Differences, Stanford, Calif.: Stanford University Press.

Nevo, B., Safir, M. P., and R. Ramraz. 1982. Sex Differences in
Intelligence Test Performance of University Applicants in Israel,
paper presented at the First International Interdisciplinary Congress on Women, Haifa, Israel, December–January.

12 SEX DIFFERENCES IN INTELLIGENCE TESTS PERFORMANCE OF JEWISH AND ARAB SCHOOL CHILDREN IN ISRAEL

Amia Lieblich

A recent review of research on sex differences in intelligence tests scores (Hyde, 1981) discusses the danger of overgeneralizing from small—even though significant—differences reported in such comparisons. However, when differences are reported, there are indeed some consistent, by now classical, findings in this area. Adolescent boys are usually better in spatial orientation and numerical ability, and adolescent girls are superior in verbal abilities. It is also accepted that no differences in overall intelligence scores of the sexes exist, they are similar in their intellectual potential as measured by the usual intelligence tests (Maccoby and Jacklin, 1974). What is the case in Israel?

From 1970 to 1975, The Human Development Institute of the Department of Psychology in the Hebrew University, Jerusalem, had been involved in the standardization of the Wechsler Intelligence Scales for the Israeli population. (Kugelmass et al., 1974; Kugelmass and Lieblich, 1975; Lieblich, et al., 1972; Lieblich et al., 1975; Lieblich and Kugelmass, 1981). The first project was the standardization of the Wechsler Preschool Primary Scale of Intelligence (WPPSI)—a test for preschoolers aged 4 to 6-1/2. A full standardization was performed for a Jewish, Hebrew speaking population. Following this, a standardization of the Wechsler Intelligence Scale for Children Form R (WISC-R) for 6 to 16 year old children, was carried out on a nationwide representative sample for both Jewish and Arab populations. Twenty-seven hundred children were individually tested in their native language. Additional background information was collected for each child, including origin of child and parents and information about socioeconomic status (SES). The results are based on the data collected in these standardization projects.

The Wechsler Scales provide a total Intelligence Quotient (I. Q.) score, plus verbal and performance I. Q. s and specific subscales' scores of 12 subtests. (Verbal subtests: general knowledge, similarities, mathematics, vocabulary, comprehension, memory span. Performance subtests: picture completion, block design, picture arrangements, mazes, coding, object assembly.) Originally, as well as in Israel, none of the items were preselected to eliminate sex differences; therefore, the test is not sex-fair. Thus it can be used as an instrument to investigate sex differences in intelligence throughout childhood and adolescence.

Comparison of WPPSI total and subscale scores for girls and boys revealed no differences. This provides an important base line for evaluation of later developments. It appears that boys and girls enter elementary school similarly equipped with the necessary intellectual function.

The situation is quite different when we turn to the results of the WISC-R. First we shall examine the results of the Jewish sample. A consistent superiority of boys over girls is found. The differences in I. Q. scores are about 3 points (total 101.7 vs. 98.5; verbal 102.1 vs. 98.3; performance 101.0 vs. 99.1), namely 1/5 of a standard deviation, and is significant at the .05 level. The same trend is apparent in the subtest scores. Boys achieve higher mean scores than girls in 11 subtests, and girls perform better only in 1, the Coding test. It is interesting to note that in verbal abilities, in which Western girls are generally found to be superior, Israeli boys are superior.

Inspection of Table 12.1 reveals that girls start their schooling at least on the same intellectual level, if not higher, than that of the boys. The boys first outpace the girls at age 9, and this difference grows through age 16 when it reaches about 12 I. Q. points. The same trends are found on the verbal and performance sections of the test. Indeed, in contrast to Western findings, boys exhibit their relatively higher achievements in the verbal subscales at 11, and later, at about 13, their superiority is manifested in the performance test as well.

How can we interpret these results? While several theories may account for the Israeli results, our preferred interpretation is based on an environmental explanation. These results reveal that both sexes have equal potential as they begin school. However, it appears that the environment throughout their school years does not provide boys and girls with the same opportunities to develop their potential, and, as a result, boys seem to benefit more from their school experience than girls do. The process by which the environment enhances or inhibits intellectual development is unclear. Parents and teachers may have different expectations of boys and girls and these expectations are transmitted to the child. Different peer group pressures and exposures to a variety of role models may all combine to create a different intel-

TABLE 12.1: Mean I.Q. scores by age and sex—Jewish sample

Age	Verbal I.Q.		Performance I.Q.		Total I.Q.	
	Girls	Boys	Girls	Boys	Girls	Boys
6	100.4	99.9	101.4	98.5	100.9	99.1
7	100.2	101.5	100.5	99.9	100.4	100.8
8	101.6	99.4	100.9	99.8	101.4	99.5
9	99.6	101.2	98.4	101.5	98.9	101.5
10	101.0	98.6	99.5	100.5	100.4	99.4
11	97.8[a]	104.4	99.2	101.8	98.3	103.4
12	96.9[a]	103.5	100.1	100.3	98.3	102.2
13	96.0[a]	105.3	99.2	101.8	97.3	103.9
14	98.9	101.2	100.2	98.5	99.5	99.9
15	93.9[a]	106.9	96.7[a]	104.0	94.8[a]	106.1
16	94.5[a]	104.7	93.8[a]	105.9	93.6[a]	105.8
Total sample:	98.3[a]	101.2	99.1[a]	101.0	98.5[a]	101.7

[a]Difference significant at $p < .05$ level.

lectual environment for growing boys and girls. The outcome of all of these processes may be a lower need to achieve in girls than in boys. On a more general level, children of the two sexes may develop different motivational make-up and also accumulate greatly different intellectual experiences.

As the child develops, these different factors and experiences accumulate to create a growing gap between boys and girls. This gap is maximal (in our studied age range) at adolescence, when the environment seems to put a lot of pressure on girls to be popular and attractive, and on boys to perform well in order to be accepted in the most desirable career choices.

While no biological-maturational process seems to be adequate to account for these findings, some other possible interpretations should be mentioned. First, the research design was not longitudinal but cross-sectional. We cannot rule out the possibility that boys and girls who were born in the late 1960s, our younger age groups, have been brought up in a more egalitarian environment than that of the groups born in the late 1950s. Such an alternative explanation seems less plausible than the former, as supported by the following results.

A growing age gap in I.Q. between subgroups of the sample, was noted in two other comparisons. When Jewish children of Sephardic (Middle Eastern and North African) origin are compared with Western

(European or U.S.) origin, the former tend, on the average, to get lower scores. (The Sephardic culture is more traditional and Middle Eastern.) Breaking the sample into age groups, produces a gap that grows steadily with age. The same phenomenon is observed between SES groups in Israel, where a larger cross-status difference is found for the older than for the younger age groups. These results can also be interpreted by the environmental-developmental hypothesis, namely that the environment throughout school years (including also the home environment, of course) is more beneficial to the intellectual development of boys, of higher SES children, and of children of Western origin.

In addition to the mean comparisons presented above, analyses of variance assessed the separate and interactional effects of sex, origin, and SES of the subjects. While all the main effects were significant, effect of sex was the smallest. The largest effect was that of the child's origin and the second—of the family SES. This finding provides a general perspective on these results. As noted, sex difference effects, even when significant and consistent, tend to be small. In our study, they are clearly smaller than those produced by other, more social subdivisions of the sample, namely those of origin and status of the family.

These results were all based on the Jewish standardization sample. Arab society is even more traditional than Jewish society. This led to the hypothesis that Arab results would reveal an even greater gap between the two sexes.

The findings for the Arab population are highly similar to those of the Jewish children. Boys achieve higher scores than girls on all the subtests except Coding. The differences in I.Q. scores are of about four points, namely nearly a third of a standard deviation (total 102.3 vs. 98.2, verbal 101.9 vs. 97.6, performance 101.6 vs. 97.3). When the results are analyzed separately for the different age groups, the trend seems to be very similar to the former one, namely, Arab girls start their schooling with higher scores than boys, but, with age, the boys outpace the girls. At the age of 15, Arab boys score on the average 8.8 I.Q. points more than the girls. At the age of 16, this difference is maximal, reaching 10.4 points.

Interestingly, for Arabs as well as for Jews, sex is the third factor in magnitude of effect on intellectual measures. For Arabs religion has the largest effect (Christians are higher than Moslems), second is the SES of the family, and sex is third in magnitude, although still significant.

As suggested in the discussion of the Jewish results, our findings can be attributed to different life experience of and environmental effects on boys and girls. This hypothesis is at least as feasible for the Arab culture as it is for Jewish culture in Israel. Indeed, the results of the Jewish sample were more surprising to us. Israelis tend to believe that they are egalitarian in values and practice, and are reluctant to accept results indicating a different state of affairs. However, studies of the intellectual development of boys and girls in Israel (Cais, 1981; Nevo et al., 1981) using completely different measures and approaches, have all verified our own conclusion, namely that Israeli girls do not receive equal intellectual opportunities to those of boys. Obviously, much work has to be done in order to produce changes in this area, including work with parents, teachers, and the media, as well as with the children themselves. This may be one of our most important social projects for the future.

In conclusion, results in the United States indicate equality of the two sexes in their intellectual performance and the Israeli Jewish and Arab data reveal differences favoring the boys. When a culture comes to believe in the equality of the sexes, as has happened in the United States in recent years, the sexes may also tend to behave in a more similar fashion. If this is the case, then decreasing sexist attitudes in society and increasing opportunities for and acceptance of women as equals are the keys to the desired change.

REFERENCES

Cais, J. 1981. Teach Thy Daughter The Torah: the Verbal Behavior of Israeli Boys and Girls. Paper presented at the International Interdisciplinary Congress on Women, Haifa, Israel.

Hyde, J. S. 1981. How Large Are Cognitive Gender Differences? American Psychologist, 36, 891-901.

Kugelmass, S., Lieblich, A., and Bossik, D. 1974. Patterns of Intellectual Ability in Jewish and Arab Children in Israel. Journal of Cross-Cultural Psychology, 5, 184-98.

Kugelmass, S., and Lieblich, A. 1975. A Development Study of the Arab Child in Israel. Scientific report, Ford Foundation Grant 015.1261.

Lieblich, A., Ninio, A., and Kugelmass, S. 1972. Effects of Ethnic Origin and Parental SES on WPPSI Performance of Pre-School Children in Israel. Journal of Cross-Cultural Psychology, 3, 159-68.

Lieblich, A., Kugelmass, S., and Ehrlich, C. 1975. Patterns of Intellectual Ability in Israel II: Urban Matched Samples. Journal of Cross-Cultural Psychology, 6, 218-26.

Lieblich, A., and Kugelmass, S. 1981. Patterns of Intellectual Ability of Arab Children in Israel. Intelligence, 5, 311-20.

Maccoby, E. E., and Jacklin, C. M. 1974. The Psychology of Sex Differences. Stanford, Calif.: Stanford University Press.

Nevo, B., Safir, M. P., and Ramraz, R. 1981. Sex Differences in Intelligence Test Performance of University Applicants in Israel. Paper presented at the International Interdisciplinary Congress on Women, Haifa, Israel.

13 SOME ASPECTS OF FEMINISM IN THE SOUTH AFRICAN CONTEXT

Gill Straker

Feminist theory and research which are based on U.S. experience is not readily transferable to women in South African context. A basic tenet of this chapter is that for both black and white women in South Africa, the issue of racial division tends to take priority over sexist division. This presentation has three components, one dealing with feminism in the case of white women, one dealing with feminism among black women, and one dealing with the possibility of their uniting across social and class lines to protest injustice.

WHITE WOMEN IN SOUTH AFRICA

White women in South Africa seem particularly unconcerned with feminist issues. They do not see themselves as oppressed but on the whole seem to be satisfied with the status quo in regard to their position in relation to men. Since identification with any liberation movement presupposes that the individual experiences a sense of oppression, the South Africa woman's position confirms Lewis' basic premise (1977) that individual's perception of the cause of their subordinate position will determine their sense of identity with a liberation movement to change it. Lacking such perception, white South African women are not attracted to feminist movements.

Perhaps one reason for their lack of any perception of oppression lies in the fact that to fully acknowledge their own oppression, these women would have to acknowledge the oppression of others in the system, a challenge of frightening proportions. I would suggest that there is also a deeper reason for white South African women's apparent disregard for the women's movement, a reason embedded in the answer to a question all liberation movements must ask themselves, namely: from what and for what are we liberating the individual?

Before exploring this question, the premise that feminism is currently a nonissue in the South African context must be substantiated. A study by J. Cock in 1980 reported that when asked if they had heard of the women's movement, 86 percent of a sample of 50 white women said that they had heard of it but only 6 percent thought it was a good idea. The white women interviewed seemed not only to feel no vested interest in promoting women's issues but actually to feel a vested interest in not doing so. This in spite of the fact that they are at least economically dependent on their husbands and relegated to the domestic sphere.

While it is a sine qua non of the feminist movement that women's oppression is embedded in male domination, there is an increasing acknowledgment of the fact that there are widely different experiences of that oppression. These vary for different societies at various periods of history and for different social classes. Lewenhak (1980) has explored the changing nature of women's oppression by tracing work history from the days of hunter-gatherers to modern times. Similarly, Barrett (1980) has attempted to show how state, ideology, racism, systems of government (i.e., socialist or capitalist), and technology, etc. all affect the form oppression will take and how it will be experienced.

What the women's movement at any time and place is trying to accomplish can vary greatly. Claudie Broyelle (1977), writing on women's liberation in China, states that liberation had to take place in five spheres, viz. the particular relationship women have to (1) social labor, (2) housework, (3) children, (4) the family, and (5) sexuality. My review of feminist literature indicates that these areas indeed seem most often cited as the locus of women's oppression, keeping women from political autonomy based on economic independence—although the terms used and emphases may have differed (Greer, 1971; Rowbottom, 1973).

However, I still believe that a basic question needs to be answered: To what end is political autonomy and economic independence desired? This basically is a philosophical question concerning the good life and freedom. Based on my survey of feminist literature, it is assumed that political autonomy and economic independence are necessary to promote the individual's right to self-determination. Freedom then is the right to determine how personal time and energy are employed. Such freedom is inferred to be the common denominator of the various definitions of liberation in feminist literature.

It is the contention of this chapter that many white women in South Africa, despite their limited political autonomy and economic independence, are free to determine use of their time and energy.

Thus it is possible for these women to subjectively experience freedom or at least a lack of oppression, even without full potential autonomy and economic independence. This raises questions of means and ends. Are political autonomy and economic independence ends in themselves, or means to acquire that elusive idea of liberation? If they are the means and not the end, are they the only means?

In the South African context, the answer to the question of whether political autonomy and economic independence are the only means to the subjective experience of oneself as unoppressed, the answer definitely seems to be negative for white women.

Accepting the notion that women's domestic labor serves two functions, the cheap reproduction of the labor force and the relain this reproduction. She looks at reproduction in two main categories, generational reproduction and day-to-day reproduction. Generational viz. generational reproduction: day-to-day reproduction. Generational reproduction involves biological reproduction, the control of sexuality, and child care. Day-to-day reproduction involves numerous tasks such as shopping, cleaning, cooking, washing, etc. Cock examined the roles of black women in white households. She found that black women made a contribution in every single one of these areas except in actual biological reproduction and the control of sexuality. In many of the areas, especially those pertaining to day-to-day reproduction, the responsibility for these tasks, e.g., cooking, washing, and cleaning was the sole responsibility of the black domestic. The white woman, by employing a black domestic, has been freed from many of the tasks involved in day-to-day reproduction.

That white women experience this kind of domestic chore as oppressive is reflected in their responses to questions of why they employed a domestic servant. These answers on the whole reflected the women's dislike for this type of work plus their relief at having been freed from it, and their desire to work and become wage earners themselves, albeit at lower salaries than males, or to indulge themselves in whatever leisure activities they desired.

If one returns to and examines Broyelle's (1977) five areas of oppression of women in the light of Cock's findings, it becomes clear that by employing black women, white women have become totally free or partially free from tasks related to housework, child rearing, and the family. The major area in Broyelle's (1977) classification within which white South African women are notably unliberated is in the area of their relationship to social labor. In nearly all sections of the economy, there are wage differentials based on sex. There are few women in top industrial posts, only one woman judge, and no women in government cabinet posts. A high percentage of white women do not work at all. That women in South Africa, including white women, are not liberated in terms of their relationship to social labor and their participation in the public sphere cannot therefore be disputed. Despite this, white women do not feel oppressed.

It would appear that one's own position in relation to social labor is not in itself the crucial factor in determining one's sense of oppression. If by extension, one occupies a favorable position in relation to the means of production, e.g., through a family tie, one may fail to experience a subjective sense of oppression. Perhaps it is stating the obvious to comment that it is rather the quality of one's day-to-day life which determines one's sense of oppression. Contrasts with theoretical concepts which state that the relationship to social labor and the means of production usually determine quality of life, as well as political, social, and economic independence are not the only determinants of the experience of freedom. Conversely the attainment of this independence is not a guarantee of a sense of freedom. Indeed, women who achieve some measure of economic freedom because of State-run crèches and house-cleaning teams may not experience themselves as free and may not find that the quality of their life has been greatly improved.

It is the quality of daily life which is the issue. How to achieve a good quality life for all, remains a perennial problem. Certainly, at this point, neither communism, socialism, nor capitalism seems to have provided a satisfactory answer. The South African reality seems to be the achievement of a good quality of life for some white women at the expense of others. For black women that expense is inestimable.

BLACK WOMEN IN SOUTH AFRICA

Black South African women are the victims of triple oppression—sexist, racial, and class—whether they reside in the rural homeland, or the urban areas, although their experience of this will differ. Women in the rural areas, living in traditional male-dominated societies, may be most intensely aware of sexist oppression. However, they are subject to both race and class oppression, being prevented on racial grounds from owning the land they work. In urban areas, blacks are more exposed to white privilege and feel even more keenly the restrictions placed on them on racial grounds.

Cock (1980) also tapped 175 black women's experiences of themselves as workers, as blacks, and as women. These women worked as domestics for the 50 white South African women discussed above. All the women interviewed expressed feelings of being exploited in all three areas. Regarding their exploitation as workers, the following statements were made: "We should be counted as people"; "Our employers should treat us as people not animals"; "It would help if our madams could be interested in knowing their servant's circumstances. Many madams don't know how many children their maids have" (p. 108). Such statements reflect the black domestic worker's intense subjective experience of oppression, she is dependent on her employer on almost every conceivable level. The domestic worker usually resides on the premises of the employer. Because of influx control and the pass laws, she may even be dependent on her employer to legitimize her presence in a particular urban area. Her powerlessness vis à vis her employer who determines her wage, her working hours, and her working conditions without a written contract, is therefore just about complete.

That the black domestic worker sees her oppression in racial terms is again reflected in statements such as "The whites are greedy." "South Africa should be ashamed of itself for the way they treat non-whites." "The whites are sitting on our heads, so we are inferior." "Whites have all the power." "We are more capable than the whites. That is why they try by all means to keep us under their feet." "We pay for school books and white children don't." "We earn less just because we are black" (p. 109). From these quotes it is clear that black domestic workers are keenly aware of the racial nature of their oppression.

Despite the emphasis on racial oppression, Cock did find that there was an awareness also of the sexist element in their oppression. Some women were quoted as saying "We work hard like men but we are paid less." "We get no maternity benefits." "The men just go to work and come home. They do not worry about children and other things." "Our men treat us badly." "We have to manage our children." "You seldom see a man trying to cope alone with his children" (p. 110). However, Cock states that for black domestics, indignation about discrimination against them as women is overshadowed by an awareness of discrimination against them as blacks. Cock found that only 24 percent of the 175 black maids interviewed had heard of the women's movement, and without exception they approved of the idea.

That the women's movement is perceived so differently by white and black women in the South African context affirms the move away from simplistic models of oppression to models that are more differentiated and produce a clearer and more complex analysis of the issues involved in women's oppression, than that obtained by previous models.

It is interesting to note that although feminism has been accused of being a product of the middle class (Barrett, 1980), in Cock's South African sample the feminist issues were not championed by the women employers but rather by the lower-class blacks. However, for these black women, racial and class oppression were felt to supersede sexist oppression, a view that contradicted Firestone's (1972) notion that sexual oppression is the primary one and hence is the priority for political liberation.

WHITE AND BLACK WOMEN IN ASSOCIATION

While the women's movement does not seem to enjoy popular support in South Africa, there are nevertheless a few women's groups which do serve as rallying points for social and political change. The names of some of these groups illustrate their broader political intentions, i.e., "Women's Movement for Peace," "Women for Peaceful Change Now." Not all the women's groups are as dedicated to peaceful change. Some believe that nonviolent change is not possible and are more militant in their outlook. That women in movements in South Africa are committed to broader social change is not a unique phenomenon. Various women's groups in the United States were champions of the Civil Rights movements. Political change in both Russia and China were aided by intensive efforts at uniting women.

That women in South Africa are capable of uniting against oppression and indeed do so, is nowhere more movingly expressed than in the following letter to the Prime Minister on August 9th, 1956. August 9th is National Women's Day and in 1956 20,000 women of all races and social classes marched to the Government Houses in Pretoria to protest the pass laws. Their protest was framed as follows:

"THE DEMAND OF THE WOMEN OF SOUTH AFRICA FOR THE WITHDRAWAL OF PASSES FOR WOMEN AND THE REPEAL OF THE PASS LAWS"

We the women of South Africa have come here today. We represent and we speak on behalf of hundreds of thousands of women who could not be with us. But all over the country, at this moment, women are watching and thinking of us. Their hearts are with us.

We are women from every part of South Africa. We are women of every race, we come from the cities and the towns, from the reserves and the villages. We come as women united in our purpose to save the African women from the degradation of passes.

For hundreds of years the African people have suffered under the most bitter law of all—the pass law which has brought untold suffering to every African family.

Raids, arrests, loss of pay, long hours at the pass office, weeks in the cells awaiting trial, forced farm labour—this is what the pass laws have brought to South African men. Punishment and misery—not for a crime, for the lack of a pass.

We African women know too well the effect of this law upon our homes, our children. We, who are not African women, know our sisters suffer.

Your Government proclaims aloud at home and abroad that the pass laws have been abolished, but we women know this is not true, for our husbands, our brothers, our sons are still being arrested, thousands every day, under these very pass laws. It is only the name that has changed. The "reference book" and the pass are one.

In March, 1952 your Minister of Native Affairs denied in Parliament that a law should be introduced which would force African women to carry passes. But in 1956 your Government is attempting to force passes upon the African women, and we are here today to protest against the insult to all women. For to us an insult to African women is an insult to all women.

We want to tell you what the pass would mean to an African woman, and we want you to know that whether you call it a reference book, an identity book or by any other disguising name, to us it is a PASS. And it means just this:

That homes will be broken up when women are arrested under pass laws. That children will be left uncared for, helpless and mothers will be torn from their babies for failure to produce a pass. That women and young girls will be exposed to humiliation and degradation at the hands of pass-searching policemen. That women will lose their right to move freely from one place to another.

In the name of the women in South Africa, we say to you, each one of us, African, European, Indian, Coloured, that we are opposed to the pass system.

We, voters and voteless, call upon your Government not to issue passes to African women.

We shall not rest until ALL pass laws and all forms of permits restricting our freedom have been abolished.

We shall not rest until we have won for our children their fundamental rights of freedom, justice and security."

PRESENTED TO THE PRIME MINISTER - AUGUST 9th, 1956

Their protest fell on deaf ears. Twenty years later we are feeling the effects of those broken homes and abandoned children. As the generation of children reared under the pass law system are now growing to maturity, so too is the pressure for radical change. In this struggle for change it is vital that women unite across racial and class barriers and, as women, obtain the right for self-determination. It is vital that women remain united in the rigors of the class struggle. Too often women successfully participated in struggles against class oppression, only to find that they themselves as a group remain oppressed, albeit by new masters and that the quality of their life remains unchanged.

This chapter has attempted to show that the subjective experience of oppression is more linked to day-to-day experience than to some objective reality separate from it. Women can also be as exploitative as men in class terms. Despite this, it has also illustrated that women are capable of uniting across social and class barriers. However, it is equally true that women by virtue of their identity as women do have unique problems which they do not necessarily share with other oppressed groups. It is vital in women's struggle that it is they who determine to what ends the means of economic independence and political autonomy should be used.

REFERENCES

Barrett, M. 1980. Women's oppression today. Problems in Marxist feminist analysis. London: Verso Editions.

Broyelle, C. 1977. Women's liberation in China. London: The Harvester Press Ltd.

Cock, J. 1980. Maids & Madams. A study in the politics of exploitation. South Africa: Raven Press.

Firestone, S. 1972. The Dialectic of sex. The case for feminist revolution. London: Paladin.

Greer, G. 1971. The Female Eunuch. New York: McGraw-Hill.

Lewenhak, S. 1980. Women and work. Great Britain: Fontana Paperbacks.

Lewis, H. 1977. A Response to Inequality: Black Women, Racism and Sexism. Signs: Journal of Women in Culture and Society, 2, 355-65.

Rowbottom, G. 1973. Woman's consciousness, man's world. London: Pelican.

14 SIMILARITIES BETWEEN HUMOR RESPONSES OF MEN AND WOMEN AND ISRAELI JEWS AND ARABS

Ofra Nevo

The first to focus on the subject of sex differences in humor was Freud (1905). He saw the joke as socially legitimate to the release of sexual or aggressive instincts. He considered humor to be a triangular situation in which a man, blocked by inner or external inhibitions from approaching a woman, finds another man and tells him an obscene joke where the woman is usually disparaged. In this way both men succeed in circumventing social taboos. From Freud's description one would assume that telling jokes is the prerogative of men. In fact, Grotjahn (1957) extended Freud's analysis and claimed that women do not have a sense of humor, they do not know how to tell or initiate jokes, and that their humor is less witty and less aggressive than the humor of men.

This chapter was stimulated by research on the differences in the humor of Israeli Jews and Arabs (Nevo and Nevo, 1983). The similarities of sex differences in humor to those of Jews and Arabs was provocative and led to the present analysis.

In order to present these similarities, results concerning humor of men and women will be presented first and then the results on Arabs and Jews.

Early studies of sex differences in humor focused on the comparison of <u>preferences of different contents</u> of jokes and especially on the amount of aggression. Researchers agreed that women prefer less aggressive, more absurd and neutral jokes as compared to men (Landis and Ross, 1933; O'Connell, 1960; Groch, 1974; Terry and Ertel, 1974; Hassett and Houlihan, 1979). Later research replaced the question of content with a more significant question: <u>Who is the butt of the joke</u> and to whom is aggression directed? (Gutman and Priest, 1969). Chapman and Gadfield (1972), rightly claimed that most aggressive jokes are created by men, for men, and against women. They also found that aggressive cartoons which did not imply the superiority of men were equally preferred by both sexes. Other studies have found that both sexes prefer jokes with women as target (Losco and Epstein, 1972; Cantor, 1976). Cantor (1976) questioned whether the "anti-feminine bias" in humor, that is, preference for jokes against women is still found in the United States, with the spread of new ideas about women's rights. Her content analysis of journals, television, and laboratory studies showed that this bias is still expressed. The woman is the preferred butt in the press, on T.V., and in the laboratory.

When active aspects of humor were examined, that is, telling or producing jokes and not just appreciating them, it was found that women initiate fewer humorous remarks in groups (Middleton and Molan, 1959; Coser, 1966, Pollio and Edgerly, 1976; Ziv, 1980). The humorous remarks made by women in groups were found to be less aggressive and less sarcastic in comparison to those made by men. In addition, Brodzinsky and Rubien (1979) found that men, in contrast to women, were more successful in assigning a funny caption to aggressive and sexual cartoons but that there was no sex difference for a neutral cartoon. Levine (1976) in an analysis of male and female U.S. comedians' humor found that women comedians created much more self-aimed humor than men.

The question of whether women prefer self-aimed humor was raised by Stocking and Zillmann (1976). They presented humorous stories to women and men in which the butt of the story was either the teller, a friend, or an enemy. Women preferred stories in which the butt was the self while men preferred stories in which the butt was an enemy, regardless of the sex of the butt.

The only results contradicting the "anti-feminine bias" in humor were found using the attitude toward women's liberation as a modifier. Women and men with more liberal attitudes did not display such a bias (La Fave et al., 1976; Losco and Epstein, 1972).

Since Arabs in Israel are low in status economically as well as socially, they have similar social characteristics to women in the western world. Therefore, one could hypothesize differences in humor between Arabs and Jews in the following areas:

Content: Arabs will prefer less aggressive humor.
Production: Arabs will produce less aggressive humor than Jews.
Butt: The preferred butt of humor for both Arabs and Jews will be an
    Arab.
Attitudes: Attitude toward Arabs will determine humor preferences.
Self-aimed: Self-aimed humor will characterize Arabs' humor.

PRESENT STUDY

Two independent samples of male high school seniors, each containing Jews and Arabs in Israel, were tested. The first sample was tested for joke preferences while the second sample was tested for production of humor. (Nevo and Nevo, 1983).

Content

When subjects were asked to rate 35 prejudged jokes, including aggressive and nonaggressive jokes, it was found that Arabs preferred nonaggressive jokes, while Jews preferred aggressive jokes.

Production

Subjects were asked to produce humorous answers in response to cartoons depicting two men in a conversation in which one was frustrating the other. A blank space, next to the other figure, was left for the subject, to complete as if they were present in the situation and as humorously as they could (Nevo and Nevo, 1983; Nevo, 1982). Half of the subjects received cartoons with an Arab frustrator and the other half, with a Jewish frustrator. The Jewish subjects expressed more aggression in their humor responses while Arabs tended to use more neutral and nonaggressive remarks toward the Arab frustrating figure, who became the butt of the humor.

Butt of Humor

The ratings by Jews and Arabs of five jokes with a Jewish butt and five jokes with an Arab butt were compared. The Jewish subjects preferred jokes that disparaged Arabs while no consistent preferences were found in the Arab sample. In the production sample, as mentioned above, both Jews and Arabs created more aggressive humor toward an Arab butt than toward a Jewish butt so that one may speak of an "anti-Arab bias" in humor in Israel, at least in the sample of high school students we tested.

Attitudes

It was difficult to assess the influence of attitudes on humor preferences and production in our samples partly because the Jewish sample was homogenous and partly because the questions used were not sensitive enough. It was found that Arabs who answered positively to the question "Are you satisfied being an Israeli citizen?"—preferred jokes with an Arab butt.

Self-Aimed Humor

Finally, Arabs produced more aggression toward an Arab target while Arabs who identify with Israel also preferred jokes with an Arab butt, which means Arabs laugh at themselves more than Jews. (More detailed examination of the question of self-aimed humor can be found in Nevo, 1982.)

DISCUSSION

There appears to be a similarity between the humor responses of the "minority" groups. Women and Arabs display similar humor responses as do men and Jews. Both Arabs and women prefer and produce less aggressive humor, prefer a target belonging to their own group, and use more self-aimed humor. The only research finding which was not completely replicated concerned the moderating effect of attitudes toward the target group. It was found only partially in the Arab sample.

These results may be interpreted as a reflection of status relations. Lower status seems to be the common denominator between Arabs in Israel and women in the western world. Humor is nothing but a reflection of social realities, and lower status subjects show less aggression in humor than high status subjects. They also internalize the stereotype accepted by the majority and show more aggression toward themselves. The fact that the similar findings were produced by Arabs and Jews in Israel makes a strong case that the "anti-feminine bias" in humor is socially determined. This seems to support McGhee's (1979) conclusion that "regardless of whether one's social power is the outcome of early childhood characteristics or experiences (e.g., role of men and women) or stems from events or circumstances in adulthood, those who have social power tend to be drawn to humor as a subtle means of exercising control over others" (McGhee, 1979).

Having said all of this, the question of whether or not women have a sense of humor, appears to be a meaningless question. They do indeed have a sense of humor but it is expressed somewhat differently from members of high status groups. While their sense of humor may be less aggressive or more self-aimed, this appears to be a reflection of their social status and not of an intrinsic quality, called sense of humor. A society that laughs at women and a society that laughs at Arabs reflects their lower status. Humor can be considered as a sensitive index of prevailing social conditions.

Jewish humor has been labeled as self-aimed, self-punishing humor (Riek, 1962). Yet new social conditions in Israel have created different humor habits. Israeli Jews no longer behave in humor as a minority. They use more aggression toward the minority and less aggression toward self. Following this evidence, one can assume that in different social conditions, women will show more aggressive humor in general, more aggressive humor toward men, and less toward themselves. Recent studies have supported this assumption. Mitchell (1977), Datan (1979), and Neitz (1980), showed that radical feminists express more aggression in humor toward men and less toward themselves, thus confirming the conclusion that different social conditions can change humor responses.

REFERENCES

Brodzinsky, D. M., and Rubien, J. 1979. Humor production: a function of sex of subject, creativity and cartoon content. Journal of Consulting and Clinical Psychology, (Aug.), Vol. 44 (4), 547–600.

Cantor, J. R. 1976. What is funny to whom. Journal of Communication, 26, 164–72.

Chapman, A. J., and Gadfield, N. J. 1972. Is sexual humor sexiest? Journal of Communication, 26, 141–53.

Coser, R. L. 1966. Laughter among colleagues. Psychiatry, 23, 81–95.

Datan, N. 1979. "Humor in No-Man Land: Women, Identity and Laughter," paper presented to symposium, Women and Society, St. Michael's College Vermont.

Freud, S. 1960. 1905. Jokes and their relation to the unconscious. London: Hogorth.

Grotjahn, M. G. 1957. Beyond Laughter. New York: McGraw-Hill.

Groch, A. S. 1974. Generality of response to humor and wit in cartoons, jokes, stories and photographs. Psychological Reports, 35, 835–38.

Gutman, J., and Priest, R. F. 1969. When is aggression funny? Journal of Personality and Social Psychology, 12, 60-65.

Hassett, J., and Houlihan J. 1979. Different jokes for different folks. Psychology Today, 12 (8) 64-71.

La Fave, L., Haddad, J., and Maesen, W. A. 1976. Superiority, enhanced self esteem, and perceived incongruity humor theory. In Humor and Laughter: Theory and Research, and Applications, edited by A. J. Chapman and H. C. Foot. London: Wiley.

Landis, C., and Ross, J. W. H. 1933. Humor and its relation to other personal traits. Journal of Social Psychology, 4, 156-75.

Levine, J. B. 1976. The Feminine routine. Journal of Communication, 26, 173-75.

Losco, J., and Epstein, S. 1972. Humor preferences as a subtle measure of attitudes toward the same and opposite sex. Journal of Personality, 43, pp. 321-34.

McGhee, P. E. 1979. "Humor as a means of controlling social interaction." Unpublished manuscript.

Middleton, R., and Molan, J. 1959. Humor in Negro and White Subcultures. A study of jokes among university students. American Sociological Review, 24, 61-69.

Mitchell, C. A. 1977. The sexual perspective in the appreciation and interpretation of jokes. Western Folklore, 36 (4), 303-29.

Neitz, M. J., Aug. 1980. Humor hierarchy and the changing status of women. Psychiatry, Vol. 43, 211-23.

Nevo, O. 1982. "Self-aimed humor. The case of Jews and Arabs in Israel," unpublished manuscript.

Nevo, O., and Nevo, B. 1983. What do you do when asked to answer humorously? Journal of Personality and Social Psychology, Vol. 44, No 1.

O'Connell, W. E. 1960. The adaptive functions of wit and humor. Journal of Abnormal and Social Psychology, 61, 263-70.

Pollio, H. R., and Edgerly, J. 1976. Comedians and Comic Style. In Humor and Laughter: Theory Research and Applications, edited by A. Chapman and H. C. Foot. London: Wiley.

Riek, T. 1962. Jewish Wit. New York: Ganut Press.

Stocking, S., and Zillmann, D. 1976. Effects of humorous disparagement of self, friend and enemy. Psychological Reports, Vol. 39.

Terry, R. L., and Ertel, S. L. 1974. Exploration of individual differences in preferences for humor. Psychological Reports, 34, 1031-37.

Ziv, A. 1980. L'humour en Education: Approche Psychologique, Les editions E.S.F. 17 Rue Viete, 75017, Paris.

15 PERSONAL APPEARANCE AND SOCIAL CONTROL

Rhoda Kesler Unger

Since feminists have been well aware of the pernicious effect that the stress on personal appearance has had on women, it might appear strange to assert that physical attractiveness has become an important variable in the study of women. There are several reasons for feminist interest in this variable. First, it is clear that physical attractiveness is in the "eye of the beholder." No objective standards for evaluation appear to exist. Moreover, perceptions of physical attractiveness are socially labile—standards vary widely among cultures and within the same culture over time. Thus, physical attractiveness represents a pure example of a stimulus effect, an effect which operates by way of differential perceptions, cognitions, and attributions produced by variations in that stimulus. To the extent that such perceptions are found to be similar between individuals, we may think of such effects as social variables and they are frequently studied under the term "stereotype."

Physical attractiveness may serve as a model for a more important social variable—the sex of the stimulus person. Perceptions are based on the external properties of the person and differentiation between persons is maintained by relatively unconscious social norms about how individuals with such characteristics do and should behave. There is a great deal of social consensus involving these expectations.

This article will discuss what we know about physical attractiveness as a psychological variable. I will summarize some past findings in the area and review some recent work that I have been conducting in collaboration with students and colleagues. The purpose of this review is to: (1) define some of the properties of physical attractiveness stereotypes; (2) discuss the social nature of such stereotypes; (3) outline contextual relationships uncovered in our investigations; and (4) discuss the impact of social assumptions about attractiveness on men's and women's perceptions of themselves and the activities in which they engage. The purpose of this discussion is to demonstrate how self-fulfilling prophecies are generated and maintained and to illustrate the extent to which perceptual processes create behaviors as well as reflect them.

THE CONTENT OF PHYSICAL ATTRACTIVENESS STEREOTYPES

Enough positive assumptions about physically attractive individuals exist that Dion et al., (1972) were able to coin the phrase "What is beautiful is good!" Physical attractiveness has been found to be associated with perceptions of greater social influence, ability to succeed, competence, and likability. In general, perceptions are similar regardless of whether males or females are the stimulus persons evaluated or the subjects doing the evaluation. Physical attractiveness stereotypes do appear to be more strongly applied to females, although ratings of the two sexes are generally in the same direction (Wallston and O'Leary, 1981).

Negative social judgments associated with lower degrees of attractiveness also exist. Less attractive individuals are more likely to be selected as showing symptoms of psychopathology (Jones et al., 1978) and are even seen as more likely to have epilepsy (Hannson and Duffield, 1976). These findings are consistent with those that indicate that clinicians view more physically attractive patients of either sex as having a more favorable prognosis (Barocas and Vance, 1974). Less attractive applicants are also considered less desirable candidates for high status employment than their more attractive counterparts (Cash et al., 1977; Dipboye et al., 1975).

The finding in this area that has attracted the most attention is that of Goldberg and his associates (Goldberg et al., 1975) in which they showed that individuals of both sexes selected photos of less attractive women as perceived supporters of feminism. This result was interpreted as due to a generalized negative prejudice against women. The interpretation is consistent with a later finding which showed that both males and females perceived that less attractive women need feminism (Jacobson and Koch, 1978).

THE SOCIAL NATURE OF PHYSICAL ATTRACTIVENESS STEREOTYPES

Physical appearance appears to be an important dimension of social reality in the United States. When males and females are asked

to rate the photographs of other males and females on a numerical
scale of physical attractiveness, there is considerable agreement
about each photograph and a high correlation between the ratings of
male and female subjects (Lemay and Unger, 1982; Unger et al., 1982).
Children as young as eight to ten years of age evaluate attractiveness
in much the same manner as adults (Madar, 1984).

Subjects rarely refuse to rate photos for attractiveness or appearance, even though they appear to be largely unaware of the basis
on which they are making judgments. Few differences have been found
among raters. For example, neither feminist ideology nor self-per-
ceived sexual identity has been found to predict the extent to which
individuals differentiate between attractive and unattractive stimulus
persons (Kupecky and Hilderbrand, 1979; Kurland and Wirth, 1978;
Madar, 1984). Combined with the level of male and female agreement
in most studies, the evidence suggests that judgments based on physical attractiveness are a part of a generalized social consensus process.

PHYSICAL ATTRACTIVENESS AND SOCIAL DEVIANCE

Less attractive individuals of both sexes appear to be more likely
to be sorted into categories representing a variety of forms of social
deviance. In this context, deviance is defined in terms of people's perception of behavior rather than as a characteristic of the behavior itself. Deviance is seen to occur when (and to the extent that) people
who are in a position to impose their judgments find other people's
behavior unacceptable in one way or another (Suchar, 1978). Thus,
the aspect of feminism that leads to its association with female unattractiveness, may be its link with an unusual sociopolitical stance,
rather than its ideology per se.

To test for a link between perceptions of physical attractiveness
and perceptions of social deviance, Unger et al. (1982) used a procedure similar to that developed by Goldberg et al. (1975). We required
our respondents to sort photographs that had already been rated for
physical attractiveness into two equal groups. They were informed
that half of the individuals in the stimulus photographs possessed some
characteristic of a socially deviant nature whereas the other half were
characterized as part of a socially acceptable comparable group. The
deviant labels explored were chosen as having a potential cognitive link
with feminism since the original studies had found attractiveness stereotypes in this area. In other words, we wished to find out whether the
finding that less attractive women were perceived to be feminists was
the result of a put-down of women or of a negative social judgment
about feminism. We also wished to explore what characteristics of
feminists induce these negative stereotypic effects.

College students were asked to sort photos using four different labels involving minor levels of social deviance. These labels were: (1) feminists versus nonfeminists, (2) members of the International Committee against Racism (INCAR) (they were additionally told that INCAR was a radical campus organization) versus members of the student government, (3) homosexuals versus heterosexuals, and (4) individuals aspiring to careers in dentistry or engineering (stereotypically masculine occupations) versus those aspiring to careers in nursing or library science (stereotypically feminine occupations). The labels were chosen to represent a form of political deviance, a form of sexual deviance, and a form of achievement-related deviance, as well as the feminist-nonfeminist categories.

Overall, deviants were significantly more likely to be selected from the less physically attractive stimulus photographs than were nondeviants. With a few exceptions, the men and women in our sample responded similarly to the photographs. However, only some of the conditions were statistically significant. Both male and female raters categorized less attractive women as significantly more likely to be political radicals than to be members of the student government. Less attractive women were also more likely to be seen as homosexual than as heterosexual. On the other hand attractiveness was not related to feminism or to masculinity of career aspiration.

As with the female photographs, our sample of men and women categorized less attractive men as significantly more likely to be political radicals but viewed less attractive men as having stereotypically feminine occupational aspirations significantly more often than attractive males. The men and women in our sample did differ in their evaluation of male homosexuality. Women rated male homosexuals as significantly less attractive than heterosexuals; the men did not make this differentiation. There was no distinction in the attractiveness ratings for male feminists versus nonfeminists.

These results suggest a great deal of consensus between the sexes in terms of the applicability of physical appearance stereotypes. The findings also suggest that feminism may no longer be viewed as socially deviant—at least not by college students in the Northeastern United States.

We have also applied the photo rating technique to the evaluation of minor levels of physical stigma (Unger et al., 1983). We were interested in determining whether physical attractiveness stereotypes would extend into areas in which stimulus persons were perceived to have no choice. Because of the general stigma associated with menstruation in U.S. culture (Unger, 1979; Weidiger, 1975), this condition would appear to be a likely target for perceptions involving lack of attractiveness. Our previous research suggested that perceptions of unattractiveness affect both females and males although conditional differences may exist. It is important to determine whether such biases are more common when females are the targets than when males are. It is impossible, of course, to provide a plausible control condition using male targets for menstruation, therefore, we decided to use a second condition—the common cold. This condition is roughly as common a phenomenon as menstruation and affects men and women equally. Comparison of the effects for the two physical labels might also indicate the strength and extent of negative social judgments associated with menstruation.

As in the earlier deviance studies, physical stigma also proved to have a significant effect. However, in our sample, both sexes made no distinctions based on attractiveness when sorting photos using the menstruation-nonmenstruation label, but less attractive men and women were selected as those who had had colds when photographed.

These data may indicate that menstruation has ceased to serve as a social stigma, at least among college-educated populations. Since the cold-no-cold label did produce differential sorting based on attractiveness, it may be argued that this lack of effect is real; e.g., not due to the failure of the manipulation. While it is hopeful that these findings suggest that negative evaluations of the menstruating woman have begun to disappear, several other studies suggest alternative interpretations. Several attempts by my students for example have failed to demonstrate attractiveness stereotypes for peculiarly "feminine" forms of deviance. Thus, subjects of both sexes did choose more or less attractive photos when informed that half of the stimulus persons were members of "Fascinating Womanhood"—an organization that advises women to be superfeminine (Kurland and Wirth, 1978). Nor was there a distinction between individuals who were said to be promiscuous or to be pregnant out of wedlock (Maret, 1982).

It is important to stress that physical attractiveness stereotypes persist throughout a broad spectrum of behavioral and situational domains. Their absence, therefore, may be just as informative as their presence. A number of studies have begun to find a close relationship between perceived attractiveness and perceived gender. Physically attractive males are seen as much more masculine and physically attractive females are seen as much more feminine than their less attractive counterparts (Gillen, 1981; Lemay and Unger, 1982). Unattractive women are also rated as more masculine, motivated, unemotional, and decisive than attractive women (Heilman and Saruwatari, 1979). In other words, attractiveness stereotypes appear to be particularly important in the regulation of socially desirable behaviors associated with appropriate gender roles.

SOCIAL DEVIANCE AND THE EYE OF THE BEHOLDER

The connection between physical attractiveness and conformity with sex-appropriate gender roles is strengthened by studies showing that under some conditions strongly sex-typed individuals are more responsive to level of physical attractiveness than are those who are less strongly sex-typed or androgynous (Andersen and Bem, 1981). High scorers on a Macho Scale developed by Touhey (1979) also indicated more and different judgments about the personality traits of members of the opposite sex than did low scorers. Hilderbrand (1982) has found that individuals of either sex who score high in political conservatism (sometimes associated with negative attitudes toward women) are significantly more likely to sort photos of unattractive women into politically radical categories than those who hold less conservative political beliefs. Unlike the previously cited studies, her subjects showed the effect only when observing women.

THE IMPLICATIONS OF ATTRACTIVENESS ATTRIBUTIONS

A number of conclusions may be drawn from these studies. If we regard these perceptual judgments as veridical expressions of social norms rather than individual idiosyncrasies, we can put together a picture of sex-related social reality. This picture indicates that while physical attractiveness may be a factor in judgments about men as well as women, the role of gender in these attributions produces effects that are more often harmful to women. Masculinity carries with it assumptions about the person's ability to function effectively in the world as well as superior societal status (Unger, 1978), but less attractive (hence, less masculine) men are assumed to aspire to predominantly feminine occupations.

Such perceptual processes perpetuate sex-bias which persists because the definition of role-appropriate traits and behaviors for women and men differ. Masculinity is seen to involve activity and instrumentality whereas feminity is seen to require expressivity and affiliation. These traits are not equally socially desirable either as evaluated by others or in societal payoffs. Interestingly, attractiveness stereotypes do not appear to operate when women engage in peculiarly feminine forms of deviance especially when these activities involve sexuality. Thus, the sexism in these processes stems from the inherent inequality of the categories rather than from the evaluation process itself.

Physical attractiveness stereotypes represent a clear example of how self-fulfilling prophecies and double-binds work against women. Women are expected to maintain a high standard of attractiveness and, indeed, physical appearance is a more important aspect of successful heterosexual social relationships for women than it is for men (Unger, 1979). Attractive women appear to be the recipients of more cues to successful social interaction than are less attractive women (Andersen and Bem, 1981; Snyder et al., 1977). Attractive women rate themselves as more likely to be skilled at social tasks than less attractive women, but do not see themselves as better at skills requiring intellectual competence (Abbott and Sebastian, 1981). And, finally, they may come to possess more social skills than less attractive others (Goldman and Lewis, 1977)—thus, confirming the "truth" of the stereotype.

Conversely, there is the widespread social assumption that less attractive women are more masculine than attractive women. They may be permitted some rewards of autonomous achievement as a recompence for their failures of femininity or their inability to get a man. However, they are also expected to engage in minor forms of social deviance such as homosexuality, political radicalism, or, sometimes, feminism. The ambivalent nature of attributions about unattractive women clearly exemplifies the/nature of a "double-bind." If a woman aims for attractiveness in the hope of social rewards, she leaves herself vulnerable to assumptions about lack of ability. If she ignores the issue of attractiveness, she becomes vulnerable to a number of severe social penalties with no assurance that her achievements will be rewarded. This no-win situation is a result of the ambivalent definition of femininity and its strong association with female attractiveness.

Since attractiveness attributions operate in both directions— what is beautiful is good, but what is good is also beautiful (Gross and Crofton, 1977)—presumptions involving attractiveness may also serve as a social control mechanism to keep women out of gender inappropriate occupations and political activities. Attractiveness stereotyping is a particularly subtle form of social control; although it appears to be universal, it is rarely explicitly recognized or discussed.

Attractiveness stereotyping is a subtle form of violence against women—keeping them in their place without giving them anything to react against. It is an especially pernicious form of social control because the definition of attractiveness comes from the outside—it begins with the eye of the beholder. The victim can do little to alter her position on the subjective scale of beauty, has few alternative sources of societal esteem than do men, and may even be blamed for her vanity and self-concern. When the attractiveness evaluations of others are incorporated, the victim's behaviors serve to validate perceptions about her and maintain the stereotype. It is these subtle nonconscious mechanisms that may prove the most resistant to change.

REFERENCES

Abbott, A. R., and Sebastian, R. J. 1981. Physical attractiveness and expectations of success. Personality and Social Psychology Bulletin, 7, 481-86.

Andersen, S. M., and Bem, S. L. 1981. Sex typing and androgyny in dyadic interaction: Individual differences in responsiveness to physical attractiveness. Journal of Personality and Social Psychology, 41, 74-86.

Barocas, R., and Vance, F. L. 1974. Physical appearance and personal adjustment counseling. Journal of Counseling Psychology, 21, 96-100.

Cash, T. F., Gillen, B., and Burns, D. S. 1977. Sexism and "beautyism" in personnel consultant decision making. Journal of Applied Psychology, 62, 301-10.

Dion, K. K., Berscheid, E., and Walster, E. 1972. What is beautiful is good. Journal of Personality and Social Psychology, 24, 285-90.

Dipboye, R. L., Fromkin, H. L., and Wiback, K. 1975. Relative importance of applicant sex, attractiveness, and scholastic standing in evaluation of job applicant resumes. Journal of Applied Psychology, 60, 39-43.

Gillen, B. 1981. Physical attractiveness: A determinant of two types of goodness. Personality and Social Psychology Bulletin, 7, 277-81.

Goldberg, P. A., Gottesdiener, M., and Abramson, P. R. 1975. Another put-down of women? Perceived attractiveness as a function of support for the feminist movement. Journal of Personality and Social Psychology, 32, 113-15.

Goldman, W., and Lewis, P. 1977. Beautiful is good: Evidence that the physically attractive are more socially skillful. Journal of Experimental Social Psychology, 13, 125-30.

Gross, A. E., and Crofton, C. 1977. What is good is beautiful. Sociometry, 40, 85-90.

Hannson, R. C., and Duffield, B. J. 1976. Physical attractiveness and the attribution of epilepsy. Journal of Social Psychology, 99, 233-40.

Heilman, M. E., and Saruwatari, L. R. 1979. When beauty is beastly: The effects of appearance and sex on evaluation of job applicants for managerial and non-managerial jobs. Organizational Behavior and Human Performance, 23, 360-72.

Hilderbrand, M. 1982. Attributions about political affiliation as a function of perceived physical attractiveness, gender, and sociopolitical attitudes. Unpublished master's dissertation, Montclair State College.

Jacobson, M. B., and Koch, W. 1978. Attributed reasons for support of the feminist movement as a function of attractiveness. Sex Roles, 4, 169-74.

Jones, W. H., Hannson, R. C., and Phillips, A. L. 1978. Physical attractiveness and judgments of psychopathology. Journal of Social Psychology, 105, 79-84.

Kupecky, I., and Hilderbrand, M. 1979. The relationship between physical attractiveness in males and their perceived support of the feminist movement. Paper presented at the meeting of the American Psychological Association, New York City.

Kurland, L., and Wirth, D. 1978. Unpublished manuscript, Montclair State College.

Lemay, M. F., and Unger, R. K. 1982. The perception of females and males: The relationship between physical attractiveness and gender. Paper presented at the meeting of the Eastern Psychological Association, Baltimore.

Madar, T. 1984. Physical attractiveness and perceptions of occupational aspirations of adults by children. Unpublished master's dissertation. Montclair State College.

Maret, S. 1982. Unpublished manuscript, Montclair State College.

Snyder, M., Tanke, E. D., and Berscheid, E. 1977. Social perception and interpersonal behavior: On the self-fulfilling nature of social stereotypes. Journal of Personality and Social Psychology, 35, 656-66.

Suchar, C. S. 1978. Social deviance: Perspectives and prospects. New York: Holt, Rinehart & Winston.

Touhey, J. C. 1979. Sex-role stereotyping and individual differences in liking for the physically attractive. Social Psychology Quarterly, 42, 285–89.

Unger, R. K. 1978. The politics of gender: A review of relevant literature. In Psychology of women: Future directions of research, edited by J. Sherman and F. Denmark. New York: Psychological Dimensions.

Unger, R. K. 1979. Female and male: Psychological perspectives. New York: Harper & Row.

Unger, R. K. 1981. Sex as a social reality: Field and laboratory research. Psychology of Women Quarterly, 5, 645–53.

Unger, R. K., Brown, V. H., and Larson, M. V. 1983. Physical attractiveness and physical stigma: Menstruation and the common cold. In Menarche: An interdisciplinary view, edited by S. Golub. Lexington: Heath.

Unger, R. K. Hilderbrand, M., and Madar, T. 1982. Physical attractiveness and assumptions about social deviance: Some sex by sex comparisons. Personality and Social Psychology Bulletin, 8, 293–301.

Wallston, B. S., and O'Leary, V. E. 1981. Sex and gender makes a difference: The differential perceptions of women and men. In Review of personality and social psychology, volume 2, edited by L. Wheeler. Beverly Hills: Sage.

Weidiger, P. 1975. Menstruation and menopause. New York: Knopf.

16 SEXUAL HARASSMENT IN THE U.S. FEDERAL WORK FORCE

Sandra S. Tangri, Martha R. Burt, and Leonor B. Johnson

This chapter reports preliminary findings from a study of sexual harassment which was mandated by the U.S. Congress in 1980. Since many social scientists desire to do more work with potential policy impact, we think it is important to articulate the ways in which practical policy considerations affected decisions about the study design. The chapter begins by discussing some conceptual, methodological, and organizational issues that shaped the research design and research outcome; and then presents findings from the national survey of the U.S. federal work force.

CONCEPTUAL ISSUES

Sexual harassment has only very recently surfaced as a term and as an issue in the United States. Its timeliness is both the reason Congress mandated a study of it, and the reason why the study posed so many conceptual issues. It's hard to study a moving target—the very knowledge one wants to have at the end of the study (what is sexual harassment?) is also needed at the beginning, in order to circumscribe the study's scope and approach. Furthermore, the U.S. Merit Systems Protection Board (MSPB)—the agency designated to carry out the study—had to use the definition of sexual harassment promulgated by another agency—the U.S. Office of Personnel Management (OPM).[2]

At the individual level, people are still in the process of making up their minds about sexual harassment. Those who have experienced incidents in their working lives which made them uncomfortable, but which remained unlabeled, have begun to reexamine their experiences. Others resist this process of redefinition, preferring the older boundaries between acceptable and unacceptable behavior. Almost everyone in our pretests believed that better communication and shared perceptions could reduce a great deal of sexually harassing behavior. By this, they meant that sender and recipient probably do not agree about what particular behaviors mean, and that better communication would clarify what is offensive and thereby eliminate it. They were thus willing to define sexual harassment as undesirable, but most were unwilling to see it as deliberate, power-motivated, exploitive behavior.

The great variety and changing nature of individual positions on sexual harassment prompted us to take a multi-pronged approach to assessing attitudes and definitions. We wanted to document responses to sexual harassment as an issue—people's overall view of the nature of the problem. We also wanted to know which behaviors they would consider to fall within the OPM definition of sexual harassment. Finally, we wanted to ask people about incidents that they considered to be sexual harassment.

A set of "attitude" items designed to obtain a range of views about the issue of sexual harassment focused on sex at work and sexual harassment. Also included were four definitional items. These measured the degree to which sexual harassment was seen as an exaggeration, as women's vindictiveness or overreactivity, as a male power move, or as the result of misunderstanding and miscommunication. These items gave respondents a chance to state their own positions, and this—our pretests demonstrated—made even avowed "sexists" more comfortable with the questionnaire. Thus individuals' positions were a legitimate response category, and it also provided a broader picture of the range of opinion regarding sexual harassment.

A section on formal definitions of sexual harassment, i.e., behaviors that respondents would include under the sexual harassment rubric, followed the attitude items. These definitions further differentiated whether the behavior came from a person's supervisor or from their coworker(s). This approach established the boundaries of the label "sexual harassment," by finding out which behaviors are included and which are excluded from the category.

We faced the obvious problem of which behaviors to ask about—the six eventually chosen, and the wording for them, reflect previous usage reported in the literature, the advice of an Advisory Group, and pretest experience.

METHODOLOGICAL ISSUES

Response Rate

We were especially concerned that the men's response rate would be low if they saw the subject as either a joke or an insult. To answer Congress's question as to whether women were more victimized than men, we had to administer identical questionnaires to both men and women so that valid comparisons could be made. Devising a questionnaire that motivated both sexes to answer all questions proved extremely difficult, since vis-à-vis sexual harassment, women and men live in different worlds, with very different interests and motivations. We learned through a long series (15) of pretests that men were eager to tell what they thought of the issue as an issue, and were also moderately interested in questions about behaviors that should be included in the definition of sexual harassment. They had much less to say about specific incidents, and had some opinions about remedies, while women were interested in all aspects of the topic.

We tried to promote a high response rate by ordering topics on the questionnaire so that those in the beginning appealed to the maximum number of people. We put attitudes first, because men had shown the most positive reactions to these items, and women also thought them important. Then came definitions and other topics we knew were relevant to both sexes (e.g., remedies). Only after spending 15 to 20 minutes on the questionnaire did respondents come to sections asking them to describe their own experience with sexual harassment. If they had nothing to report (more than 50 percent of the women and over 80 percent of the men did not report such an experience), the end of the questionnaire was only about five minutes away. Question wording was sex-neutral, and instructions specifically included both men and women.

The second approach to achieving a high response rate relied on factors specific to the federal government. The initial letter requesting their participation came from the federal government personnel office (OPM), and the questionnaire came from the federal office responsible for ensuring that all employees are protected by the merit system (MSPB). The cover letter spoke of the Congressional mandate to conduct the study, the study's historic, first-of-its-kind nature, and the potential improvement in work conditions that could result from the study's findings. Complete confidentiality was assured. These measures were effective and we attained an 85 percent response rate.

Confidentiality

We took elaborate measures to preserve respondent's confidentiality, and to eliminate any possibility of negative consequences to respondents as a result of study participation. Questionnaires were sent to home addresses and returned to a private research firm so no one in the government would know who got or responded to the questionnaire. These efforts to assure confidentiality were carefully explained. Finally, we took care to place potentially identifying information (e.g., grade level, agency, geographic region, job classification) in categories broad enough so no one could, by cross-classification, identify the respondent to an individual questionnaire.

Sample Size, Sampling, and Format Constraints

MSPB was committed to survey 1 percent of the civilian federal work force. A potential "universe" of almost 3 million was reduced to about 2 million by excluding inaccessible agencies (e.g., the FBI, CIA) and the Post Office (now a quasi-federal organization). That still left a projected sample size of 20,000. So the questionnaire had to be short, mailed, and without any open-ended questions. Thus, we could not fully explore this very complex and under-researched topic. Yet, we had to include certain politically motivated questions (e.g., about geographical region, federal agency) which could contribute little to any theoretical understanding of sexual harassment, but which took up almost an entire page of an 11-page questionnaire. It also had to discover respondents' definitions of, attitudes toward, experiences with, and repercussions from sexual harassment, and their perceptions of what the government could and should do about reducing it and/or alleviating its consequences. Clearly, the dimensions of this problem called for excellent formatting and the flexibility and space-saving features of typeset copy.

Finally, sampling proved a formidable task for two reasons. First, previous nonrandom studies provided no solid clues about how certain key variables were distributed in the population (e.g., sexual harassment experiences, formal complaints, or remedies tried). Second, the federal work force is extremely skewed on key population parameters (sex, age, grade, salary, agency, minority status, probationary status). It was clear that we would have to use a stratified random sample. We ended up with 60 cells in a 2(sex) x 2(minority status) x 3(agency) x 5(salary) sampling design, and drew equal numbers for each cell. To compensate for the agony of choice imposed by foreknowledge of skewness, the federal government has the advantage of having a completely enumerated universe. So after the strain of making sampling decisions, respondent selection was relatively easy.

ORGANIZATIONAL ISSUES

The organizational issues that arose were educational in and of themselves. For instance, we, with our university research backgrounds, were shocked that our independent nonprofit institute vetoed the research by refusing to submit the contract proposal. The study, of such potential richness, was seen as a politically "hot topic" and required breaking new ground methodologically. We therefore, with regret, did the study as independent consultants to MSPB. Also, several men whom we asked to serve as statistical consultants either declined immediately, or backed out after a few days. They stated various reasons which boiled down to discomfort with the issue. We never mentioned the study's topic to the man who finally served as our statistical consultant, and he never asked. He did do an excellent job.

The central organizational issue was the reality of working for and with a federal agency that had a Congressional mandate to fulfill. Of course there was the tremendous advantage we gained in access to resources and cooperation. OPM supplied information about parameters of the work force upon request, pulled the entire sample to MSPB specifications, directed its agency personnel officers to provide work station addresses for the first mailing requesting home addresses, and made personnel officers available to organize pretests. Agencies gave release-time to more than 400 people to participate in pretests. Key federal people in several agencies served on MSPBs advisory board, and several of these people also helped with debriefing pretest participants in postquestionnaire discussion groups. It would be hard to imagine outside researchers gaining such thorough and invaluable access to any work setting.

On the other hand, the constraints imposed by the mandate, MSPB's organizational need to stay within its bounds, and the political sensitivity of the topic often led to hard bargaining between the agency's pragmatic concerns and our desire to do a study with as much conceptual significance as possible. We have already described the machinations necessary to achieve two fairly incompatible things simultaneously—using OPM's definition of sexual harassment in the questionnaire, and finding out what respondents thought the definition of sexual harassment ought to be. Other incompatibilities also arose because of MSPB's multiple objectives.

For example, MSPB initially hoped to have a questionnaire that would teach as well as be a research instrument, that is, to both tell respondents what remedies were available and ask them what remedies they were aware of; to inform respondents of OPMs definition of sexual harassment and its implications for relief, as well as ask them what their definition was. The latter dilemma was solved by using the cover letter. The former dilemma was resolved in favor of research, which also coincided with the Congressional mandate. Ultimately, we trusted in respondents' self-interested reactions to the list of remedies to spread the word that help was available.

Another dilemma was that the Congressional mandate and MSPB placed a heavy focus on remedies, but since most respondents had not heard of most available remedies, opinions about their effectiveness were largely guesswork. Policy makers would have to be quite tentative about any decision they made based on these opinions.

Fourth, the mandate stipulated that the study was not to explore "sex in the office," but was to focus specifically on sexual harassment. But where does one stop and the other start? Further, what is sexual harassment from women's viewpoint often appears to be "just" sex in the office from men's perspective. Had we had a looser mandate, our approach to definitions and discovering the boundaries of acceptable behavior might have been quite different. On the other hand, a more broadly defined conceptualization of the study would probably have aroused strong political and civil libertarian protest.

Finally, the "hotness" of the topic and the public spotlight on it prevented us from engaging interested legislators in a dialogue which might have helped to shift priorities. Such ongoing discussion could save an agency from an overstrict interpretation of a mandate when professional judgment and further study may suggest more fruitful lines of inquiry than initially envisioned by the legislature.

The second part of this article presents preliminary results of the study, which provide answers to the questions raised by the Congressional mandate.

RESULTS[3]

Definitions and Attitudes

Respondents were asked whether they would consider each of six behaviors sexual harassment: (1) uninvited pressure for sexual favors; (2) uninvited and deliberate touching; (3) uninvited letters, phone calls, or materials of a sexual nature; (4) uninvited sexually suggestive looks or gestures; (5) uninvited pressure for dates; and (6) uninvited sexual teasing, jokes, remarks, or questions. The first three were considered sexual harassment by most respondents and are therefore grouped as "more severe." The latter three were somewhat less frequently considered sexual harassment and are referred to as "less severe." Rape and attempted rape or assault are referred to as the "most severe."

The majority of both men and women considered behaviors 1-4 sexual harassment, although women were more likely to perceive these behaviors as harassment. While the majority of women stated that pressure for dates, suggestive looks, and sexual remarks constituted harassment, the majority of men agreed only with the first. Interestingly, the majority of men and women considered all six behaviors as sexual harassment when initiated by a supervisor, a finding consistent with the view that sexual harassment is an abuse of power and authority. Although coworkers can affect one's job performance, they do not have the formal power to control job outcomes that supervisors have.

The use of the terms "unwanted and uninvited" preceding each behavior, which had to be inserted to be consistent with OPM's definition, may have created a methodological artifact. That is, although respondents showed high consensus that they considered all of the behaviors sexual harassment when they are "unwanted and uninvited," we do not know when they would in fact perceive the behavior to be unwanted and uninvited. As we know from rape research, people think rape is terrible, while at the same time denying that many individual instances are really rape. We need to know what clues people use to decide whether a particular situation is uninvited and unwanted. This information could be used as the basis of training programs to increase sensitivity to sexual harassment and help managers deal with it constructively.

Most workers did not regard a behavior as sexual harassment if the person doing it did not mean to be offensive. However, victims, supervisors, and more educated workers were less likely than nonvictims, nonsupervisors, and less educated workers to consider motives. While half the men felt that people should not be so quick to take offense when someone expresses a sexual interest in them, only one-third of the women agreed with this view. This is as expected: since women are more likely to be victimized, they should also be more likely to identify with the victim than with the perpetrator.

Incidence

Previous studies provide estimates that anywhere between 20 and 100 percent of U.S. working women experience sexual harassment. This variability in estimating incidence is due to lack of probability sampling, self-selected samples or cluster samples, and small sample sizes. Because the present study has overcome these weaknesses, a more accurate estimate of incidence is now available.

Within a 24-month period (May 1978-May 1980) a projected 462,000 federal employees were sexually harassed. More women (42 percent) were sexually harassed than men (15 percent). Although a small percentage had experienced attempted or actual rape or assault (1 percent of the women; 0.3 percent of the men), most victims reported at least one severe harassment incident. Sexual remarks, suggestive looks, and deliberate touching were the three most common forms of harassment. Most incidents continued for a week or more and a sizable percentage continued in excess of six months. Less severe harassment was most likely to recur repeatedly, particularly for women. Surprisingly, among victims of actual or attempted rape or assault, a higher proportion of the men than of the women reported that the experience continued for longer than six months.

Characteristics of Victim and Perpetrator

Although sexual harassment occurs among workers regardless of background, position, and geographic location, individuals with certain characteristics are more likely to be sexually harassed than others. Age, marital status, and sexual composition of the individual's work group have the strongest influence on the probability of being sexually harassed. For example, the most likely victims are under 34, unmarried, and working primarily with members of the opposite sex.

Among the factors having a weaker relationship to sexual harassment are race or ethnic background, educational level, job classification, traditionality of the employee's job, and sex of the employee's immediate supervisor. For example, educated men and women report sexual harassment at a higher rate than their less educated counterparts. For women this difference may be because more educated women tend to be more sensitive to signs of sexual harassment, or because they are more likely than less educated women to hold nontraditional jobs—a factor which was also related to higher levels of sexual harassment. Minority males, unlike their female counterparts, reported higher incidence rates than nonminority males. Nonminority males reported the lowest rate. While women were somewhat more likely to be sexually harassed if their supervisor was male, men were almost twice as likely to be harassed if their supervisor was of the opposite sex. However, only 7 percent of male victims were harassed by a female supervisor. Most harassment is perpetrated by coworkers, not supervisors. Among women the incidence rate was highest for trainees, but surprisingly, the next highest rate for women occurred among professional and technical workers, while the lowest rate was among blue-collar and service workers. Few women in the last category were in nontraditional jobs.

For both male and female victims most harassers were (1) of the opposite sex; (2) acting alone; (3) of the same race/ethnic background as their victims, except for minority men who were harassed by those of a different background more often than nonminority men; (4) coworkers (not supervisors); and (5) married. Furthermore, of the victims who knew, most said that the person who harassed them had also harassed others. Male and female victims differed on two major points—unlike the men, most women were harassed by someone older than themselves; and men were considerably more likely to be victims of homosexual harassment (22 percent vs. 3 percent for women).

Consequences and Coping Strategies

The supervisory status of the harasser and the type of sexual harassment affects the perceived consequences. For both men and women, harassers who have direct organizational control over them are seen as more coercive or threatening than those whose relationship is more distant (e.g., higher-level supervisor) or who share equal organizational power (e.g., coworker). However, individuals experiencing severe harassment, such as actual or attempted rape or assault, perceived adverse consequences regardless of whether the harasser was a coworker or a supervisor. Regardless of gender, those harassed by their supervisor were more likely to perceive adverse or beneficial consequences related to job status and pay. On the other hand, those harassed by coworkers were more likely to perceive consequences related to the quality of their personal relationships.

The effectiveness of the coping strategies used differed by gender of the victim and the severity of the harassment. Sixty-one percent of the women tried to ignore it, forty-eight percent avoided the harasser, and a small percentage went along with the behavior. While few women (8 percent) who went along with the behavior felt it improved their situation, 25 percent of the men reported that this action made things better. For women the next least effective strategy was to ignore the behavior or do nothing—only 28 percent of female victims who chose this action reported that the situation got better. In contrast, 42 percent of male victims who ignored it or did nothing reported that things got better. The most effective action was assertive and direct confrontation. The majority (54 percent) of women who asked or told the person to stop or who reported the behavior to a supervisor or other officials found that things got better. Men also found this to be an effective action. Although the most effective action was disciplining the harasser (74 percent of the women and 56 percent of the men who did this found things got better), few women were in a position to carry out this action and even for men, this was a rare response.

Relatively few victims of either sex talked with anyone about the experience, and when they did they were most likely to talk to coworkers. Generally, women who discussed their experiences with officials outside and within the agency found that the situation got better. However, for those women who experienced the most severe harassment, talking to officials (i.e., EEO or union officials) made things worse or had no effect. On the other hand, men benefited from talking to personnel officials, but received least benefit from talking to union officials. Furthermore, men experiencing rape or attempted rape or assault found that talking to outside contacts was helpful and talking to unions or EEO officials had no effect.

Remedies

Respondents were asked to report on their awareness of remedies and their effectiveness. Five formal remedies were presented: (1) filing a discrimination complaint under Equal Employment Opportunity Commission guidelines; (2) filing a grievance or adverse action appeal under the negotiated grievance procedures of a union contract; (3) requesting an internal investigation by the employing organization; (4) requesting an investigation by an outside agency (e.g., Special Counsel of the Merit Systems Protection Board); and (5) filing a complaint through special channels set up for sexual harassment complaints. For each type of formal procedure, respondents were asked if they were aware of this remedy and if they felt it was effective in helping employees.

Most Federal workers were relatively unaware of formal remedies, though male victims and supervisors were more familiar with remedies than their female counterparts. More than half of the supervisors did not know employees could request internal or external investigations, and fewer than two-thirds knew about filing an EEO complaint. And in any case, four in every ten victims and supervisors did not think filing a formal complaint per se was the most effective strategy.

Despite the lack of faith in formal action, most respondents felt that management could ameliorate the problem by publicizing management policy regarding sexual harassment and instituting tougher sanctions and enforcement.

The Cost: Personal and Organizational

Victims experiencing sexual harassment are vulnerable to economic, psychological, physical, and social consequences. If the harasser is a supervisor, economic consequences can be most severe, for all recourses have the potential to seriously affect the subordinate's immediate job and long-term career.

Our respondents were asked specific questions concerning personal and job-related costs. With the exception of the most severe sexual harassment, the majority of respondents did not report a decline in personal well-being and job morale or productivity. However, a fifth to two-fifths of the victims of severe and less severe harassment reported that their feelings about work and their emotional or physical condition worsened.

Women tended to experience more negative impacts on personal and work-related behavior than men did, regardless of type of harassment. Among those experiencing the most severe form of harassment 82 percent of the women and 53 percent of the men reported worsened emotional or physical conditions. Even for the less severe forms of harassment a substantial minority of both sexes reported worsened emotional or physical health (21 percent of the women; 17 percent of the men).

With regard to feelings about work, 62 percent of the women and

27 percent of the men experiencing the most severe sexual harassment reported a worsening in their feelings about work. Smaller but still very substantial numbers of victims of severe harassment (41 percent of the women; 20 percent of the men) and less severe harassment (24 percent of the women and 17 percent of the men) also reported a worsening in their feelings about work.

Despite these negative outcomes, victims judged their own work and their work group's performance and productivity to be unaffected by their experience with sexual harassment. This is a puzzling finding, especially for those experiencing rape or attempted rape or assault. Forty-eight percent of the women and 22 percent of the men reported that because of their experience their use of time and attendance at work became worse. Yet, 89 percent of the women and 87 percent of the men in this same group claimed that their productivity was unaffected. Perhaps to admit low productivity is difficult in a work culture which believes that personal affairs must not enter the work arena. Further research is needed to unravel this puzzle.

In dollar terms, [4] the cost of sexual harassment has to take into account the costs of: (1) replacing those who left their jobs because of sexual harassment; (2) paying medical insurance claims for employees who sought psychological and medical help; (3) paying sick leave; and (4) absorbing the costs associated with reduced productivity. Based on these factors, it is estimated that sexual harassment cost the U.S. government $189 million during the period May 1978 to May 1980. It is clear that sexual harassment is not only a problem, but a financial, psychological, and emotional drain on the U.S. federal work force. There is every reason to believe that the same is true outside of federal employment.

CONCLUSIONS

This study, despite its dilemmas and limitations, was a privilege to be involved in and a source of pride in its completion and contribution to knowledge and consciousness. It seems quite incredible that any employer would permit, let alone order, such an inquiry which, if it found anything, would likely find situations damaging to the employer. Indeed, since the ruling that sexual harassment is sex discrimination under U.S. law, discovery of sexual harassment means that employers maintain illegal working conditions. It is hard to imagine any private company allowing a study like this among its employees since that ruling. Thus, the MSPB study may stand as a landmark, a one-of-a-kind exploration of the basic and, we hope, changing, facts of sexual harassment.

NOTES

1. This study was conducted by the U.S. Merit Systems Protection Board, Office of Merit Systems Review and Studies, Patricia A. Mathis, Director. Project Director was Cynthia Shaughnessy.

2. The OPM definition of sexual harassment is "Any deliberate or repeated unsolicited verbal comments, gestures or physical contact of a sexual nature that is considered to be unwelcome by the recipient."

3. Additional analyses of these data are presented in <u>Sexual Harassment in the Federal Workplace. Is It a Problem?</u> Washington, D.C.: Government Printing Office, March 1981. A more theoretical discussion of sexual harassment by these authors is presented in "Sexual Harassment at Work: Three Explanatory Models," <u>Journal of Social Issues</u>, Vol. 38, No. 4, 1983.

4. The estimates of economic cost were designed and carried out by Dr. Joel D. Chananie.

17 CONTEMPORARY PORNOGRAPHY AS A CONTRIBUTOR TO SEXUAL OFFENSES AGAINST WOMEN

John H. Court

One of the objections raised against pornography is that distortion is used to present a completely false impression of sexuality. The worst kinds of chauvinistic stereotypes are maintained by the exaggerations of female availability and male dominance. The distortions do not end with the pornography itself. There are many examples of scientific reports that are also guilty of ignoring important evidence and disregarding adverse effects, while presenting reassuring data which allow pornography to circulate unhindered.

The U.S. Commission on Obscenity and Pornography (1970) is still widely quoted as if it had presented the last word on the subject and given pornography a clean bill of health. From the many objections that have now been directed at the research, let me quickly summarize objections to some of the more widely circulated myths.

On the basis of research by Gebhard et al. (1965) the commission argued that it could find no difference between sex-offenders and others in their exposure to pornography. An important finding if true, but note this. All the evidence for the book had been obtained by 1960 and most of it "between 1941 and 1955." Interviews were conducted with offenders who were asked to cast their minds back to the 1930s and 1940s to determine whether pornography had influenced them to commit offenses. Indeed it is because such antiquated material is often quoted, that I have referred in my title to "contemporary" pornography.

We are told that exposure to pornography will bring satiation. Hence given free access to it, interest will be lost. This must surely be the pornographers' favorite finding. It comes from the laboratory study of Clifford Reifler et al. (1971) in which 23 male students were shown the <u>same</u> pornographic materials for 90 minutes a day. After three weeks they reported and showed reduced interest—not too surprising. The authors were themselves critical of their study especially in relation to generalizability. Others have been willing to extrapolate widely. It has since been shown that the study as designed necessarily produced extinction of responsiveness (Schaefer and Colgan, 1977). Also, had there been an opportunity for sexual response their results might have been very different.

According to the Commission Chairman, Cody Wilson, pornography is actually therapeutic, on the basis of a survey conducted for the Commission (Wilson, 1978). He has claimed that "one million adults (in the United States) have had the personal experience of obtaining relief from a sexual problem by means of exposure to pornography." In the survey, 2,469 adults were asked about their responses to sexually explicit materials (the word 'pornography' was carefully avoided, so we have a major problem of definition). Fifteen of the women and twenty men claimed they had received help with their sex problems. Extrapolating to the whole population produced the figure of 1 million. The dishonesty of the advocacy of pornography is amplified by what was not reported. In the original data (Abelson et al., 1971) in addition to the 1 percent of women and 2 percent of men claiming this benefit, there were 47 percent of men and 51 percent of women who thought pornography might lead some people to commit rape.

Studies of Schmidt and Sigusch (1980) in Germany, presented to the Commission, concluded that sexual disinhibition was not a risk. In September 1980 an article by these authors appeared in the British Journal of Sexual Medicine; "Contrary to widespread public fears our experiments gave no indication of any kind of an increase in uncontrolled sexual activity or of reduced effectiveness of controlling mechanisms. . . . There is therefore no question of a sexual disinhibition." Such statements would generally be taken as authoritative and up-to-date. There is no reason why the medical audience, to whom the article was addressed, should question such statements. However, because I have been following the recent research on disinhibition, I found reason to challenge the material. I wrote to the authors and to the journal editor and confirmed what I had suspected. Although this appeared to be a 1980 article by Schmidt and Sigusch, the journal editor had actually revived a conference paper presented in Czechoslovakia in 1972 which described experiments conducted in the late 1960s and published in 1980 (Schmidt and Sigusch, 1980). The editor was evidently unaware that by 1975, the same authors had reported two further experiments, including by this time sexual themes with aggressive content. Their more recent conclusions were very different, e.g.:

> Strong aggression in films of sexual content does not inhibit either men's or women's ability to react with sexual

arousal. The aggression may even have an added sexually
stimulating effect. (Schmidt, 1975, p. 359)

Their findings have since been confirmed in numerous studies
by other workers (Court, 1981). In particular, Malamuth and his colleagues have tested the disinhibition hypothesis quite fully and shown
that disinhibition can and does occur (Malamuth et al., 1980). For
example, a study in which normal males became sexually disinhibited
by listening to tapes of rape victims experiencing both orgasm and
pain found that "within pornographic depictions of rape the victim's
arousal constitutes an important component of these stimuli's appeal"
(Malamuth et al., 1980, p. 406). Specifically invoking conditioning
principles: "The elicitation of sexual arousal within a violent context
may result in a conditioning process whereby violent acts become
associated with sexual pleasure, a highly powerful unconditioned
stimulus and reinforcer" (op. cit., p. 407).

"Evidence" that deserves challenge more than any other is that
relating pornography and sex-crimes. An extended case, starting in
1970, has been made on the basis of very dubious data from Denmark,
that sex-crimes go down when pornography becomes freely available.
Kutchinsky's data (1970, 1971, 1973) have been very widely quoted
ever since the U.S. Commission publicized it (Ward and Woods, 1972;
MacNamara and Sargarin, 1977; Williams, 1979). My own objections
(Court, 1977) to the findings have served to inspire many rebuttals
(e.g., Cochrane, 1978; Williams, 1979; Biles, 1979) but I remain
convinced that the effects found in the laboratory studies of researchers like Donnerstein (1980), Zillmann (e.g., Zillmann et al., 1981) and
Baron (Baron and Bell, 1977) provide parallels that suggest that sexual assaults may not only be increasing, but that this increase is in
part influenced by the theme promoted by pornography. If it was acceptable in 1970 to take sex crime figures as an indication of an effect
of pornography, as those who follow Kutchinsky claim, then I ask that
we take such evidence further.

It is now clear that minor sex-crime reports declined in Copenhagen but, as Kutchinsky himself acknowledged, rape did not. In fact,
since he reported, the trend has steeply risen (Figure 17.1). The
same is true in Sweden (Figure 17.1).

Some of the reasons for this have been discussed by Geis and
Geis (1979). They relate increased rape reports to social attitudes
toward sexuality and increasingly permissive expectations by men
regarding what they can do. It is popular to argue that such increases
arise from increased reporting rates borne of greater public awareness. I believe that argument is overstated by those who wish to deny
the association with pornography. Greater access to Rape Crisis Care
and similar facilities has undoubtedly allowed many women to come

FIGURE 17.1: Reports of rape and attempted rape in Copenhagen and Stockholm (based on police figures, 1979)

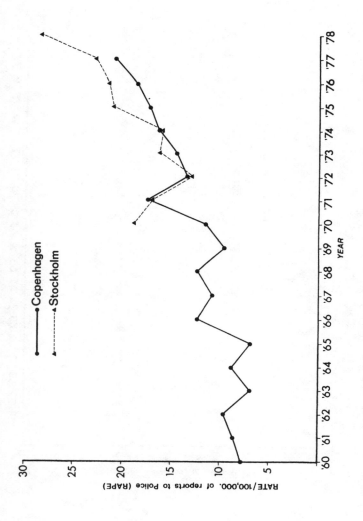

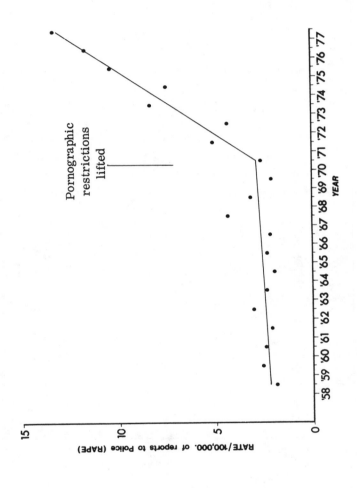

FIGURE 17. 2: Rape reports to police in South Australia

FIGURE 17.3: Rape reports in Hawaii. (Pornography restricted in 1974 and freed again in 1976)

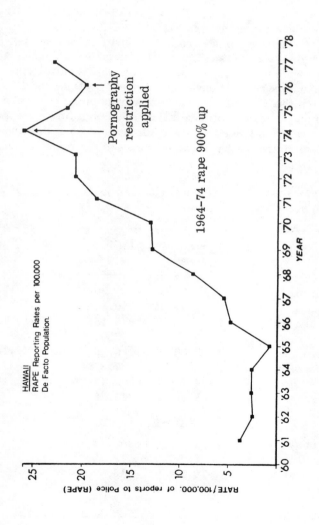

169

forward but I have yet to find evidence that they are going to the police more than before, indeed rather to the contrary (Court, 1977; Bush, 1977). In South Australia (Figure 17.2) pornography restrictions were lifted in 1970, but public awareness has become pronounced only since 1975. In Hawaii the rise in reports closely parallels (Figure 17.3) changes in pornography control. One cannot readily explain a <u>downturn</u> by arguments on reporting rates.

Data on rape reports have been obtained in parts of the world where access to pornography is relatively restricted and compared with places known for ready availability of pornography. Table 17.1 illustrates the striking separation between such places.

What I am stressing here is that undifferentiated sex-crime data are thoroughly unreliable. Too many procedural difficulties exist for them to provide an adequate account of what is really happening. Where sex-crimes appear to go down, the biggest contribution to the decline comes from the offense of carnal knowledge being no longer reported. For example, total sex offense reports in South Australia are going down. Carnal knowledge reports contribute most of this trend. Rape reports are rising so that these now exceed the minor offense reports.

TABLE 17.1: Rate/100,000 population of rape reports for high and low pornography locations

| | High Pornography: 1964–76 | | |
	1964	1974	Annual % change
United States	11.00	26.30	+13.9
California	20.00	40.60	+10.3
England and Wales	1.10	2.13	+9.4
London	0.70	2.04	+19.1
Australia	2.35	6.10	+16.0
South Australia	1.88	7.27	+28.7
New Zealand	4.40	9.12	+10.7
Copenhagen	8.88	16.32	+8.4
	Low Pornography		
North Dakota	7.00	7.80	+1.1
Queensland[a]	2.83	3.22	+3.0
South Africa	10.80	13.87	+2.8
Singapore	2.01	3.40	+6.9
Japan[a]	11.50	5.85	−4.9

[a]1965–75.

One cannot afford to ignore the seriousness of this by talking of the general reduction in sex crime reports.

Finally, since I am suggesting that the evidence in this area is often faulty, I refer to the recent British Report on Obscenity and Film Censorship (Williams, 1979). The report maintained that evidence for harm from pornography was not forthcoming, and cited in support of this conclusion a literature review by Yaffe, but Yaffe himself wrote: "These results extend available evidence dealing with fantasy aggression and offer some empirical support for the existence of a connection between sex and aggression. . . While our attitudes and ideologies may lead us to think that media sex can do no harm, it is possible that sexual materials may actually increase the likelihood that a few persons will carry out bizarre and deviant actions" (Yaffe, 1979, p. 36).

I have criticized the work of various authors of the last decade. Every one of them happens to be male. I find the most appropriate summary for the position I have been advocating is expressed in words from Diana Russell, who writes: "The point about the relationship between pornography and rape is this: pornography even at its most banal, objectifies women's bodies. Women become things. . . . An essential ingredient of much rape, particularly between strangers, is the objectification of the woman. This is not just rhetoric. It means that women are not seen as human beings, but as things. Men are reared to view females in this way, pornography thrives off this, and feeds it, and rape is one of the consequences" (Russell, 1977, p. 7).

REFERENCES

Abelson, H. , Cohen, R. , Heaton, E. , and Suder, C. 1971. Public attitudes towards and experiences with erotic materials: Findings. Technical Reports of the Commission on Obscenity and Pornography, Vol. 6, Washington, D.C. , U.S. Govt. Printing Office.

Baron, R. A. , and Bell, P. A. 1977. Sexual arousal and aggression by males: Effects of erotic stimuli and prior provocation. Journal of Personality and Social Psychology, 35, 2, 79-87.

Biles, D. 1979. Minor sexual offences in Australia: A research note. Australian and New Zealand Journal of Criminology, 12, 33-40.

Bush, P. E. 1977. Rape in Australia, Melbourne: Sun Books.

Cochrane, P. 1978. Sex crimes and pornography revisited. International Journal of Criminology and Penology, 6, 307-17.

Court, J. H. 1977. Pornography and sex-crimes: A re-evaluation in the light of recent trends around the world. International Journal of Criminology and Penology, 5, 129-57.

Court, J. H. 1981. Pornography update. British Journal of Sexual Medicine, 8, 28.

Donnerstein, E. 1980. Aggressive erotica and violence against women. Journal of Personality and Social Psychology, 39, 2, 269-77.

Gebhard, P. H., Gagnon, J. H., Poneroy, W. B., and Christenson, C. V. 1965. Sex Offenders: An analysis of types. New York: Harper & Row.

Geis, G., and Geis, R. 1979. Rape in Stockholm: Is permissiveness relevant? Criminology, 17, 3, 311-22.

Kutchinsky, B. 1970. Studies on pornography and sex crimes in Denmark. New Social Science Monographs, Copenhagen.

Kutschinsky, B. 1971. Towards an exploration of the decrease in registered sex crimes in Copenhagen, Technical Reports of the Commission on Obscenity and Pornography, Volume 7. Washington, D.C., U.S. Govt. Printing Office.

Kutchinsky, B. 1973. The effect of easy availability of pornography on the incidence of sex crimes. The Danish experience. Journal of Social Issues, 29, 3, 163-81.

Lederer, L., editor. 1980. Take Back The Night. New York: W. Morrow and Co.

MacNamara, D. E. J., and Sargarin, E. 1977. Sex, Crime and the Law, New York: Free Press.

Malamuth, N., Heim, M., and Feshbach, S. 1980. Sexual responsiveness of college students to rape depictions: Inhibitory and disinhibitory effects. Journal of Personality and Social Psychology, 38, 399-408.

Reifler, C. B., Howard, J., Lipton, M. A., Liptzin, M. B., and Widman, D. E. 1971. Pornography: An experimental study of effects. American Journal of Psychiatry, 128, 5, 573-82.

Russell, D. E. H. 1977. Pornography: A feminist perspective, Symposium paper, San Francisco. (see L. Lederer, editor. 1980).

Schaefer, H. H., and Colgan, A. 1977. The effect of pornography on penile tumescence as a function of reinforcement and novelty. Behavior Therapy, 8, 938-46.

Schmidt, G. 1975. Male-female differences in sexual arousal and behavior during and after exposure to sexually explicit stimuli. Archives of Sexual Behavior, 4, 453-65.

Schmidt, G., and Sigusch, V. 1980. Sex differences in responses to psycho-sexual stimulation by films and slides. Journal of Sex Research, 6, 4, 268-83.

Schmidt, G., and Sigusch, V. 1980. The effects of pornography. British Journal of Sexual Medicine, 7, 3-6.

U.S. Presidential Commission Report on Obscenity and Pornography. 1970. New York: Bantam Books.

Ward, P., and Woods, G. 1975. Law and Order in Australia. Sydney: Angus and Robertson.

Williams, B. 1979. Report of the Committee on Obscenity and Film Censorship. London: HMSO, Cmnd 7772.

Wilson, W. C. 1978. Can pornography contribute to the prevention of sexual problems? In The Prevention of Sexual Disorder, edited by C. B. Qualls, J. P. Wincze, and D. H. Barlow, New York: Plenum Press.

Yaffe, M. 1979. Pornography and violence. British Journal of Sexual Medicine, 6, 47.

Zillmann, D., Bryant, J., and Carveth, R. A. 1981. The effect of erotica featuring sadomasochism and bestiality on motivated intermale aggression. Personality and Social Psychology Bulletin, 7, 1, 153-59.

18 WOMEN WHO KILL THEIR BATTERERS

Anne Jones

Women are regarded as "natural" victims. We aren't troubled to inquire into the situation when women are the victims of homicide. It's only when women commit homicide that some sort of explanation seems to be required. Yet I find, after writing Women Who Kill, that no one is very eager to hear those explanations.

Most books on the subject of women who commit homicide are frivolous or sensational. They sport catchy titles like Fatal Femmes or The Deadlier Species and dwell upon woman's "innate" evil. Woman is seductive Eve, reckless Pandora, vengeful Medea, loathsome harpy, wicked stepmother, deadly witch. These books have nothing to do with real women. On the other hand, when Women Who Kill appeared in 1980, a law professor attacked it in print for failing to deal with bizarre, grotesque, and ghoulish cases. Women Who Kill, he complained, is about only ordinary women. And that, of course, is the point.

The title Women Who Kill seems to me to be a straightforward, objective indication not only of the contents of the book but also of the nature of the women I write about: like women who sew, women who cook, women who raise children—women who kill. This is not to say that killing is an ordinary activity, like cooking and sewing. Certainly it is a morally revolting act; yet it is an act that human beings (mostly men) from time to time perform. An implication of the title, then, is that women—ordinary women—are capable of the whole range of human activity, wrong as well as right. The woman who kills is no monster. Usually she is an ordinary woman who performs a morally repugnant act for reasons we can understand if we try. To make this effort is not to condone a homicide but to seek ways to prevent others.

My thesis is that throughout U.S. history, women have killed in response to being boxed in by some kind of social repression, some means of social control. That social box was constructed at various times by religion, science, social science, the structure of the family, and the law itself. Those patterns of social control and women's responses have changed with the times. I will consider the situation of the women who are most likely to kill at the present time, namely battered women.

Today's particular box for women is to be bound, without aid or easy exit, to men who beat them. The FBI estimates that one-third of women who kill in the United States do so in self-defense—that is, usually in response to battery or sexual assault. I would place that estimate much higher. I think that perhaps two-thirds of women who kill do so in what they perceive to be self-defense; but because so many of them are nevertheless convicted of murder or manslaughter, they don't appear in the self-defense statistics.

It is important to recognize that battery of women is connected to other crimes of violence against women. Often battery and rape go together. "Both rape and wife-beating are crimes of violence against women. Both are widespread, under-reported, trivialized, and inadequately punished by the legal system. Both are acts of terrorism intended to keep all women in their place through intimidation. In fact rape is often part of wife abuse, though so far only a few states acknowledge even the possibility of rape within marriage. The chief difference between the two crimes is that while the victim of nonmarital rape must live with a terrifying memory, the abused wife lives with her assailant. Rapists are, in Susan Brownmiller's phrase, the 'shock troops' of male supremacy. Wife beaters are the home guard" (Jones op. cit., 1980, p. 282).

At the International Congress on Women (1982) Diana Scully reported on her study of convicted rapists, and Beverly Houghton reported on her work with wife beaters. The two crimes—rape and woman beating—are part of the same system of intimidation, yet while Scully's rapists are in a maximum security prison in Virginia, Houghton's wife beaters are at home in Rockland County, New York.

Woman beating is also intimately connected to homicide. Too often it is only the warm-up for murder. Though some women defending themselves kill their batterers, it is the women who are far more likely to die. Three out of four women murdered in the United States are killed by their husbands or lovers. A great many of them are simply punched and kicked to death.

Yet we hear plenty of excuses for our failure to protect women from violence within the family—and women accept those excuses. The police claim, for example, that they can't intervene and arrest batterers because they—the police—are likely to get hurt. Apply that excuse to any other kind of crime and you will instantly see its absurdity. Suppose the police tell us that they are not going to respond to bank robberies anymore because confronting bank robbers is too dangerous. "Some of our boys got hurt last year." Clearly the public wouldn't stand for it. Taking risks on behalf of the citizenry happens to be the job of the police.

Or take this case: A battered woman calls the police who come, if at all, with a clergyman or social worker in tow to cool off the situation and provide marriage counseling. Now suppose your house is burglarized. You call the police and they show up with a minister who says, "We've got the burglar right here. Let's sit down and see if we can't work this out."

Another common police excuse is that if they arrest the battering man, they will make him angry. If they prosecute him and put him in jail, they will make him angrier still—and he will come back to beat up his wife again. Suppose once again that your home is burglarized and the police say, "We know this man burglarized your house, and we know you want him arrested. But we sent him to jail a while ago, when we caught him cleaning out a house, and as soon as he got out he burglarized your house. So you see it does no good to punish him. It just makes him angry."

These common excuses applied to any other kind of crime sound perfectly ridiculous, but when it comes to crimes of violence against women, even women swallow them whole. That is a sorry measure of the value we place on women—on ourselves.

I think it's about time for somebody to do something about these batterers. Beverly Houghton (op. cit.) reports that in the past two years her agency has converted 60 batterers to nonviolence at a cost of about $1000.00 per batterer. (I think that's cheap. I'd kick in for that.) But sixty batterers in two years doesn't amount to much when the FBI tells us that 50 percent of women married to or cohabiting with a man in the United States will be battered by that man.

These men should be arrested. What they are doing is committing felonious assault. We should arrest them and prosecute them, not in the name of the battered woman, but in the name of the state. Everyone who studies family violence agrees that violence is learned in the home and passed on from generation to generation, from the home to the street. This process has created a world with completely unacceptable levels of violence—90 percent of it committed by men. We must intervene somewhere to stop it. We can intervene by calling this violence what it is—a crime—and by putting the assailants in jail. Counsel them if you will, but first let them know that their actions are criminal and will not be tolerated.

Don't get me wrong. I am not enthusiastic about punishment or imprisonment. Jails and prisons are, as a rule, miserable places; in the long run, we need alternatives to incarceration, not bigger and costlier prisons. Nevertheless, at the present time, law enforcement is the chief way in which we teach the difference between acceptable and unacceptable social behavior. As things stand now, the police don't respond when a battered woman calls, or they bring a social worker, or they simply walk the man around the block and ask the battered woman what she did to provoke him. Prosecutors discourage battered women from prosecuting. Juries won't convict. Judges won't sentence. The battering men, then, readily learn this lesson: that it is all right to do what they do. All our sophisticated psychological and sociological research must finally come up against this hard fact: men beat women <u>because they can</u>. What I heard over and over from battered women who killed was: "Nobody stopped him. Nobody stopped him."

So some of these women take it upon themselves to stop the men. I must emphasize that women, despite the violence visited upon us, are extraordinarily peaceable. We commit only about 10 percent of all crimes of violence and only 15 percent of homicides. Many (if not most) of those homicides are committed in self-defense, in last resort situations, after the women have been forsaken by every social service and criminal justice agency that should aid them—or at least they perceive that this has happened to them. An outside observer might still be able to find some other alternative, but boxed in that desperate situation, with another beating imminent, the terrorized woman may act to save herself.

The homicide that then takes place usually follows one of three patterns. In the first type, when the man is beating the woman, she grabs whatever comes to hand to threaten him and stop the beating. With no intention of killing or even harming him, she picks up a kitchen knife to hold him off. He charges and the knife happens to hit a critical artery, or the ambulance takes an hour to arrive, and he dies. There is such a strong element of chance in the death that the killing could almost be said to be an accident.

In the second type, the woman recognizes that the beating she is getting or sees coming is "different" from previous ones. This time he intends to kill her. (Often he tells her so.) In that instant, with intention to save herself, she kills him. In these cases the man often "asks" for it. In a surprising number of these "victim precipitated homicides" (as the criminologists call them), the batterer hands the lethal weapon to the woman and challenges her to use it before he does.

In the third and most rare pattern of homicide, the woman plans ahead for the killing and works at it over a long period of time, especially if she is not skilled at murder and is trying hard to get away with it. Eventually she kills the man or hires someone else to kill him.

All of these killings take place as a last resort. Usually they take place because the men will not let the women go. (Beverly Houghton

(1981) vividly described how batterers fall apart when the women leave. That should help us to understand why so many batterers won't let "their women" go.) We hear the same question asked over and over; "Why didn't she just leave?" But the fact is that in most cases these women tried to leave. In many cases they left. It is often at that point—when the woman prepares to get out or actually leaves—that the man escalates the level of violence, even to the point of homicide.

Let me give you some examples, because I think the behavior of the men is a determining factor. (Examining that behavior is a powerful antidote to querulous talk about "Why didn't she leave?")

> Battering husbands . . . are usually described by their wives as extremely possessive people. Usually they persuade or force their wives to stop working or going to school. They are cool or rude to family and friends, gradually cutting their wives off from social contacts. Some keep the car keys; some permanently sabotage their wives' cars. Others make sure their wives never have enough cash to get out. Some won't let their wives use the telephone; James Hughes used to rip the wires out of the wall if he thought Francine had used the phone, and another husband beat the telephone to splinters on the concrete floor. Some lock their wives in; others follow them when they leave the house. Some make their wives literal prisoners. During a five-month marriage, Gary Bartosh of Charlotte, North Carolina, never let his wife, Eileen, out of his sight except for some "monitored trips to the bathroom." When he finally turned his back, she shot him. A study that analyzed how victims and offenders in marital homicide perceived their sex roles found that men were more than ten times as likely as women to define their spouse as "an object of personal property" and to treat her accordingly. And it is hardly surprising that men who do so may be killed (Jones, op. cit., pp. 297-98).

What happens to these women after they commit homicide? The women who were battered by their husbands are subsequently battered by the legal system. The law of self-defense is applied inequitably to men and women because it uses the standard of a hypothetical "reasonable man" and assumes that he is involved in an altercation with another man of relatively equal physical training and strength. The reasonable man is entitled to counter an assailant's force with "like force" and no more. Thus, when a woman picks up the weapon she feels she needs to defend herself against a larger and stronger man, she is meeting an assault not with like force but with deadly force. She is committing an act not of self-defense but of murder. She will be prosecuted for murder.

Contrary to what you may have heard—because the cases of some women who killed in self-defense and were acquitted have received enormous publicity—most women who commit homicides of this sort are convicted of murder, or at least of voluntary manslaughter, and serve long prison sentences. Some informal prison surveys suggest that in some states perhaps as many as 80 or 90 percent of women serving time for homicide are serving long terms for killing in what they describe as self-defense. The law simply does not take their perceptions into account. [1]

The women who kill, battered by their husbands and battered by the law, go to prison. They serve long terms. How do they feel about their crime and their punishment? How do they adjust? This passage from Women Who Kill addresses those questions.

> Women who kill their battering husbands or lovers almost
> always express great remorse and sorrow. They say they
> still love the dead man and grieve at his loss. Some feel
> so guilty and depressed that they try to take their own lives,
> or say that they would if they did not have children to care
> for. But at the same time, many of them experience an
> exhilarating sense of release. "Even when I knew I would
> go to prison," said one woman, "I felt as if a stone hand
> had been lifted off my head." Another said, "Suddenly I
> knew that I could take a walk, call my mother, laugh—and
> it would be all right. For the first time in eleven years, I
> wasn't afraid." Another said, "While I was out on bail wait-
> ing for trial, even though I'd done such a terrible thing, the
> kids and I had fun for the first time in years." Some women
> experience a new sense of themselves when people begin to
> treat them with a certain deference. "Even the sheriff, who
> laughed off the beatings for fifteen years, suddenly can't
> do enough to help me," one woman reported. Many of them
> use their painfully acquired self-respect to aid others
> through programs for battered women. Their message is
> always the same: "Get out—you don't have to take it." And
> some women use their power directly. One woman, who
> served eight years for shooting her husband to death, was
> asked what she would do if she found out that her daughter
> was being battered by a husband or boyfriend. "I think I'd
> just take the man aside and have a little talk with him about
> nonviolence," she said. "And then I'd tell him who I am"
> (Jones, 1980, pp. 320-21).

NOTE

1. For analysis of the exceptional Wanrow decision [State v. Wanrow, 88 Wash. 2d 221, 559 P. 2d 548 (1977)] see Jones, pp. 285-86. This decision, which takes the woman's perceptions into account, has not been widely applied.

REFERENCES

Houghton, B. 1981. Spouse Abuse: Origins and Remedies. Presented at The First International Interdisciplinary Congress on Women, Haifa, Israel.

Jones, A. 1980. Women Who Kill. New York: Holt, Rinehart & Winston.

Scully, D. 1981. Convicted Rapists' Attitude Toward Women. Presented at The First International Interdisciplinary Congress on Women, Haifa, Israel.

PART 4

EARTH TREMORS

A tremor of the earth contains the implication of agitation, excitement, and upheaval in what ought to be the most stable aspect of our lives. Thus it is fearsome. The women's liberation movement is such an earth tremor. The articles in this section deal with some of the political, social, and intellectual consequences of such movements in various times and various cultures. A common thread is the shifting image of women's world that has emerged. The search for a valid view of this world has been the heart of the recent feminist struggle. It is a search that has proceeded through unfamiliar layers of consciousness by way of paths that had not been previously explored. Early studies were descriptive, compelled by the realization that women's reality had been ignored or even suppressed. Current scholarship has moved beyond description to analysis, a level of discourse that is well illustrated in these chapters. The common theme, one which is perhaps at the heart of the fear of earth changes, is an effort to understand both the powerless character of the situation of most women and the dynamics of change. These chapters also demonstrate the importance of culture, of history, of social context, also basic to an accurate revision of personal consciousness.

Atsumi presents a succinct summary of the history and current status of feminism in Japan. She tells of a feminist movement that has existed for many decades and that the early Japanese feminists had already recognized in the saying that "in the beginning woman was the sun, now she is the sickly pale moon. . . . " Her account illustrates the elusiveness of empowerment. Apparent victory, achievement of constitutional recognition of women's rights, coopted the movement of the early twentieth century and diverted the quest for power realignment. Atsumi argues, too, that Japanese culture, e.g., in its denigration of egoism and autonomy, places constraints on the attainment of some feminist goals.

Eleanor Lerner analyzes the New York City woman's suffrage vote at the turn of the century, teasing out the ethnic, family, and work-related factors that influenced the vote of the men of that period. The results reveal the web of personal relations that affected men's willingness to vote for the political empowerment of women. At a very simplistic level they show that working side by side with women, particularly with commonly perceived goals, made a difference in men's political behavior. This may indicate that while the movement for a comparable worth analysis of pay scales may lead to fairer wages, insofar as there is continued segregation of the work place, it will not lead to a change in power relations between the sexes. At the very least this uncovers a tension between different approaches to equity that deserves attention.

Ilse Schuster traces the history of female participation in the political life of Zambia from precolonial to modern times. Her analysis of the impact of colonialism on female consciousness shows that change can produce a powerless condition even when such change is defined as progress in Western terms. Schuster shows how women's powerless status was actually used in the Zambian battle for independence. Women's role, as socialized in the Colonial era, allowed them to help, but in a way that did not allow self-definition or the development of woman-defined solidarity. This in turn guaranteed that postindependence political participation by women would be limited to mere tokenism.

The study by Alice Eagley on supposed sex differences in conformity, moves us to another level, that of understanding the female psyche. The received truth about the female character has included the idea that women are more conformist and influencible than men. She shows us, in an illuminating example of recent feminist intellectual revisionism, that this supposed trait, with all of its connotations of immutability and innateness, is in fact the result of the almost universal isomorphism of gender and status in the mixed sex world. She also cautions that the laboratory world and the real world differ, particularly with respect to the genders' real power and status in each domain.

Nancy Henley also questions received knowledge about female consciousness. While focusing on the area of nonverbal communication, her points are more generalized, as she outlines the positive aspects of the so-called feminine nonverbal style. Like Eagley, she argues that the social context creates behaviors that are then viewed as innate. Her notion that women are "immigrants to man's world" leads again to a tension between integration and separation, certainly a central problem of defining women's world.

Finally, Barbara Wallston argues that the generation of knowledge is in itself a path to power and that the scientific model is a method that should not be, as some feminists have argued, rejected. Instead we must examine, in the light of an understanding of power relations and sexism, the questions we ask, the values undergirding the research process, and the implications of various methodologies. But the tools for learning must all be exploited as the servants which they are.

Each of the chapters in this section speaks to the issue of power and the possibilities of new definitions of the world which women inhabit. The changes envisioned surely validate the image of a tremor of the earth.

19 WOMEN'S LIBERATION IN JAPAN: WHAT DOES MODERNIZATION MEAN FOR WOMEN?

Ikuko Atsumi

Though it seems difficult for many Westerners to imagine active women's movements in Japan, there have been many such movements for over 70 years and they still exist even today. As early as 1911 a magazine, Seito, or Bluestocking, began to try to raise women's consciousness with a manifesto that stated: "In the beginning, woman was the sun. Now she is the sickly pale moon, reflecting only the light of others." Its editor, Hiratsuka Raicho, joined other women in 1920 to form the New Women's Society, the first nation-wide politically oriented women's organization in the country.

The history of the women's movement in Japan since then may be subdivided into three periods. The first in the prewar period, roughly 1920 to defeat in World War II and U.S. occupation; the second in the postwar 1950s and 1960s; and the third in the 1970s.

In the first period, Seito and later feminist groups in prewar Japan were much inspired by the ideals of women's movements in other nations and were linked to the first world-wide wave of feminism. Their main goals were to gain women's political rights, to combat prostitution, and improve the working conditions of women. But the rise of prewar militarism led to the suppression of all such efforts.

In the second period, Japan's defeat in World War II led to occupation by the United States and the creation of a new constitution which granted women the right to vote and at least theoretical equality with men. Ironically enough, under this constitution Japanese women have the equivalent of the constitutionally protected equality which women in the United States still have not achieved. But this had the effect of breaking up the upper middle-class feminist movement which became more or less coopted. This left the field to left-wing women's groups and grass-roots consumers' groups which took center stage in the 1950s and 1960s when Japan was making rapid economic gains.

In the third period, during the 1970s, the new women's liberation movements were stimulated by the importation of U.S. women's liberation views, and profited from the existing grass-roots movements and from the new consciousness surfacing in the student movements. It went further than either the prewar or postwar movements which limited their demands to more legal rights. Present day feminists in Japan do not incorporate the class-struggle ideology, for Marxist feminist theory no longer fits the reality of present-day Japan where about 90 percent of the people have come to have middle-class consciousness and a middle-of-the-road lifestyle. What does seem urgent to them, in a country with a long male-oriented tradition, is cultural reform, especially with respect to the sexual division of labor. Thus, since 1975, the first year of the United Nations Decade for Women, Japanese feminists have generally agreed their priority should be nothing less than to change the current strict division of labor by sex.

The strategic difficulty lies in the fact that Japan's explosive economic growth has been based precisely on this division of labor which exploits women as low-paid menial workers or as unpaid homemakers who use most of their energy to take care of their husbands and educate male children to make them future dedicated workers. What had modernized Japan has forced Japanese women to remain in an unmodernized status, a process that has been going on for more than a century.

Ever since Japan began modernizing after the Meiji Restoration of 1868, it has been competing fiercely to catch up and even surpass Western countries. And it succeeded. Now it ranks among the world's leading nations; only the United States and the Soviet Union have a larger Gross National Product. Yet such impressive economic growth has relied to a great extent on cultural values and their expression that still survives from a feudal past. Three of these cultural items are: the ideas of prewar "family state" expressed in "family-style businesses"; traditional Asian views on the nature of human relationships; and the categorization of women's roles.

"FAMILY-STYLE BUSINESSES" ORGANIZATION BASED ON IDEALS OF THE PREWAR "FAMILY STATE"

The young leaders who guided Japan's early modernization were mainly from the warrior-bureaucrat class and most believed in strict social control. Thus, Japan's constitution of 1889 strongly promoted the concept of a "family state" with the emperor as the "father" with patriarchal households as the basic social units. Of course the present constitution does not employ these concepts, but much of the "family state" ideology has been taken over by Japan's huge companies, which consider themselves "family-style businesses" calling for selfless devotion from their workers. Meanwhile, "defense of the home" has always been considered women's proper role, according to Confucianism. Such ideas, coupled with the life-time employment and seniority system in Japan tend to keep men tied to their work and women tied to their households.

TRADITIONAL ASIAN VIEWS ON HUMAN RELATIONSHIPS

The importance of mutual dependence and mutual reliance are emphasized in Japan, and developing interpersonal relations is regarded as an end in itself. This so-called "interpersonalism," contrasts with the "individualism" emphasized in the west. The Japanese feel that they are welded together into the already fixed infinite human networks, an idea originating in Buddhism. This is combined with the Confucian view of the universe, divided into Yin and Yang, night and day, male and female. Thus harmonious human relationships are considered of highest importance. The sexual division of labor embodies such a view. Thus, according to a study of women's consciousness in 1981, 80 percent of Japanese women believe that division of labor by sex is essentially beneficial in maintaining a harmonious partnership between men and women.

CATEGORIES OF WOMEN'S ROLES

Wives have been traditionally viewed as vessels for bearing children while other women in entertainment districts could be considered objects for pleasure. The "myth of the sacred mother" was emphasized under the prewar Emperor system, and motherhood still regarded as a full-time job. This makes women feel guilty whenever they leave home for work, although women actually account for around one-third of Japan's workforce, and 65 percent of all women workers are married. The mothers' main role is to educate their children, fiercely pressuring them to succeed, and to serve as substitute mothers for their husbands, who can also receive entertainment and sexual comfort from women in the entertainment districts. Japanese women almost all assume they must eventually marry (the marriage rate is 98 percent) and raise children. The number of lesbians is very small and the impetus for solidarity among women is weak.

With this cultural ambience, it would be impossible to simply copy the tactics of the U.S. liberation movement. Thus, instead of starting with reforms of domestic law and other institutional changes, Japanese feminists may have to first concentrate on the creation of a "women's culture" and on attempts to have women's views incorporated into the social mainstream. Since in Japan it is always necessary to achieve national consensus in order to make any institutional changes, the only possible course is to raise consciousness with respect to legal change. One way to do this is by pointing out that sex prejudice causes Japan to lose face when compared with the other advanced countries.

Despite the emphasis on "women's culture," feminist separatism would not work. Japanese men must also be involved in order to achieve nation-wide consensus. Another way is by emphasizing women's creative power. It is characteristic of Japanese feminism that open hostility between the sexes is relatively rare.

Since 1975, more serious and practical groups, such as the Women's Action group, have been founded and women's studies have begun to be introduced. And since the Japanese government in 1980 was obligated to sign the Convention on the Elimination of All Forms of Discrimination against Women at the United Nations Conference for the Decade of Women, a main focus of Japanese feminists has been one of urging the government to change certain domestic laws that prevent parliamentary ratifications of this document. They have also made remarkable progress these past few years with the dissemination of new information about feminism from other countries. The 1978, Japanese Government's Action Plan for improving women's status is currently being implemented on the local administrative level, with emphasis on adult education programs, and some companies now appeal to an improved self-image for women in their advertising.

But, again, the question arises: What does modernization mean for women? For men it has meant industrialization and, concomitantly to some extent, greater individualism, a concept imported from the West. For women it should mean a transition to a society allowing a greater range of options. But as Japan's economic growth slows down and features of the "post-industrial" age emerge, certain old Japanese views—such as, for example, "interpersonalism" and "corporativism"—the idea of symbiosis between a group and its components—are being reevaluated as unique traits to be presented for the new era. Such developments do not make for free choice.

Nevertheless the Japanese women's liberation movement should strive against the current sexual division of labor and seek women's independence in a society that has traditionally sought interdependence. It may seem, by Western standards, that forces of modernization and antimodernization are both operative at the same time. This is the difficult reality with which the Japanese movement must cope. It is such contradictions that make the Japanese case a useful one when considering the meaning of modernization from a non-Western or male-centered perspective.

20 POLITICAL WOMEN: THE ZAMBIAN EXPERIENCE

Ilsa Schuster

The political talents of women and their desire for power have been limited to the domestic sphere in so many world civilizations, and for so many centuries, that their exclusion from formal political roles in the wider society is often seen as biologically based. Indeed, it was to criticize the view that by nature women were apolitical that early feminist anthropologists emphasized that when women were leggally excluded from formal political offices and activities, they were still political actors, albeit in the domestic domain (Collier, 1974). But in societies that grant equal rights and obligations to both men and women to participate in extradomestic politics, this concentration on domestic politics is a side issue, since even in such societies women are less committed to political activity than are men. At best we find only a handful of female politicians—never more women than men. If we view their apparent lack of interest in politics as biologically based, no further analysis is necessary. If such an explanation seems less than satisfactory, then we must analyze the conditions necessary for women to undertake extradomestic political roles and the constraints under which political women operate.

The Republic of Zambia, a Central African state, is a fertile arena for the study of political woman. [1] Precolonial traditions of matriliny and female leadership, colonial history of female freedom fighters, and postcolonial experience of female office holders demon-

---

A fuller analysis is available in Schuster, I, "Constraints and opportunities in political participation: The Case of Zambian women." Geneve-Afrique, XXI (2), 1983, 7-37.

strate a relatively consistent high level of female involvement in the political process. Yet even in Zambia, women's involvement is less than men's. This chapter analyzes why such is the case.

PRECOLONIAL SOCIETIES

Ethnographic descriptions of traditional precolonial Zambian societies provide tantalizing hints of female political activity. [2] Among the Ila, Bemba, Chewa, pre-Lunda, Luapula, and Lozi peoples, societies were organized as chiefdoms or kingdoms; women were sometimes chiefs, priests, and prophets. In acephalous societies, which had no formal political offices, such as the Plateau Tonga, economically successful, personally charismatic women were able to gain communities of followers (cf., Colson, 1958, 33; Smith and Dale, 1920, 380-81; Roberts, 1970, 527; Richards, 1940, 93; 1951, 168-69; Poewe, 1981, 108; Marwick, 1965, 144; Ntara, 1973, 14, 33-34, 36-38; Gluckman, 1951, 19 ff.).

No anthropologist or historian has more than casually mentioned these precolonial female leaders. Scholars have only now begun the task of restudying precolonial social formations based on orally transmitted clan histories. Whether they will make the effort to include women in their studies depends on their perceptions of historical process; some consciousness-raising may be necessary to motivate them to seek out women's traditional political roles (e.g., Lebeuf, 1971).

It is particularly unfortunate that female leadership roles have been neglected in the study of precolonial Zambia, because most of the societies were matrilineal. Matriliny is important because it is a social mechanism that maximizes women's options for autonomous choice, a basic condition for the political actor. In precolonist Zambia, women had not only theoretical access to power and leadership in the extradomestic domain, but some actually held power. This contrasts with many societies elsewhere in which women's political activity was confined to women's issues (Hoffer, 1972; Okonjo, 1976), or was indirect, with formal political office holding or informal leadership reserved exclusively for men (Okeyo, 1980).

The limited data we have on women's participation in precolonial Zambian politics suggest that only a minority of women were active in traditional political processes of office holding and leadership. In some societies, the institutional constraint on access to leadership roles was the structural incompatibility of marriage and leadership. Among the Ila, for example, only unmarried women could become chiefs. Since all women spent at least part of their adult lives married, a structural brake on individual achievement was built into the system. In other chiefdoms, fewer women than men were eligible for political

office, and territories controlled by royal women, as in the Bemba
and Lozi cases, seem to have been smaller than those controlled by
men. Thus formal offices were not equally available to the genders.

The central concerns of the majority of women reflected their
primary civic responsibilities in social and economic production. Most
of their adult lives were dominated by the production of crops and children, and not by public affairs. Yet because of their responsibilities
in the production and distribution of goods and services, and the interdependence of the genders, women influenced public policy. In both
acephalous and hierarchical societies, the legitimacy of women's expression of interest in politics was unquestioned. Thus while a majority were neither leaders nor chiefs, women had the right to seek power
and to address wider social concerns; assertive women exercised this
right.

THE COLONIAL PERIOD

The imposition of colonial rule by Britain in the early twentieth
century was marked by the unification of previously independent tribes
and kingdoms into a single nation. In the process, the legitimacy of
women as political actors suffered. The entire colonial political super-
structure was composed of British males. At the local level, African
male kings and chiefs became salaried provincial or district chiefs;
in formerly chiefless societies African male "warrant chiefs" were
appointed by the government. At the village level, appointed leaders
were exclusively African men. Only where female chieftaincies were
firmly fixed in local tradition were these retained. But apart from
these, the social mechanisms which had previously made it possible
for assertive women to gain positions of political power were removed.

Women were distinctly disadvantaged by the time Africans began
their anticolonial political mobilization efforts to achieve independence
from Britain. By the 1950s, decades after colonial rule began, a modern urban economic sector based on copper mining which provided jobs
for men alone had been created. The limited educational facilities that
had been made available for Africans were mostly for boys. A new
tradition had been created, in which women who managed, despite the
difficulties involved, to migrate to town were denied access to its modern amenities (Epstein, 1958), and all political institutions that had
evolved in the towns to serve Africans were exclusively male domains
(Epstein, 1958). In turn women's roles were redefined as unemployed,
dependent housewives, while rural women struggled for sheer physical
survival because the healthy young men who used to share the workload
were now working in town (Richards, 1940). Thus, most women had
neither the facility in English nor the direct experience of contact with

Europeans through employment to enable them to act independently in the anticolonial struggle. The economic interdependence of the genders that had been characteristic of precolonial society had changed to economic dependence of women on men. This was reflected in the redefinition of political roles. The essential maleness of the colonial experience politically and economically meant that most Zambian women came to see politics as an activity suitable for men alone (Harries-Jones, 1975).

The early anticolonial struggle was marked by the spread of Christian separatist sects. Such movements are frequently interpreted as protest against European rule, arising when overt, legitimate political expression is blocked. It is significant that among the most successful sects was one led by a charismatic female leader of the late colonial period, Alice Lenshina, based on her visionary experiences (Roberts, 1970). Her Lumpa church attracted a large male and female following in the rural north, Chinsali District, and in the mining towns. Although initially supporting the protest campaigns of nationalist leaders in Chinsali, by the time Zambia achieved independence, Lenshina was instructing her followers not to participate in the political organization headed by the newly elected President of Zambia, Kenneth Kaunda. The political significance of the Lumpa movement is suggested by its brutal suppression, after independence, by order of President Kaunda, a former classmate of Lenshina.

The creation of the church was an outlet for a talented charismatic but uneducated woman to exercise a form of leadership, as the head of a religious protest movement. This was closed when Lenshina was arrested and the church broken up by orders of the President. Its destruction symbolized the closure of meaningful political opportunities for relatively uneducated rural women.

As often occurs in revolutionary movements, Zambian male nationalists came to appreciate the importance of recruiting women for the anticolonial struggle. Working behind the scene, women could mobilize other women and men, raise funds, hide male leaders who faced arrest, organize protests, and continue the work of arrested leaders. Their activities would arouse little suspicion by the colonial authorities precisely because they defined women as "apolitical." Those women who volunteered their services tended to be atypical cases of unmarried individuals with personal experience of contact with Europeans in work or school, and thus with strong motivation to correct the injustices they had witnessed. Julia "Chikamoneka" Mulenga, Losa "Nawatwika" Lukanda, and Zeniah "Ken" Ndhlovu were such cases. Princess Nakatindi defied her royal family in order to participate. Foster Mubanga said she felt she was chosen by God to engage in political mobilization. Married women, such as Chibesa Kankasa, were drawn into politics through their husbands' political activity.[3]

Volunteer activists faced almost unrelenting hostility and condemnation by both men and women. Foster Mubanga was denied food and water by communities she visited and never received the bicycle or subsistence allowance she had been promised by the male leaders. Her husband was ridiculed by neighbors. Zeniah Ndhlovu was the victim of vicious gossip. Princess Nakatindi was thought of as "mad." Zambians had come to accept that the only legitimate role for a woman was as a dependent wife, and the most important role of a wife was to be available to her husband to provide hot water for his bath and a well-cooked evening meal. Thus there was no legitimate reason for a woman to talk to strangers.

"Talking to strangers" is a key concept in the problem of women as political actors. It refers to the notion of morality. Though free to use public space and unrestricted in physical mobility—there is no tradition of seclusion of adult women—the moral woman should not talk to men outside the kinship circle. A woman who "moves" with men in the course of working together in modern activist politics, is "talking and moving with strangers." It is widely assumed that a woman who "talks to strangers" is arranging a sexual encounter and is therefore immoral. Because women were now so dependent on men's incomes, it was important for them to be thought of as moral, to define their primary responsibilities as wives and mothers, to limit their encounters with strangers, and to confine themselves to the home. Whereas female political activity was institutionalized precolonially, the withdrawal of institutional support under the impact of colonialism made politics for women "immoral."

The nationalist leaders recognized that there would be safety in numbers for women. The burning issue of women's morality might be reduced, though not eliminated, if there was a separate women's organization which they could join. Thus the men created a "Women's Brigade" (Zambia Daily Mail, September 30, 1974). The Brigade had great appeal to both urban and rural women. Now, as a group, women could engage in mass rallies and demonstrations to protest not only European colonial rulers, but the African chiefs and village headmen who symbolized colonial authority. Their protests were sometimes violent, sometimes symbolic expressions of disgust, such as stripping to the waist (Heisler, 1974, 79; Times of Zambia, February 25, 1973). Brigade women worked on literacy drives to aid voter registration, and organized town funerals to broaden appreciation of the power of the major political party, UNIP (the United National Independence Party) (Harries-Jones, 1975, 64, 101, 103-4). They supported the men in labor strikes and prepared food for male activists when they met in private homes. Heisler (1974) claims that it was their support of the freedom struggle that earned women citizenship under the 1962 constitution, and thus political emancipation. Nevertheless, such back-

stage roles limited women by channeling their energies away from
direct involvement. Brigade activity was sporadic, did not conflict
with the primary duties of a housewife and mother, and did little to
legitimize the moral right of women to seek power outside the Brigade.
Since the Brigade's activities were determined by male leaders, women
did not develop an organization that would represent their interests as
women, except to the extent that their interests coincided with those
of men.

THE FIRST DECADE OF INDEPENDENCE: 1964-74

In October 1964, Britain handed over the reigns of government
to UNIP and Zambia was born. [4] The new political power of men was
different from that which they had enjoyed under precolonial conditions.
It was greater since it was backed by their control of modern western
institutions: military, education, economic, communication. Although
granted citizenship and the right to vote, women were clearly disadvantaged. They had the right to stand for office, for example. But with
few women sufficiently educated, and few women working in the modern sector, few were available to do so. Thus the political equality of
women was more theoretical than real. Having the vote did not mean
having equal access to power. It created the illusion of equality without its substance.

The ruling elite continued to consider the cooperation of female
citizens necessary to consolidate its power and used several strategies
to gain their support. One was to immediately promote some from
among the tiny handful of educated women who had been elected to
Parliament. Another strategy was to appoint outstanding women to
positions of national prominence, and a third strategy was to appoint
relatively uneducated female party activists to the UNIP Central Committee. Thus women seemed nicely represented in view of their disadvantaged position.

A favorite theme of politicians' speeches was that, as voters
and full and equal citizens of Zambia, women had both the right and
obligation to participate simultaneously in political activity and economic development (Schuster, 1979, 1982). At the local level women
were encouraged to enter politics. A few were elected as town coun-
cillors and appointed as regional secretaries. Women had the rather
negative distinction of being jailed for anti-UNIP activity as they had
rarely been under the colonial government. Many joined the UNIP
Women's Brigade, especially in the line-of-rail towns. In the periurban shanty towns, Brigade members served as agents of social control. As guardians of traditional morality they settled disputes and
judged the suitability of people wishing to build houses. As housewives,

traders, and "mothers of the nation," they were important symbols of change and continuity. The symbol of continuity was the emphasis on the virtues of wife-and-motherhood. The symbol of change was that these roles could be incorporated into newly defined urban-based political activity (Schuster, 1979, 160-64).

Constraints in political expression were similar for all politicians because of the necessity of working within UNIP, particularly after it became the sole legal party. The fundamental responsibility for policy decisions was retained by President Kaunda. The task of the leaders within the government and the party was mostly to interpret the President's decisions to the public. As elected or appointed officials or as members of the Women's Brigade of UNIP, women played their part in these political functions. But the pattern of their involvement was the same as in the colonial system; they worked through the male-controlled organization, propagandizing and implementing policies formulated by UNIP men.

One of the casualties of UNIP male control was the fate of women's rights legislation. At all levels of society, from the poorest to the top elite, women were united in their view that the legal system had to change (Mindolo, 1970). Yet in the first decade of independence, virtually none of the legislation so widely desired by women was passed. This legislation would have lessened male control of women and would have influenced women's participation in politics by increasing their capacity for autonomous action.

Whether women were high in the UNIP hierarchy as elected or appointed officials or illiterate members of the Women's Brigade at the grass roots level, the tendency was for their political influence to become marginalized. The Brigade became embroiled in scapegoating the first generation of educated women employed in modern jobs (Schuster, 1979, 161-62), and even failed to represent the interests of the market women who were the majority of its members (Schuster, 1982). Women elected or appointed to top positions were often posted abroad. Those who remained became politicians-who-happened-to-be-women, or, alternatively, symbols of what women could achieve. They developed a conservative style of comportment and dress, distinguishing themselves from other young educated feminist women, gaining prestige and the support of male politicians rather than using their power to improve the position of women. They were trapped by the very institutional structures which promoted their personal positions. Since they represented official views, they could not address the underlying causes of women's relative lack of interest in politics; the failure of government to represent women's interests could not be corrected, and women's political representation could not be increased. The majority of women, particularly among the educated, then became alienated from politics, which was seen, quite

correctly, as belonging to men, for even electing women to office
did little to alleviate their problems.

CONCLUSIONS

In traditional Zambian matrilineal societies, women had the
legitimate right to participate in extradomestic politics, either by
inheriting chieftaincies or achieving positions of leadership. Colonial
rule both denied women legitimate political functions and defined them
as dependent housewives. Because of their dependence on men's incomes, most men, and the women themselves defined the "moral"
woman as the housewife, and condemned the few women who, as individual activists, entered the political foray, thereby discouraging
more participation. The Brigade provided safety in numbers, because
women could act as a group. The Brigade's activities were sporadic,
and they participated with enthusiasm. After independence, government encouraged their continued participation both as individuals in
top positions and as members of the women's organization. However,
political women represented the policies of the male ruling elite rather
than the interests of women. Anticipated legislative reforms were not
forthcoming. Therefore most women became disinterested in politics.
They perceived that they could improve their lives only by pursuing
personal goals, seeking educational and employment opportunities,
and leaving politics to the men.

NOTES

1. Fieldwork in Zambia was conducted in 1971-74, under grants
from NIMH and the University of Zambia, and in 1975-76.
2. Ethnographic descriptions date from the 1920s-1950s—after
colonial rule was already imposed. Traditional political forms evolved
from about the sixteenth through the nineteenth centuries in the majority of cases—only Tonga and Ila seem to have an earlier history
of settlement dating back about 1,000 years.
3. See Times of Zambia, May 30, 1971, February 25, 1973,
March 17, 1974; Poewe, 1981; Harries-Jones, 1975.
4. The analysis is confined to the period of intensive participant-
observation fieldwork in Zambia. Personal communication with Zambians in subsequent years indicates the situation described for the
first postindependence decade remains unchanged today.

REFERENCES

Collier, Jane Fishburne. 1974. Women in Politics. In Women, Culture and Society, edited by Michelle Rosaldo and Louise Lamphere, pp. 89-96. Stanford: Stanford University Press.

Colson, Elizabeth. 1958. Marriage and Family among the Plateau Tonga. Manchester: Manchester University Press.

Epstein, A. L. 1958. Politics in an Urban African Community. Manchester: Manchester University Press.

Epstein, A. L. 1981. Urbanization and Kinship. London: Academic Press.

Gluckman, Max. 1951. The Lozi of Barotseland. In Seven Tribes of British Central Africa, edited by Elizabeth Colson and Max Gluckman, pp. 1-93. Manchester: Manchester University Press.

Harries-Jones, Peter. 1975. Freedom and Labour: Mobilization and Political Control on the Zambian Copperbelt. Oxford: Basil Blackwell.

Heisler, Helmuth. 1974. Urbanisation and the Government of Migration: The Inter-relation of Urban and Rural Life in Zambia. London: C. Hurst and Co.

Hoffer, Carole. 1972. Mende and Sherbro Women in High Office. Canadian Journal of African Studies, VI, 2, 151-64.

Lebeuf, Annie M. D. 1971. The Role of Women in the Political Organization of African Societies. In Women of Tropical Africa, edited by Denise Paulme, pp. 93-119. Berkeley: University of California Press.

Marwick, M. G. 1965. Sorcery in its Social Setting. Manchester: Manchester University Press.

Mindolo Ecumenical Foundation. 1970. Women's Rights in Zambia: Report of a Consultation. Kitwe: Mindolo Ecumenical Foundatior

Ntara, S. J. 1973. The History of the Chewa. (Mbiri Ya Achewa). Wiesbaden: Franz Steiner Verlag GMBH.

Okeyo, Achola Pala. 1980. Daughters of the Lakes and Rivers: Coloni-
zation and the Land of Rights of Luo Women. In Women and
Colonization: Anthropological Perspectives, edited by Mona
Etienne and Eleanor Leacock, pp. 186-213. New York: Praeger.

Okonjo, Kamene. 1976. The Dual-Sex Political System in Operation:
Igbo Women and Community Politics in Midwestern Nigeria. In
Women in Africa: Studies in Social and Economic Change, edited
by Nancy Hafkin and Edna Bay, pp. 45-58. Stanford: Stanford
University Press.

Poewe, Karla. 1981. Matrilineal Ideology, Male Female Dynamics
in Luapula, Zambia. London: Academic Press for the International African Institute.

Richards, Audrey. 1940. The Political System of the Bemba Tribe.
In African Political Systems, edited by M. Fortes and E. E.
Evans-Pritchard, pp. 83-120. London: Oxford University Press.

Roberts, Andrew. 1970. The Lumpa Church of Alice Lenshina. In
Protest and Power in Black Africa, edited by R. I. Rotberg
and A. A. Mazrui, pp. 513-70. London: Oxford University Press.

Schuster, Ilsa. 1979. The New Women of Lusaka. Palo Alto: Mayfield
Publishing Company.

Schuster, Ilsa. 1982. Marginal Lives: Conflict and Contradiction in
the Position of Female Traders in Lusaka, Zambia. In Women
and Work in Africa, edited by Edna Bay, pp. 105-26. Boulder,
Colo.: Westview Press.

Smith, Edwin, and Dale Andrew Murray. 1920. The Ila-Speaking Peoples of Northern Rhodesia Vol. 1. New Hyde Park: University
Books (1968 edition).

Times of Zambia

Zambia Daily Mail

21   THE NEW YORK WOMEN'S SUFFRAGE MOVEMENT: ETHNICITY AND FEMINIST POLITICS

Elinor Lerner

New York State was pivotal in the struggle for votes for women in that it was the first eastern, industrial state to grant women the franchise prior to the 1920 federal amendment. For many years a major debate had been whether to continue costly and often unsuccessful state campaigns or to work solely on passage of a federal constitutional amendment. For Carrie Chapman Catt it was a tactical question of having women's suffrage in enough states to convince Congress to take action on a federal level. As early as 1909 when she took charge of the New York City movement, formed the Woman Suffrage Party (WSP), and began to implement her detailed plan carrying New York through eight years of campaigns, Catt believed that for suffragists "On one State hung all their hopes for winding up referenda campaigns and compelling federal action by Congress. That State was New York" (Catt and Schuler, 1969, p. 280).

With past victories for suffrage occurring mainly in western, predominantly rural states, New York suffragists believed their base of support was not in Eastern urban centers with largely Jewish and Catholic, working-class populations, but rather in rural small towns and with farmers. Suffragists believed that the greatest opposition came from working-class and immigrant men, while U.S.-born men were considered to be more modern and progressive with respect to rights for women. In 1911, the WSP stated that those areas "which may now be counted upon as opposed to woman suffrage are known as tenement-house districts. They are occupied mainly by foreign speaking people and these represent almost every known nationality in the world. The families by the thousands in these districts are occupied in the lower ranks of labor" (New York Woman Suffrage Party, January 1911, p. 2). Suffragists considered that "from old world conditions, old time traditions concerning women have been imprinted on our immigrants" (New York Woman Suffrage Party, February 1910, p. 2).

However, results in the two New York State elections show that this analysis was incorrect. In 1915 voters defeated a suffrage referendum, with many urban areas voting more in favor than most rural ones. In 1917 woman suffrage passed in New York State, with New York City voting heavily in favor of suffrage and rural areas voting against. In other words, it was New York City, with its immigrant, working class, Catholic and Jewish population which carried the state for suffrage.

In both elections Manhattan suffrage sentiment crossed class and racial lines and was sharply divided by ethnicity and religion. The largest, strongest, and most consistent support came from the Jewish community, both middle- and working-class Jews living in Harlem and on the Lower East Side. The strongest and most consistent opposition came from working- and middle-class Irish neighborhoods. Italians were not unified on suffrage; most voted against, but the heart of Italian Greenwich Village was solidly and consistently prosuffrage (New York City, 1915; New York City, 1917).

Votes of middle- and upper-class native-born men hovered around the average for Manhattan. They were as a group neither very opposed nor very much in favor of woman suffrage. The only nonworking class, nonimmigrant areas that were strongly prosuffrage were the intellectual, professional neighborhoods around Columbia University and an area in upper Manhattan inhabited largely by members of New York City's literary, artistic, theatrical community. These voting patterns show that the mass base for support of woman suffrage in Manhattan did not correspond to the usual stereotype of the U.S. suffrage movement: middle-class, Anglo-Saxon Protestant.

Given this, why were Manhattan's Jews and some Italians so in favor of woman suffrage, and what distinguished prosuffrage Italians from those voting against suffrage? Analysis of samples from the 1915 New York State census shows that certain internal, demographic community features made it possible for Jews and some Italians to create a strong base for support of suffrage (Lerner, 1984). These factors were the economic and social position of women in the community and the interconnections between family and work for both men and women. Factors that built upon this demographic base and were crucial in creating community support for suffrage were the extent of suffrage organizing activity, and the position of community organizations such as religions, neighborhood settlements, labor groups, and political parties. All of these functioned as intermediary links between the suffrage movement and its constituency, helping to interpret the issue and set the community context. Those factors which produced prosuffrage sentiment in the Jewish community were also those which were significant in the prosuffrage Italian areas, particularly the garment unions, the Socialist Party, and the settlement houses.

Jewish and prosuffrage Italian areas shared important demographic characteristics that set them apart from antisuffrage Italian and Irish communities. First, prosuffrage areas were more family oriented in that more men and working women lived in family households, as opposed to the more usual boarding houses in antisuffrage areas. Voters in prosuffrage areas were more likely to be married and more likely to live in a household with a working woman than voters in antisuffrage areas. Second, prosuffrage areas had a higher density of working women; women who worked, significantly, in predominantly unionized trades. In the Jewish community 53 percent of working women were employed in the garment trades. In the prosuffrage Italian areas 65 percent of working women were garment workers as opposed to only 35 percent in the antisuffrage Italian areas. Since large numbers of both Jewish and Italian men were garment workers, these were areas where many men and women worked together in the same industry and lived together in the same household.

They also shared the same union and union struggles. By 1915 Italians were approximately one-third of the garment workers, most other garment workers being Jewish immigrants. Most of these workers, both men and women, had been involved in the garment unions through strikes, memberships, and organizing activity. Thus Jewish and prosuffrage Italian neighborhoods were distinguished by large numbers of men (particularly voters) and women who worked in the same industry, lived in the same household, and shared the same union struggles. In other words, men and women tended to have the same economic and political interests. Given this demographic base, organizations could effectively push for suffrage support from male voters, by convincing them that women's rights were to their own advantage.

Garment unions were an important support for woman suffrage. New York City was a center of union activity, with relatively more unions and more union members than other New York State areas. These union members were concentrated in the garment and textile trades, and construction and transportation industries, with about one-half of New York City union members in the garment trades. Practically all unionized women were in these industries. To varying degrees, depending on ethnicity and trade, unions were one of the focal points in community life and were often connected to political parties in terms of personnel and interests. This combination produced a multiplying effect for union influence (Hourwich, 1922, pp. 326-28; New York State, 1915, pp. 1, 4, 6, 9).

Unions had different functions and served various purposes within different ethnic communities. For most Jews and the Italians who were unionized, unions provided a focal point for community expression and individual social mobility. Alice Kessler-Harris has argued that because of the language barrier, non-English speaking immigrants relied heavily on community, ethnic organizations such as unions for outlets for social grievances and expressing community needs. Unions also provided a means for individuals to become community leaders, a means for upward mobility and realization of personal ambition. For these reasons unions were expected to become involved in social issues and their position on woman suffrage was important within the Jewish and Italian communities (Harris, 1968, pp. 157-58).

Unions provided suffragists access to large groups of working men and women. Although many unions formally endorsed woman suffrage and urged their members to vote for it, their importance was less as active campaigners than as structures through which suffrage demands could be pressed. Suffrage organizations sent delegations and speakers to every sort of union gathering, from local meetings to city and state federations, attempting to present suffrage arguments and enlist active union support. Recognizing the importance of unions in the Jewish community, the WSP, through its organizers on the Lower East Side, attempted to reach all Jewish Unions in the United Hebrew Trades and the Workman's Circle. Generally well received, suffragists reported that unions often asked for suffrage speakers (New York Woman Suffrage Party: September 1913, p. 19; January 1915, p. 21; April 1915, pp. 20-21; March 1915, p. 22).

Some unions were more sympathetic than others. Given that union membership reflected ethnic occupational concentrations in New York City, it is not surprising that the more sympathetic unions tended to be those whose ethnic constituency was more favorably disposed to woman suffrage. Unions in such trades as the carpenters, plumbers, teamsters, and longshoremen, most of whose members were Irish, tended not to be strong supporters for votes for women. In contrast, unions with predominantly Jewish membership, especially the garment trades, showed a much greater degree of support for woman suffrage. Many of these unions had substantial numbers of Italian members by 1915, which contributed to the spread of prosuffrage sentiment into the Italian community. Jewish unions were often socialist in orientation and involved in reform causes. Many male Jewish union leaders were active in the suffrage movement, at least to the extent of speaking at suffrage meetings. The Jewish press and labor press also supported votes for women. The International Ladies' Garment Workers Union (ILGWU) printed periodic short items on suffrage and the relationship of suffrage to the needs of working women.

Recognizing the support for suffrage among its female members, the ILGWU, as early as 1909, in its journal the Ladies' Garment

Worker, stated that "nearly all women who read these pages are clamoring for the right to vote" (International Ladies' Garment Workers Union, 1910.) A later editorial claimed that women trade unionists were "fully awake to the advantages to be gained by the political vote" (International Ladies' Garment Workers Union, December 1912, p. 14). As for union men, the journal stated that appeals for the right to vote for working women to "trade unionists and Socialists should be entirely uncalled for . . . And because we stand for freedom, justice and right for working women we advise our members to vote for the Suffrage Amendment on Nov. 2nd" (International Ladies' Garment Workers Union, November 1915, pp. 8-9).

Interconnections in Jewish and some Italian households between male and female occupations and union affiliation helped to facilitate the spread of feminist ideology and provided a base for women to press their demands upon men. One suffrage leader reported that the "influence of the individual girl on the men in her family and on her acquaintances was a big factor in winning the vote. Girl factory operators appealed to the men of their own race in their own tongue" (Brown, Chapter 5, p. 8).

Along with unions, political parties were very influential in forming community attitudes on woman suffrage. Judgments as to whether the passage of woman suffrage would be to their political advantage had a major impact on party and voter sentiment. Political parties' stands on suffrage were influenced by how the issue fit into party ideology and overall platform, evaluations of constituency sentiment, and assessments as to whether the passage of votes for women would benefit or harm party power and advance or hinder careers of party officials. In this complex interaction between constituency, party considerations, and individual political futures, parties in New York City took various stands on suffrage. Both the Progressive and Socialist Parties came out relatively early in favor of woman suffrage. It was not until 1916 that the state Republican and Democratic Parties expressed limited support.

These different positions can be explained by what suffrage meant to each party. Votes for women meshed well with Progressive and Socialist Parties' ideological emphasis on social and legislative reform, and political democracy. Also these parties had more women in their membership and involved in party affairs than did the Republicans and Democrats, thereby creating more internal pressure for support. Both Socialist and Progressive parties hoped to profit from woman suffrage by attracting more votes and members since they associated women with support for general reform issues.

This association, on the other hand, led Republicans and Democrats to view women voters not as allies, but rather, as challengers to their established political control. Fearing that women's votes would be used for civic and political reform, which would erode their base of political power, Democrats and Republicans were reluctant to support suffrage.

Of all New York City political parties, the Socialist Party had the most direct influence by carrying out extensive prosuffrage work in certain ethnic and immigrant communities. From 1909 on, it waged an aggressive campaign with many of its efforts parallel to work done by suffrage organizations: canvassing working-class neighborhoods; leafleting working men and women; holding numerous street meetings, conferences, and mass meetings. Much of their activity took place on the Lower East Side in Jewish and Italian areas. Many of the most important and larger socialist women's mass meetings had a suffrage theme and included as speakers some of the more prominent Party feminists and Jews such as Meyer London, Rose Schneiderman, and Meta Stern (New York Call, 25 February 1908; New York Times, 1 March 1909, 28 February 1910, 26 February 1911, 7 February 1914, 1 March 1915, 18 October 1915, and 30 October 1915).

Although the Republican Party was strong in the state, it was relatively weak in Manhattan, supported mainly by the small black community and by some affluent neighborhoods. Republicans also had scattered and occasional support among some of the newer immigrants such as Italians and Jews, depending on candidates and issues; however few of these groups voted Republican in 1917.

The Democratic Party, with its city political machine, Tammany Hall, had more of a following among Manhattan's recent immigrants. The Party's base of support was working and middle class, containing many of Manhattan's Irish. Tammany also managed to attract many Italians and some Jews from time to time; but they were never party-loyal as were the Irish. Rather they voted on issues and appeal of individual candidates. Although the state Democratic Party officially endorsed suffrage by 1915, the city political machine was considered to be opposed. Certainly its constituency was decidedly antisuffrage. In 1917 those election districts that voted the most against the suffrage amendment voted the heaviest for Tammany Hall candidates. Those Italian and Jewish election districts that most strongly endorsed suffrage tended to vote less for Republicans and Democrats and more for the Socialist Party candidates. So, there is a correlation between areas that voted strongly for suffrage, supported the Socialist Party, and had many residents connected to unions that supported suffrage. Thus attitudes of political parties and labor organizations reflected and helped to create prosuffrage community sentiment.

Together with political parties and unions, a third factor, settlement houses, helped to form community opinion on suffrage. Many suffrage attempts to reach workers and immigrants were carried out under the auspices of, and by the efforts of women connected with, settlement houses. Located mainly in immigrant neighborhoods, settlement houses became a cross-roads for reform groups, political organizations, and labor unions. Popularly supported by local residents, settlement houses became community centers, championing reform causes, opening their facilities for political meetings, and lending financial and resource assistance to labor and union causes.

Those attracted to settlements were generally socially and politically aware and eager to become involved in the numerous social and political activities offered. Members of settlement clubs were often interested in feminist issues. The University settlement reported that "investigations into the Feminist Movement occupied the attention of several girls clubs (University Settlement Society, 1912, p. 36) in 1912."

Recognizing the importance of settlements in immigrant life and the ability of settlement workers to reach large numbers of working men and women, suffragists used settlement workers as recruiters and organizers for movement events. Many settlement house workers became community suffrage leaders and suffrage events were identified by local residents as much with the settlements as with the suffrage movement.

Since most settlement houses were in areas inhabited by recent, non-English speaking immigrants, their influence was felt more by these groups than by the Irish. Most Jewish and Italian areas had at least one settlement house and many settlement suffrage activities were directed specifically at these groups. Frequently meetings were conducted and speeches given in Italian or Yiddish and often featured as speakers local leaders such as an Italian newspaper publisher or a Jewish garment union leader. Sometimes ethnic social events would accompany a suffrage meeting as in 1915 when Greenwich House held a meeting with an Italian dance following. The Henry Street Settlement had an active Jewish suffrage club that sponsored dances, social gatherings, and meetings (New York Times: 19 July 1915, 18 July 1915, 30 October 1915, 29 October 1915; New York Woman Suffrage Party: August 1915, p. 22; September 1915, p. 23).

As an intermediary link between local residents and the suffrage movement, settlements were important for mobilizing local resources and as an information outlet for suffrage news. These three connecting links between the suffrage movement and the communities—unions, political parties, settlements—existed independently of the suffrage organizations and affected how communities interpreted the issue of votes for women. Their stands of suffrage depended largely on whether they perceived women voting as beneficial to themselves and their constituents.

All three of these institutions in the Jewish and certain Italian communities were sympathetic to suffrage and helped to carry this to

their constituencies. Garment unions, with predominantly Jewish and
Italian membership, felt that women voting would increase their power
by increasing the number of members and voters supporting prolabor
legislation. The Socialist party also felt that women voting would increase their membership and base of support. Most settlement house
workers were liberal and reform oriented, most were women, and
many were feminists. All three of these organizations had relatively
large numbers of women members; women, who by force of numbers
or position of power, were able to push for suffrage within their
groups.

As noted earlier, the analysis given by suffrage leaders concerning the base of support for suffrage in New York bore very little relationship to the actual voting patterns. Suffragists tended to portray the
situation in New York as a battle between enlightened, modern, democratic Americanism versus backward, patriarchal, ignorant peasant
reactionism (New York Woman Suffrage Party, November 1914, p. 11).
Catt illustrated this mistaken analysis when she contrasted suffrage
movement members as having "American birth, education and ideals,"
who had "in their childhood homes learned the meaning of political
freedom and had inherited other ideas of progress." She considered
most of the City's voters unlikely to support suffrage since they were
"untrained, and . . . foreign-born. . . , mainly uneducated, with
views concerning women molded by European tradition" (Catt and
Schuler, 1969, p. 162). However, in some sense, it was the least
Americanized, most recent immigrant who supported votes for wom-
en, while Anglo-Saxon, native-born Americans and earlier immigrants were the least supportive.

However, the usual distinction between rural-peasant values
versus urban-modern-industrial ones does not hold. On the whole,
Manhattan's native-born population was not a major support for
woman suffrage and the more recent the group, the more likely it
was to support votes for women. So, support for suffrage cannot be
considered to be a consequence of modernization, urbanization, or
Americanization. Clearly one must be wary of attributing political
opinions and actions to past cultural, social behavior, and beliefs.

Instead, the results indicate that structural, institutional community factors encouraged or limited possibilities for support of feminist issues. Male voters in a community made what were to them
reasoned decisions based on what they perceived to be their personal
and group interests. Voting largely in terms of self-interest, not
ethnic heritage, male voters were influenced by economic and political factors, which in part reflected the relative strength of women
within their communities. In both the Jewish and parts of the Italian
Manhattan communities, women, largely by virtue of their employment in politicized and unionized industries and by their relatively

large participation in community social and political life (through the settlements, unions, and the Socialist Party) were able to convince men that it was in their economic and political interest to support votes for women.

REFERENCES

Brown, G. No date. On account of sex. Woman Suffrage Papers. Sophia Smith collection. Smith College. Northampton, Mass.

Catt, C. C., and Schuler, N. R. 1969. Woman suffrage and politics. Seattle, Wa.: University of Washington Press.

Harris, A. K. 1968. The lower class as a factor in reform: New York, the Jews and the 1890's.(Doctoral Dissertation, Rutgers University).

Hourwich, I. 1922. Immigration and labor. New York: B. W. Huebsch.

International Ladies' Garment Workers Union. The Ladies' Garment Worker. New York.

Lerner, E. 1984. Structures familiales, typologie des emplois et soutien aux causes feministes à New York (1915-1917) [Family structure, work patterns and support for feminist issues in New York, 1915-1917]. In Strategies des Femmes, edited by M.-C. Pasquier, M. Marini, F. Ducroq, G. Fraisse, and A.-M. Sohn, pp. 424-42. Paris: Tierce.

New York Call.

New York City. Board of Elections. 1915. Official canvass of votes cast in the city of New York, Nov. 2, 1915. New York.

New York City. Board of Elections. 1917. Official canvass of votes cast in the city of New York, Nov. 6, 1917. New York.

New York State. Department of Labor. 1915. "Labor organizations in in 1914." Bulletin, 74.

New York Times.

New York Woman Suffrage Party. The Woman Voter. New York.

University Settlement Society. 1912. 26th annual report. New York.

22 STEREOTYPES ABOUT THE INFLUENCEABILITY OF WOMEN

Alice Hendrickson Eagly

In the United States and in many other cultures, people believe that women are easier to influence and more submissive, conforming, persuasible, and suggestible than men. Before examining the origins of this stereotypical belief, I will contrast it with research findings on how easily people are influenced, so that we can compare the cultural stereotype to behavioral data. The relevant research consists primarily of laboratory experiments on conformity and persuasion. Reviews of this research literature (Eagly, 1978; Maccoby and Jacklin, 1974) found that the majority of studies reported no significant sex differences. However, among the minority of studies in which significant differences were found, almost all of these differences indicated that females were more influenceable than males.

More recently both Cooper (1979) and Eagly and Carli (1981) conducted meta-analytic reviews of sex differences in how easily people are influenced. In a meta-analysis, a quantitative summary is made of the results of independent studies testing the same hypothesis. These meta-analyses established that in laboratory research there is an overall sex difference such that women are more easily influenced than men, yet this overall sex difference is quite small in magnitude. In terms of the standard score unit known as <u>effect size</u>, Linda Carli and I estimated that the size of the sex difference is approximately one-fifth of a standard deviation. With a sex difference of this size, subjects' gender accounts for only 1 percent of the variation in subjects' persuasibility and conformity. Because effects as small as this may not even be discriminated by observers, it may be puzzling that the cultural stereotype that women are easily influenced is so clear and persists.

One reason for the discrepancy between the gender stereotype about influenceability and research findings is that laboratory research draws on a different data base than perceivers do in their daily lives. In the natural settings where perceivers learn about gender, men are more likely than women to have higher status roles. For example, within most organizations, the positions held by men tend to be higher in hierarchies of status and authority than the positions held by women, and, in family settings, husbands generally have an overall power advantage. In contrast, in most research settings, especially experimental laboratories, females and males are assigned the exact same role—that of subject. In the research setting, then, there is rarely any formal status inequality between men and women, whereas such inequalities are typical of natural settings.

These formal status inequalities that exist between men and women in daily life produce the sex differences in influenceability that perceivers observe and represent in their gender stereotypes. Status inequalities bring about behavioral sex differences in influenceability, because power and legitimate authority are inherent in higher status roles. Individuals higher in a hierarchy have the right to exert influence by virtue of their positions in the social system, and individuals lower in the hierarchy have the obligation to comply with the demands that are made. Women tend to hold lower status positions than men, so they more often have to comply with others' demands.

The "kernel of truth" underlying perceivers' beliefs that women are easily influenced may be, then, that in most organizations men tend to hold higher status positions than women. If this theory about the origins of this stereotype is correct, it should be possible to demonstrate that perceivers' beliefs about how gender affects social influence stem from perceived sex differences in the distribution of people into roles. In other words, we should find that perceivers believe in the stereotypical sex difference that women are easily influenced to the extent that they believe that the men and women they observe are related through hierarchical roles that give men higher status. Let me turn to some recent research that I carried out with Wendy Wood that tests these hypotheses (Eagly and Wood, in press).

Our research proceeded by presenting each respondent with a written scenario describing two employees interacting in a familiar organizational setting. In each scenario, one employee (whom I will call the communicator) attempted to influence another employee (whom I will call the recipient) on a policy issue relevant to the organization. For example, for scenarios that were set in a bank, the policy issue was whether employees ought to dress more formally, to improve the bank's image. Each scenario concluded by having the communicator ask the recipient whether he or she "goes along with" the policy recommended by the communicator. Our subjects predicted the recipient's response.

In our first experiment, each scenario was set in a bank or supermarket. Either a man was said to be trying to influence a woman or a woman was said to be trying to influence a man. In some experimental conditions, subjects knew the sex of the communicator and recipient and lacked any more valid information for discerning the relative status of these stimulus persons. We predicted that these subjects would perceive that a male employee has higher status than a female employee, since subjects' knowledge of the differing distributions of men and women into organizational roles should cause them to infer a sex difference in status. Subjects did infer that the men in the scenarios had higher status than the women, as demonstrated by the higher salaries and higher-level job titles they ascribed to the male communicators and recipients. We hypothesized that this inference that men hold higher status jobs would lead perceivers to conclude that a male communicator is more successful in influencing a female recipient than a female communicator is in influencing a male recipient. Table 22.1 presents findings on perceived compliance with the recipient's recommendation. In the conditions in which subjects were given only the information about gender of the communicator and recipient, the communicator's recommendation was considered more likely to induce compliance when the communicator was male and the recipient female than when the communicator was female and the recipient male.

To examine the effects of information that are more directly related to status than are gender, we gave other subjects in this experiment information about the job titles as well as the gender of the communicator and recipient. We used both high status job titles (bank vice president and supermarket manager) and low status job titles (bank teller and supermarket cashier). In these experimental conditions, subjects were expected to base their predictions about compliance on the job title information and not on the gender of the communicator and recipient. As shown in Table 22.1, these subjects considered successful influence more likely to occur with high status communicators and with low status recipients.

Wendy Wood and I carried out two more experiments using this scenario methodology. In a second experiment, scenarios omitting job titles described an influence attempt between same- or opposite-sex persons. This experiment showed that both the communicator's and the recipient's sex contributed to the greater perceived compliance of women to men than of men to women. In a third experiment, this perceived sex difference in compliance was shown to occur only when the communicator and recipient were employed by the same organization and thus were perceived to be in a superior-subordinate relation in which men generally have greater access to resources and control over sanctions.

TABLE 22.1: Mean perceived likelihood of recipient's behavioral compliance

Sex of dyad members	Scenarios omitting job title information	Comparison scenarios (including job title information)			
		Low status communicator		High status communicator	
		Low status recipient	High status recipient	Low status recipient	High status recipient
Male communicator addressing female recipient	9.02	7.61	6.51	10.60	8.23
Female communicator addressing male recipient	7.44	7.51	5.64	11.08	7.76

Note: Higher numbers indicate greater compliance (15-point scale).
Source: Eagly and Wood, 1981.

In these experiments, then, our subjects appeared to reason as if they had a theory of how gender affects behavioral compliance in the work settings described by our scenarios, even though they probably could not state their theory in abstract terms. This implicit theory was shared by male and female subjects, whose judgments differed very little. According to this theory, a man is likely to obtain behavioral compliance with the expectations that he conveys for persons who occupy positions in the same hierarchy in which he holds his position, and a woman is likely to comply behaviorally with the expectations of other persons in the same hierarchy. We assumed that these ideas about compliance stemmed from perceivers' belief that men occupy higher status positions than women within organizational hierarchies—an assumption supported by correlational analyses of the data as well as analyses of variance that compared subjects' responses to the various scenarios.

The gender stereotype that women are easily influenced is important because it can function as a self-fulfilling prophecy, producing conformity sex differences that confirm the stereotype even in the absence of formal status differences between men and women. Studies of behavior in task-oriented groups, especially those by Berger and his associates (1980) suggest that attributes such as gender which convey information about social status affect behavior because people have expectations about their own and others' competence, based on these characteristics, and these expectancies cause them to interact with others in ways that produce confirmation of their expectancies. In particular, individuals whose characteristics convey high status both are given and take more opportunity to state their own views and to exert leadership. Such persons have more influence over other group members and, in turn, are less influenced by them.

The tendency for stereotypes to be self-fulfilling may explain why laboratory experiments, where male and female subjects have equal-status roles, reveal a small sex difference such that females are more persuasible and conforming than males. In this regard, it is noteworthy that our meta-analysis (Eagly and Carli, 1981) showed that the tendency for women to be more easily influenced than men is somewhat stronger in experimental settings involving on-going interaction—namely, in group pressure conformity experiments, an experimental paradigm stemming from the work of Muzafer Sherif, Solomon Asch, and other investigators. In such studies, the influence induction consists of presenting subjects with other group members who hold beliefs or attitudes discrepant from subjects' own positions. These other members have surveillance over subjects' responses to their influence induction—that is, these other members know (or appear to know) whether subjects have conformed to their views. The importance of surveillance was confirmed in a recent conformity experiment in which Wendy Wood, Lisa Fishbaugh, and I manipulated whether group members had surveillance over one another's opinions (Eagly et al., 1981). We found the stereotypical sex difference in conformity only with surveillance. Thus, group settings where group members have surveillance over one another's behavior are especially likely to produce the stereotypical sex difference wherein women yield to other members' opinions and men are relatively independent.

The importance of the group and of the opportunity it provides for surveillance is noteworthy in terms of the theory that stereotypes have self-confirming properties. If stereotypes affect behavior, they do so primarily through their effects on social interaction (Darley and Fazio, 1980). Therefore, stereotypical sex differences are particularly likely to occur in interactive contexts that allow men and women to observe and react to one another.

In summary, according to the theoretical analysis and the empirical findings I have presented, a social structural perspective is needed to understand why there is a gender stereotype about social influence. The greater concentration of men in high status roles and the legitimate authority inherent in such roles explain why in natural settings women are more easily influenced than men. Women play social roles in which they are more often subordinates than superiors, so they have to comply with others' wishes and demands. Our social stereotypes reflect the effect that this status inequality has on social influence.

To understand the effect that this stereotype has on behavior, I have proposed a social psychological analysis based on the idea that gender stereotypes function as self-fulfilling prophecies. Thus, individuals' stereotypes, which are based primarily on their everyday experiences in groups and organizations, affect their behavior in new social settings, especially in settings where men and women have surveillance over each other's behavior. Because stereotypes affect behavior, even those groups that lack formal status inequalities on the basis of gender tend to develop a weak version of the status-correlated sex differences that exist in the larger society. The tendency for women to be influenced by other group members and for men to be more independent of group pressure is one of these sex differences. Because such sex differences continue to characterize female and male behavior, societal social structure is echoed in every new group that is established, and the inequalities between men and women are maintained.

REFERENCES

Berger, J., Rosenholtz, S. J., and Zelditch, M., Jr. 1980. Status organizing processes. In Annual Review of Sociology (Vol. 6), edited by A. Inkeles, N. J. Smelser, and R. H. Turner. Palo Alto, Calif.: Annual Reviews.

Cooper, H. M. 1979. Statistically combining independent studies: A meta-analysis of sex differences in conformity research. Journal of Personality and Social Psychology, 37, 131-46.

Darley, J. M., and Fazio, R. H. 1980. Expectancy confirmation processes arising in the social interaction sequence. American Psychologist, 35, 867-81.

Eagly, A. H. 1978. Sex differences in influenceability. Psychological Bulletin, 85, 85-116.

Eagly, A. H., and Carli, L. L. 1981. Sex of researchers and sex-typed communications as determinants of sex differences in influenceability: A meta-analysis of social influence studies. Psychological Bulletin, 90, 1-20.

Eagly, A. H., Wood, W., and Fishbaugh, L. 1981. Sex differences in conformity: Surveillance by the group as a determinant of male nonconformity. Journal of Personality and Social Psychology, 40, 384-94.

Eagly, A. H., and Wood, W. Gender stereotypes as a product of inferred sex differences in status: Stereotypes about social influence. Journal of Personality and Social Psychology, 43, 915-28.

Maccoby, E. E., and Jacklin, C. N. 1974. The psychology of sex differences. Stanford, Calif.: Stanford University Press.

23 WOMEN'S NONVERBAL BEHAVIOR: UNDERLYING ASSUMPTIONS IN THE ADMONITION TO CHANGE

Nancy M. Henley

What is the nature of women's nonverbal world? And why should we be concerned with it, in the international context of women's poverty, illiteracy, inadequate education, hunger, poor medical treatment, and subjection to violence? It is my opinion that nonverbal behavior, as far removed as it may seem from these overwhelming concerns, is not trivial but is part of the overall pattern of domination, control, and discrimination from which these injustices result. Relations of power between groups, as between women and men, exist at various levels. In particular, there are both a macropolitical level, at which, for example, public policy is exercised, and a micropolitical level, realized in interpersonal interaction between individual members of the groups. We have studied too little the relationship between these levels. But we cannot understand one without the other: the thousand daily gestures of deference and dominance help to keep in place that structure which incorporates rape, woman battering, female unemployment and poverty, and other aspects of women's subordination. [1]

There are several reasons why nonverbal communication is particularly important to women taken in the international context: first, the comprehensive research program of Rosenthal and his colleagues (1979) demonstrates that in a wide variety of cultures of the world, women are more sensitive than men to nonverbal communication cues. Adding to this the knowledge that nonverbal communication is of major importance in interpersonal communication, estimated to carry from two-thirds to four-fifths of the message in a communication, and yet it is unnoticed and little understood, we may come to the conclusion that studying women's nonverbal world is critical to understanding women, especially in the context of power.

Women are immigrants to men's world, and like immigrants anywhere they face the issue of cultural assimilation versus preservation of group identification. As immigrants from a dominated culture, they feel the pressure placed on any subordinate group to assimilate, to adopt not only the cultural style, but the beliefs and attitudes of the dominant group—in this case, to become like men are supposed to be, both nonverbally and interactionally. The rewards are clear when women are told that their "weak" language or gestures keep them from fitting in or advancing in, for example, management. But what really is typical "women's" nonverbal behavior, and how does it differ from "men's"? Must we adopt "masculine" forms (e.g., staring, touching, interrupting, invading personal space) in order to succeed in our work? And what costs might there be to such change? This chapter will take up these questions in the framework of "women's world."

THE NONVERBAL WORLD OF WOMEN

On the one hand, women's nonverbal world is characterized externally by domination by men, and on the other hand, it is characterized internally by the prescription to behave in certain ways. These two aspects are related; but let us first look at them independently.

Male domination is experienced through various verbal and nonverbal controlling behaviors, such as interruption, staring, touching, and postural displays of superiority by males (Henley, 1973b, 1977; West and Zimmerman, 1983; Zimmerman and West, 1975). Those are part of women's nonverbal experience, the experience of external domination. Another aspect of women's nonverbal experience is the internal prescription, often nonconscious, to behave in certain ways. Examples of this prescription are the nonverbal norms of condensing the body, taking up little personal space, lowering the eyes, smiling, cocking the head, and canting the body (Goffman, 1979; Henley, 1977). A third aspect of women's nonverbal world, one we know little about, is that of behavior not associated with external domination or internal prescription—the behavior emitted by women for their particular needs and expressing their particular attitudes and values.

These behaviors associated with women have been demonstrated to correspond to the behaviors of subordinates, while the behaviors associated with men have been demonstrated to correspond to the behaviors of superordinates (Frieze and Ramsey, 1976; Henley, 1973a, 1977). Women's behaviors thus have been seen as "powerless" compared to men's more "powerful" behaviors.

In a similar way, women's typical language use has been characterized as "weak," and men's as "strong." The U.S. linguist Robin Lakoff (1973, 1975) has named such usage as "inappropriate" question intonation, the use of so as an intensive, tag questions, excessive politeness, and hedges as "women's language," and suggested that this language does not have the power of men's more direct speech. Her analysis, a preliminary speculation at the time, has been accepted as fact without testing by many, and widely understood as supported by research (e.g., Miller and Swift, 1976; Yaguello, 1978). In fact, subsequent empirical testing of her hypotheses has produced mixed results (see Kramarae et al., 1983, especially sections IV and V).

Beliefs about the source of accepted behavioral differences lead to beliefs about appropriate remedies. Women's nonverbal behavior, like their alleged speech, is often believed to emerge from personality characteristics rather than from the social context or from an interaction of the two (e.g., Exline, 1963; Lakoff, 1975, 1979). The origins of such characteristics are seen to lie in female socialization and the impetus for female socialization is seen to be the female "sex role," i.e., the restriction of females to certain spheres and the prescription of certain concerns and behaviors for women within their relationships to others (Frieze and Ramsey, 1976; LaFrance and Mayo, 1979; Weitz, 1976).

Various writers have suggested, explicitly or implicitly, that women should adopt "masculine" forms, i.e., in language should use interruption, speak with more assertions and fewer questions, without inappropriate question intonation, without hedges, without "empty adjectives" and needless intensifiers, without excessive politeness (e.g., Lakoff, 1975), and nonverbally, should invade personal space, touch, stare, not cock the head, lower the eyes, or cant the body, and so on (Henley, 1977).

A more recent prescription for women, a twist on the older one, is the prescription to become "androgynous," to combine the socially desirable behaviors attributed to both women and men in their behavioral repertoires (Bem, 1974, 1975). The existence of such advice acknowledges the importance of our nonverbal behavior, and points out that we may question its appropriateness as an expression of our opinions and feelings, and may intentionally change it. However, much of the advice, and indeed much of the analysis, carries with it subtle messages that bear closer examination.

NEW QUESTION—A NEW ANALYSIS

(1) There is a common belief that we know much about women's behavior, and that there are significant sex differences. But studies have failed to demonstrate alleged sex differences in many areas (Birdwhistell, 1970; Grady, 1979; Henley, 1977; Kramarae, 1981, 1982; Kramer, 1974; Macauley, 1978; Maccoby and Jacklin, 1974).

And furthermore, we must acknowledge (especially in light of the failure to find hypothesized sex differences) that we know less about women's behavior, and about men's, than we think (Bernard, 1981; LaFrance and Mayo, 1979). Therefore many conclusions that we might draw based on assumptions about these behaviors are premature. If we don't know for certain that women do use, for example, tag questions (and also do not know for sure that tag questions are a weaker form), we should not at this point direct women to drop the use of tag questions.

(2) Personality traits are not necessarily the source for a given behavior. Women's situations often demand or encourage certain behaviors or attitudes, and these forms may be responses to situational demands including nonverbal control gestures and threats, rather than personal style or habits or traits. If we accept this reanalysis, we must reconsider the analysis of socialization as a source of female subordination. Given that subordinating conditions can cause subordinate behavior, then it is not females' personalities and socialization that must be changed, but their social conditions.

(3) Many of the behaviors attributed to women as weak are ones which could as well be interpreted as reflecting positive values:

> . . . Admitting our ignorance and sharing our emotions shows the values of honesty and openness; admitting that our ideas are not all our own shows sharing and collective spirit and clarifies the collective nature of work and achievement. Responsiveness to others' moods, needs, and feelings shows sensitivity and consideration for others. Being supportive and nurturing to others shows lack of selfishness (Henley, 1978, p. 36).

Not invading space or touching inappropriately show respect for another's bodily integrity; similarly, not interrupting shows respect for another's conversational rights; using tag questions invites the listener to respond and voice an opinion, and question intonation may do the same; hedges may be an honest expression of relative ignorance, an acknowledgment that one's information is limited but with that recognition one is going to state an opinion anyway. "Empty" adjectives and intensifiers may reflect emotion and involvement with the subject. Politeness is typically taken to be a kindness toward others. (McMillan et al., 1977.)

Although these forms may be carried to an extreme, I would nevertheless like to examine the possibility that women's use of such forms may stem not from powerlessness, but from values that are supposed to be not merely "feminine values" but societal ones. At times it is taken for granted that such forms are intrinsically weak, but they are weak only in contrast to their opposites, only within a cultural context which imputes strength to behaviors that disregard others and may be harmful. Open, sharing behaviors become weak only when another person in an interaction refuses to reciprocate them. Crying is weak, for example, only when the other person refuses to cry or accept crying as an appropriate form of expression. Confessing ignorance of some fact is only a disadvantage when with someone who claims to be all-knowing and never wrong. Being sensitive to another's needs is a disadvantage only when the other is insensitive to our needs. Revealing emotions is only a disadvantage when others are being reserved and refusing to share, or even to feel emotions, in a culture that prefers to hide and deny emotions.

In women's world behaviors labeled as weakness may be strengths. Sharing emotion, admitting ignorance, showing hesitation or openness, and sacrificing for others, when they are reciprocal, bind the community and affirm the person. The powerlessness of so-called "feminine" actions exists only relative to the power of so-called "masculine" ones. To recognize this fact is to recognize that power depends on two manifestations. When we consider only the necessity for women to change their behavior, we ignore the other side of the equation and focus on only one of the manifestations.

(4) The accusation that women exhibit such behaviors out of weakness is based on an inadequate analysis. It tends toward a form of blaming the victim (Ryan, 1971), that is, focusing on the behavior of the victim in a situation or relationship rather than analyzing the oppressor or the structure of the situation. Blaming the victim is a notoriously inadequate approach to understanding any phenomenon, and is used to justify and maintain the status quo. It ignores such issues of context as class, sex, race, and age dominance, as well as pressures of expectancy due to relationship, cultural factors, etc. Blaming the victim fails to recognize the interactive nature of submissiveness and dominance, particularly the dominance side of the interaction (Henley, 1980). In fact, in women's world the values underlying behaviors labeled as weak and feminine are often strengths. Therefore there is nothing inherently weak about the behaviors and no reason to attribute women's situation to the inadequacy of female interaction styles.

(5) The admonition that women should change their behavior is detrimental to them. The blame implies inadequacy and guilt, and to label as inadequate behaviors that are simultaneously labeled as characteristic of oneself or of one's group is to question deeply one's value and to stigmatize one's group. Not only can the demand to change diminish women's sense of self, it can divide them and undermine the strength of their joint action. If women's interaction apart from the world of men, exemplifies certain strengths and values, then ques-

tioning their actions and/or changing them cannot but alter the nature of that interaction, possibly for the worse. It therefore becomes quite important to be sure that the analysis about changing women's behavior is the correct one.

(6) If change is needed in the nonverbal interaction of women and men, rather than that of women, then what change ought there to be? When we consider only the necessity for women to change their behavior, we are ignoring the other side of the picture, ignoring the point that the "powerlessness" of women's behaviors exists only relative to the power of men's. Alternatives to women's change are: change in the perception of the manifestations, separatism, and change in men's behavior.

(a) Change in Perception. Recognizing the positive values of the truly strong behaviors, advocating their spread, rather than deprecating them, will assist in changing the perception of them from weak to strong and positive. It has done little toward that revised perception that so much of the labeling of women's behaviors as weak has come from the women's movement and from feminist scholarly writing. A reemphasis on the strength of female interaction style, based on a rigorous examination and understanding of it, will contribute to that reevaluation.

(b) Separatism. Another way that women's behaviors may gain in perceived and felt power is to eliminate the contrast with behaviors seen as strong. Some women choose to accomplish this through separatism; if change is not forthcoming, why waste energy struggling in a situation which has embodied within it false definitions of power and powerlessness?

(c) Change in Men's Behavior. If change in men is seen as possible, then it bears serious consideration. If we value these forms now defined as female and powerless, societies would benefit from their universal adoption. Resocialization of men on a grand scale ought to be a goal instead of the broad resocialization of women currently pressed for in many quarters. At the very least, we should advocate resocialization of both women and men with the best and most appropriate interactional styles of each. Such resocialization would aim toward developing attentive, supportive, sharing, honest, open interaction styles in men, to be used both in interaction with women and with other men. So-called "powerful" forms which are in fact harmful to others and/or to the interaction would be eliminated.

While not all women would wish to work on resocialization of men, and indeed men have a responsibility to work for their own change (and many are, individually or through the men's movement and support groups), some women may see this goal as an important one for the direction of their energies, and particularly may wish to concentrate on revising the socialization of young boys.

Change in men's behavior is not likely to come about so long as their present behavior is rewarded. If we continue to perceive and publicize certain interaction styles as strong and to urge women to adopt them, and give men who use them only positive rewards, why should men change? A first step in that resocialization program for men, and indeed for ourselves, is to reestablish our own values for the behaviors, respond positively to those we value and wish to encourage, and respond negatively—do not give power—to those we do not value.

(7) Some would regard a training program for changing both women and men as one moving both sexes to androgyny, a state of having the positive behaviors attributed to both sexes. Critiques of the concept of androgyny (Lott, 1981) have raised quite valid questions about certain aspects of this conceptualization. There has been strong pressure particularly on women to become androgynous, i.e., to add "masculine" behaviors to their "feminine" ones. Many of the benefits described concern situational adaptability, the ability to call forth from one's repertoire a behavior appropriate to a given situation one is in. As others (Rebecca et al., 1976) have pointed out, such situational flexibility assumes the dominance of the situation, and is not necessarily the most desirable response in a situation. An alternative response is not to change oneself chameleon-like to fit into any situation, but to consider whether the situation itself is one that one wants to put up with, or whether it should instead be changed.

As others have pointed out in their critique of androgyny, this concept continues to dichotomize the world and behaviors into feminine and masculine. It is not uncommon to see apologies for the use of sexual stereotyping, but it is uncommon to see it abandoned because of dissatisfaction with it.

(8) Finally, there is a difference in the meaning of change in nonverbal behavior for women and for men. Men's adoption of so-called "feminine" forms is often a matter of personal fulfillment: they will feel more complete, more whole, if they can cry, express tenderness, learn to cook, to sew, and begin to raise children. Because of society's stereotyping and bias, there are few material rewards for men who adopt behaviors that are usually the province of women, and there may be psychological costs, e.g., in scorn from other men.[2] But despite, or because of, the fact that material rewards for such change are lacking, men often reap generous interpersonal rewards, especially from feminists: we think a man working toward nonsexist behavior is a wonderful person (and indeed he is), and extend him much recognition and praise.

But women's experience of parallel change is different. Such change is motivated by survival more than by personal fulfillment needs in a male world, a world which demands male-related behaviors in many work settings. It is true that some of the behaviors can be fulfilling in themselves, such as learning to express one's anger and wishes clearly. But others, if they mean suppressing societal and personal values of sharing and concern for others, may be unfulfilling. In any case, several points may be made about the outcome of such change. It is not clear that society in general responds positively to such change in women, any more than it does to change in men—in fact, it may respond less positively; even if a woman finds success at work, she may be disliked and held back for "unfeminine" ways. Also such change does not garner the attention or praise—even from feminists—that similar change does for men. There therefore exists the situation that women are blamed for their position in life. They are admonished to change their behavior; yet the rewards for such change are often not forthcoming.

Since women's subordination, to varying degrees, seems to be a cultural universal (Webster, 1975), it should be illuminating to study the relation of nonverbal behavior, including sex differences, to women's status cross-culturally.[3] I stated earlier that women are immigrants to men's world. We have seen that this is not entirely true, and that the behaviors that distinguish the sexes are not so much differences of sex as differences of power and social context. Keeping that in mind, the immigration analogy is still relevant, and we may find the literature on immigration, assimilation, "passing," cultures in contact, or cultural identity of interest in addressing questions that arise in the admonition for women to change. We must be clear in looking at these questions that we understand the interaction of the cultural and the political. What gives value to one cultural form over another within a society is most often a matter of political domination.

Where does this leave us with the admonition for women to change their behavioral style? With more questions than answers. I do not mean to defend forms that may be inadequate for responsible and effective interaction—but I do mean to ask: do we know what women's nonverbal style really is? Do we know its efficacy? Do we understand the underlying values expressed in that style and in the style that women are urged to adopt? Which values do we wish to express? And who should change?

NOTES

1. I am not talking here of so-called "personal power," which has become for some a focus for discussing women's power. Personal power, seen as "control over one's decisions and life situations without control over others," seems to me to be a possibility only within the context of political power; as I have written elsewhere, ". . . We

would be naive to think that this simple power to move unrestrained through our own lives will be unobtrusive and will be allowed without resistance, so long as we don't attempt to control others. . . If control over my decisions means control over how I spend my share of tax money, and control over my life situations means control over whether my children have unpoisoned food to eat, or whether I in fact have children, then this 'personal' power must be very strong indeed, in the face of a society that does not now let me control those decisions or situations." (Henley, 1978, p. 35.) The power I am speaking of, then, is at an interpersonal level though it is still political, social power, power that affects others' lives as well as one's own.

2. Some believe though, that development of expressiveness in men will contribute to their physical and mental well-being and longer life; see, e.g., Jourard, 1964.

3. However, it should be noted that my observations in this chapter have been drawn almost exclusively from studies conducted in the United States (and don't apply universally even there), and are not meant to apply in the specific to other cultures.

REFERENCES

Bem, S. L. 1974. The measurement of psychological androgyny. Journal of Consulting and Clinical Psychology, 42, 155-62.

Bem, S. L. 1975. Sex-role adaptability: One consequence of psychological androgyny. Journal of Personality and Social Psychology, 31, 634-43.

Bernard, J. 1981. The female world. New York: Free Press.

Birdwhistell, R. L. 1970. Masculinity and femininity as display. In Kinesics and context, pp. 39-46. Philadelphia: University of Pennsylvania Press.

Exline, R. V. 1963. Explorations in the process of person perception: Visual interaction in relation to competition, sex, and need for affiliation. Journal of Personality, 31, 1-20.

Frieze, I. H., and Ramsey, S. J. 1976. Nonverbal maintenance of traditional sex roles. Journal of Social Issues, 32(3), 133-41.

Goffman, E. 1979. Gender advertisements. New York: Macmillan.

Grady, K. E. 1979. Androgyny reconsidered. In Psychology of women: Selected readings, edited by J. H. Williams, pp. 172-77. New York: Norton.

Henley, N. M. 1973a. Power, sex and nonverbal communication. Berkeley Journal of Sociology, 18, 1-26.

Henley, N. M. 1973b. Status and sex: Some touching observations. Bulletin of the Psychonomic Society, 2, 91-93.

Henley, N. M. 1977. Body politics: Power, sex and nonverbal communication. Englewood Cliffs, N.J.: Prentice-Hall.

Henley, N. M. 1978. Changing the body power structure. Women: A Journal of Liberation, 6(1), 34-38.

Henley, N. M. 1980, March. Body politics: Power and status patterns in inter-ethnic and inter-gender communication. Paper presented at Conference on Body Politics, Institute for Nonverbal Communication Research, New York.

Jourard, S. M. 1964. The transparent self. New York: Van Nostrand Reinhold.

Kramarae, C. 1981. Women and men speaking. Rowley, Mass.: Newbury House.

Kramarae, C. 1982. Gender: How she speaks. In Attitudes toward language variation: Social and applied contexts, edited by E. B. Ryan and H. Giles, pp. 84-98. London: Edward Arnold.

LaFrance, M., and Mayo, C. 1979. A review of nonverbal behaviors of women and men. Western Journal of Speech Communication, 43, 96-107.

Lakoff, R. 1973. Language and woman's place. Language in Society, 2, 45-79.

Lakoff, R. 1975. Language and woman's place. New York: Harper & Row.

Lakoff, R. 1979. Stylistic strategies within a grammar of style. In Language, sex and gender, edited by J. Orasanu, M. K. Slater, and L. L. Adler, pp. 53-78. New York: New York Academy of Sciences.

Lott, B. 1981. A feminist critique of androgyny: Toward the elimination of gender attributions for learned behavior. In Gender and nonverbal behavior, edited by C. Mayo and N. M. Henley, pp. 171–80. New York: Springer-Verlag.

Maccoby, E. E., and Jacklin, C. N. 1974. The psychology of sex differences. Stanford, Calif.: Stanford University Press.

McMillan, J. R., Clifton, A. K., McGrath, D., and Gale, W. S. 1977. Women's language: Uncertainty or interpersonal sensitivity and emotionality? Sex Roles, 3, 545–59.

Miller, C., and Swift, K. 1976. Words and women: New language in new times. Garden City, N. Y.: Doubleday.

Rosenthal, R., Hall, J. A., DiMatteo, M. R., Rogers, P. L., and Archer, D. 1979. Sensitivity to nonverbal communication: The PONS test. Baltimore: Johns Hopkins University Press, 1979.

Ryan, W. 1971. Blaming the victim. New York: Random House.

Webster, P. 1975. Matriarchy: A vision of power. In Toward an anthropology of women, edited by R. Reiter, pp. 141–56. New York: Monthly Review Press.

Weitz, S. 1976. Sex differences in nonverbal communication. Sex Roles, 2, 175–84.

West, C., and Zimmerman, D. 1983. Small insults: A study of interruptions in cross-sex conversations between unacquainted persons. In Language, gender and society, edited by B. Thorne, C. Kramarae, and N. Henley, pp. 102–17.

Yaguello, M. 1978. Les mots et les femmes. Paris: Payot.

Zimmerman, D. H., and West, C. 1975. Sex roles, interruptions and silences in conversation. In Language and sex: Difference and dominance, edited by B. Thorne and N. Henley, pp. 105–29. Rowley, Mass.: Newbury House.

24 FEMINIST RESEARCH METHODOLOGY FROM A PSYCHOLOGICAL PERSPECTIVE: SCIENCE AS THE MARRIAGE OF AGENTIC AND COMMUNAL

Barbara Strudler Wallston

To a psychologist, research means empiricism. Thus, I will discuss what feminism brings to empiricism. I believe the primary value of feminism to the scientific enterprise is in its perspective related to asking questions, framing inquiry, and interpreting data. I do not believe that feminism implies a single methodological approach. The agentic and communal marriage of the title characterizes a pluralistic approach to method. Exploring alternate ways of knowing and viewing them as valuable should not be done at the expense of the valuable aspects of logical positivism and the scientific method. Methods are not good in and of themselves, but only in relation to questions (Wallston, 1983). However, since the nature of our methods do shape our questions, it is important to be aware of and to value a broad range of methods to ensure that a sufficiently broad range of questions to understand human behavior are asked.

If not a specific method, then what does feminism bring? My definition of feminism goes beyond that of the dictionary, which highlights the equality of women and men politically, economically, and socially as central to feminist theory. In addition to a belief in equality, I believe feminism includes an understanding of women's oppression in society. Thus, power is a central construct, and part of feminism's contribution is an analysis of the power dynamics of the research process.

It is important to note the lack of consensus regarding feminism and methodology. Graham and Rawlings (1980), for example, present a radical position conceptualizing sexist, nonsexist, and feminist research. They conceptualize feminist research as process-oriented, qualitative, inductive, etc. They seem, to me, to be recreating anthropology or ethnography. While their emphasis on the use of women

subjects and women's experience as a source of questions would miti-
gate the sexism of the field, I believe some of the valuing of these
methods is only because they are new and different to psychologists.
Certainly anthropology and ethnography have been no less patriarchal
than psychology. Just as a sexist ethnographer will do a sexist ethnography, I contend that there can be feminist true experiments.

There are four aspects of feminist methodological discussion
to be clarified.

VALUES AND SCIENCE

First, the most agreed upon aspect is the role of values in our
work and the impossibility of doing work that is value free (e.g.,
Sherif, 1979; Wallston and Grady, in press). While objectivity is the
goal, it must be recognized that true objectivity is not possible. Feminists, then, argue for bringing values to consciousness and developing
a value-sensitive science (Wittig, 1982).

> Rather than abandon the quintessentially human effort to
> understand the world in rational terms, we need to refine
> that effort. To do this, we need to add to the familiar
> methods of rational and empirical inquiry the additional
> process of critical self-reflection. Following Piaget's
> (1972) injunction, we need to 'become conscious of self.'
> In this way, we can become conscious of the features of
> the scientific project that believe its claim to universality
> (Keller, 1982, p. 594).

POWER AND THE RESEARCH PROCESS

The second aspect, the power analysis of research, encompasses multiple facets. The power of the experimenter over the subject and, in fact, the lower power implied by the term subject rather
than participant is critical to understand. Carrying feminist advocacy
for a redistribution of power in society to the research domain implies
more equal power between researcher and participant. The Graham
and Rawlings (1980) discussion of participants as active collaborators
involved in all stages of the research process illustrates these ideas.
Unger's (1983) power analysis of research highlights positivist empiricism as defining the researcher participant relationship as impersonal
and as transforming "people into object-like subjects" (p. 11). The
human element, when it slips through, is treated as an unwanted side
effect while actually it is intrinsic to the human relationships in experiments.

The political power of research findings must also be considered when research questions are framed (Wallston, 1981). An ivory tower approach, in which we claim no responsibility for the uses of our data, is not consonant with feminist psychology. When sex differences are studied, we must be concerned whether differences that are found will be used politically to deny women access to selected roles in society. If certain findings will have negative ramifications, it may be that the research question should be reframed. Sometimes discussion of results can provide orientations to helpful rather than harmful data utilization.

CONTEXT MUST BE CONSIDERED

The third aspect is the importance of context and situational factors in understanding human behavior. Weisstein (1970), in a now classic critique of psychology, argued against the heavy emphasis on a personological approach. When women are studied, or seen as "other," personal rather than situational attributions are used as explanations for behavior. The work on fear of success, which has been reinterpreted from a situational perspective rather than as an intrapsychic motivational deficit in women (Condry and Dyer, 1976) provides one example. Women live in a society where they are punished for success in traditionally masculine areas; thus, what has been termed fear of success may instead be a realistic appraisal of the world. Similarly, Allen (1979) has argued that research on black women has focused on background characteristics relating to success rather than scrutinizing societal practices and institutional racism and sexism that deny black women the opportunity to achieve commensurate with their ability.

The focus on individual difference variables such as race and sex may cause us to ignore more fundamental situational distinctions, such as those inherent in power relations, which are confounded with these characteristics (e.g., Wallston, 1983; O'Leary et al., in press).

The feminist emphasis on context also complements the critique of experiments as context stripping (e.g., Bronfenbrenner, 1977; Petronovich, 1979). People are brought into the laboratory and their history is forgotten. In fact, Unger (1981) noted that sex differences are less likely to be found in laboratory than in field research, in part because of lost history. Such factors as growing up as a woman, being discriminated against, not being listened to, etc.—important history— are ignored in entering the artificial world of the laboratory. The unequal power relationships that underlie many sex differences have less impact in the artificial laboratory environment.[1] At a minimum, it is important to articulate the issues involved in losing context and history and to consider the implications of this loss for interpretation of data.

Additionally, context may be included rather than eliminated from laboratory experiments. For example, Aronson (1983; see also Aronson and Osheron, 1980) discussed how laboratory experiments helped understand the processes involved in the successful desegregation teaching techniques termed the jigsaw classroom. Students who had and had not been exposed to the jigsaw classroom were brought into the laboratory and this history factor was considered, not ignored. In fact, it added to the value of the findings. The field experiments on the jigsaw classroom in the schools only allow us to judge its overall effectiveness. By studying students' interactions in controlled laboratory experiments it was possible to learn more about the process involved in that students who had been exposed interacted differently from those without such exposure.

METHODOLOGICAL PLURALISM

The fourth aspect is an openness to new methods. Frequently the unfortunate labels "masculine" and "feminine" (Bernard, 1973; Carlson, 1972) have been used to delineate the distinctions between experimental quantitative and more qualitative, descriptive, and correlational methods (Wallston and Grady, in press). The phallocentric nature of the terms hard and soft, including the clear valuing of the hard or masculine has been noted by Bart (1971). In her original paper (but not in the final published version) she suggested the vaginocentric replacements of "dry" and "wet." This relabeling is helpful in clarifying some hidden assumptions in scientific terminology, but I find it just as problematic to value the wet rather than the dry. I prefer to use Bakan's terminology of "agency" and "communion" because the terms are less value-laden than any of the others.

Bakan (1966) initially distinguishes between these as follows:

Agency manifests itself in self-protection, self-assertion and self-expansion; communion manifests itself in the sense of being at one with other organisms. Agency manifests itself in the formation of separations; communion in the lack of separations. Agency manifests itself in isolation, alienation and aloneness; communion in contact, openness and union. Agency manifests itself in the urge to master; communion in noncontractual cooperation. Agency manifests itself in the repression of thought, feeling, and impulse; communion in the lack of removal of repression. One of the fundamental points which I attempt to make is that the very split of agency from communion, which is a separation, arises from the agency feature it-

self; and that it represses the communion from which it
separated itself (p. 15).

Later, Bakan continues:

The agency feature is what is involved in the process of
differentiation, specialization, and separation of function
within and between organismic units; whereas communion
is what is involved in a variety of relationships among
organismic units (p. 152).

How does this apply to research? Carlson (1972) argued that
current scientific operations including:

[S]eparating, ordering, quantifying, manipulating [and]
controlling . . . are 'agentic' features. . . . In contrast,
more communal kinds of scientific inquiry—relatively
neglected in psychology, but exemplified in ethnology,
anthropology, and in such physical sciences as geology
and astronomy—involve naturalistic observation, sensitivity in intrinsic structure and qualitative patterning of
phenomena studied, and greater personal participation
of the investigator (p. 20).

Then, qualitative methods, observation, etc. are relatively
communal and experimental techniques are agentic. By thus relabeling
them, the association of women or men with particular methods becomes an empirical question. In fact, the sex of researchers and the
novelty of the questions asked are sufficiently confounded so it is difficult to assert that women or men have an affinity for particular
methods (Wallston and Grady, in press).

A method can only be considered in relation to the question being
studied (Wallston, 1983). The issues of validity of a particular method
can only be raised in terms of validity for what. What is the goal of
the work? In my health research, internal validity (is the effect found
real?) is critical to my theoretical understanding of processes. If my
work is to have practical implications, then I must consider external
validity or generalizability before changes in the health system can
be suggested. Research involves compromise between such types of
validity (Wallston, 1983) and the nature of the compromise chosen is
related to the questions and goals of the research.

A feminist methodology repertoire must include agentic and
communally oriented approaches. We learn the most from data that
are hard and wet, the agentic and communal marriage of my title.
Illustrations of the value of including qualitative data with experimental

and other quantitative methods abound (Wallston, 1983; Wallston and Grady, in press). Most of us trained in the positivistic psychology of recent decades are most familiar with agentic methods, but we now must develop an openness to the communal. Similarly, the more communally oriented should not ignore the value of quantification and of the controlled experiment. Even those of us who consider ourselves quantitative scientists make numerous qualitative decisions at every phase of research, such as when to continue a statistical analysis, when to replicate, and when to attempt to publish findings. Research reports rarely address these qualitative aspects of the scientific enterprise. On the other hand, while feminism can bring us to an appreciation of communal methods, it does not dictate a denial of agentic methods.

SUMMARY

The feminist contribution to research has been most important in bringing to light new theories, new questions, and new interpretations of data. Feminism has also brought to the analysis of the research process: the importance of values, the power dimensions, the importance of situations and context, and the value of communal methods. While I believe that no method is inherently feminist, feminism can lead us to a true and equal marriage of agentic and communal inquiry in which both are utilized and perhaps lead to more creative science.

NOTE

1. This may appear to contradict the discussion regarding power in the experiment. The issue is not that power dynamics are inoperative but that power distinctions relevant in other contexts may be irrelevant in the laboratory. Artificial power dimensions such as experimenter-subject or roles that are delineated take precedence. Moreover, sex as a status characteristic is not inoperative in the laboratory but it appears to be less salient.

REFERENCES

Allen, W. R. 1979. Family roles, occupational statuses, and achievement orientations among black women in the United States. Signs, 4, 670-86.

Aronson, E. 1983. The jigsaw classroom. Colloquium presented at George Peabody College, Nashville, Tenn.

Arsonson, E., and Osheron, N. 1980. Cooperation, prosocial behavior and academic performance: Experiments in the desegregated classroom. In Applied social psychology annual, Volume 1, edited by L. Bickman. Beverly Hills: Sage.

Bakan, D. 1966. The duality of human existence. Chicago: Rand McNally.

Bart, P. B. 1971. Sexism and social science: From the gilded cage to the iron cage, or, the perils of Pauline. Journal of Marriage and the Family, 33, 734-35.

Bernard, J. 1973. My four revolutions: An autobiographical history of the ASA. American Journal of Sociology, 78, 773-91.

Bronfenbrenner, U. 1977. Toward an experimental ecology of human development. American Psychologist, 32, 513-31.

Carlson, R. 1972. Understanding women: Implications for personality theory and research. Journal of Social Issues, 28(2), 17-32.

Condry, J. C., and Dyer, S. L. 1976. Fear of success: Attribution of cause to the victim. Journal of Social Issues, 32, 63-83.

Graham, D. L. R., and Rawlings, E. 1980. Feminist research methodology. Paper presented at the American Psychological Association, Montreal.

Keller, E. F. 1982. Feminism and science. Signs, 7, 589-602.

O'Leary, V. E., Unger, R. K., and Wallston, B. S., editors, in press. Women, gender and social psychology. Hillsdale, N.J.: Lawrence Erlbaum.

Petronovich, L. 1979. Probabilistic functionalism: A conception of research method. American Psychologist, 34, 373-90.

Sherif, C. W. 1979. Bias in psychology. In The prism of sex: Essays in the sociology of knowledge, edited by J. A. Sherman and E. T. Beck. Madison, Wis.: University of Wisconsin Press.

Unger, R. K. 1981. Sex as a social reality: Field and laboratory research. Psychology of Women Quarterly, 5, 645–53.

Unger, R. K. 1983. Through the looking glass: No wonderland yet. Psychology of Women Quarterly, 8, 9–32.

Wallston, B. S. 1981. What are the questions in psychology of women? A feminist approach to research. Psychology of Women Quarterly, 5, 597–617.

Wallston, B. S. 1983. Overview of research methods. In Sex role research: Measuring social change, edited by B. L. Richardson and J. Wirtenberg, pp. 51–76. New York: Praeger.

Wallston, B. S., and Grady, K. E. In press. Integrating the feminist critique and the crisis in social psychology: Another look at research methods. In Women, gender and social psychology, edited by V. E. L'Leary, R. K. Unger, and B. S. Wallston. Hillsdale, N.J.: Lawrence Erlbaum.

Weisstein, N. 1970. Kinder, Kuche, Kirche as scientific law: Psychology constructs the female. In Sisterhood is powerful, edited by R. Morgan. New York: Vintage.

Wittig, M. 1982. Value–fact–intervention dilemmas in the psychology of women. Presidential Address, American Psychological Association, Washington, D.C.

PART 5

MAKING WAVES

Confronted in recent decades with the unintended effects of social changes—such as nationalism, modernization, urbanization, and suburbanization—women began to make waves of their own. The changes that have had an impact on women's lives, and women's response to the change process provide the common link of the chapters in this section. Each chapter highlights change in a different cultural and social context, and it reveals the impact of women's adult experiences on behavior.

The Bloom-Bar Josef paper shows that the military, which is a male institution, can have a strong socialization effect on the women who serve in it by empowering them intellectually, emotionally, and socially.

Social change is often accompanied by unintended and undesirable consequences for which new solutions must be sought. Suburbanization in gilded ghettos that isolate women not only from the main centers of activity but also from one another, is a case in point. Urban and community planners have rarely considered the effects of their policies and practices on women. (See also Chapter 3 by Nordström.) Sarkissian outlines the elements of a project designed specifically to reach and serve women isolated in the suburbs of an Australian metropolis. The emphasis is on the direct involvement of women in all stages of the project. Networking and social support systems proved to be effective for accomplishing the objectives of the project as well as for empowering the women to become active change agents.

That the effective transformation of women's reality requires their active involvement as change agents is argued in the chapter by Mar'i and Mar'i. They trace the evolving status of Arab women in Israel from their being passive objects of the forces of change to their achievement of positions of influence in local social and political life. The initial male response to the traumatic disruptions of the 1948 War and the resultant heightened sense of personal insecurity and loss of status was to increase their control over women. However, conditions that forced men to leave the villages and seek work in the urban centers created a vacuum which was filled by the women, who consequently increased their autonomy and influence in and around the home. Legal, political, social, and economic developments enabled women to enter the labor force and institutions of higher education, experiences which brought on a changing consciousness, and transformed women into the advocates and activists in public affairs. Still, participation in the public domain is conditional on male approval.

Abu Baker emphasizes the catalytic effects of cross-cultural contacts between Arabs and Jews on improving women's status. Although women living in "mixed" cities were for the most part newcomers to urban life (having left their villages during the 1948 War), the level of modernization they have attained during the last 30 years is significantly greater than that of women living in a nearby all-Arab town. Abu Baker attributes the difference to the greater opportunities for Arab-Jewish interaction and to modeling of attitudes and behavior in the mixed cities. Modernization was also more rapid among Christian Arab women than among their Moslem or Druze sisters. Baker explains this in terms of their "western orientation" which made them more ready to adopt the behaviors they observed during their interactions with Jews.

Writing about Egypt, El Mahairy begins by legitimating women's claim to greater equality and access to societal resources, in terms of Islamic sources. She distinguishes Islamic law, which she argues advocates equal value for women and men, from the discriminating norms of traditional culture which are a foreign import, and in fact violate the commands of the Koran. She portrays women as being under the pressure of contradictory forces, namely: (1) those pushing toward modernization and economic development, which necessitate that women be educated toward an achievement orientation and for participation in the labor market, and (2) those pulling women back to their traditional spheres, advocating education as a measure for strengthening family life.

Boneparth and Stoper close this section with a view of the future that shows how technological advances may render radical feminist revisions—in the structure of work and the work-family nexus—a general social imperative. They, like others in this section, recognize the need to ground their claims for women in terms of the dominant value system and the interests of those who control the resources for implementing the policies recommended. They conclude their chapter with the observation that the restructuring of work requires that women "persuade policy makers and business leaders that the elimination of the sexual division of labor will foster rather than hinder economic well-being."

25 STATUS AND EDUCATION OF WOMEN: A PERSPECTIVE ON EGYPT

Theresa El-Mahairy

STATUS OF WOMEN

In Egypt, the future of women is particularly bleak. They are victims of sexual and educational biases which for many begin at birth. For example, in Egypt the mortality rate for female infants is nearly 20 percent higher than the rate for male infants (Al-Azhar University, 1979). Preliminary findings of current studies suggest the reason. As long as breast milk was sufficient to meet the child's nutritional needs, no sex difference in development was observed, but during the period when the child required supplemental feeding, the incidence of mal-nutrition among girls was 40 percent higher than the incidence among boys. Most mothers of newborn girls (73 percent) believed that by giving birth to a female child they had caused unhappiness to their husbands.

Analysts of women's status in the Middle East have blamed Islamic traditions for such biases. But, it should be emphasized that Islamic law and traditional culture are not necessarily one and the same. The Koran speaks angrily about the father "whose face darkens" when he is told of the birth of a daughter and the prophet repeatedly stressed the importance of giving equal affection and care to children of both sexes.

As early as 1899, Quasim Amin (1865-1908), poet and leading figure in the movement for female emancipation, argued that the social decay of the time was not due to Islam but rather to the disappearance of the social virtues of "moral strength" and the cause of that was ig-norance. This ignorance, according to Amin, begins in the family. The relations between man and woman, between mother and child, are the basis of society; the virtues that exist in the family are those which

239

will exist in the nation. The woman shapes the morals of the nation through her role as the educator of children (Amin, 1901). Amin (1899) argued that in Muslim countries, neither men nor women are properly educated to create a true family life and the woman lacks the status necessary to play her role. Corruption penetrated Islam by converts, primarily Turks, who brought in their own "customs and illusions." They destroyed the original Islamic system of government, which defined the rights of rulers and ruled, and replaced it with the rule of despotic force. The strong learned to despise the weak and men to despise women (Amin, 1899). In other words, the degradation of women is an external phenomenon which was imported into Islamic society. The segregation of the sexes, however, appears to be an indigenous part of Islamic religion as it is of Orthodox Judaism.

Islam in itself is not an oppressor of women and within Islamic tradition, there were and there are those who advocate equality in the sense of equal value.

The interrelationship between Islamic ideals, education, feminism, and professionalism warrants further examination in order to understand the development of female emancipation in Egypt. There are roughly two views of the goal and nature of education for women: the traditional perspective and the modern or Western perspective. Both are concerned with improving women's status and well-being. One way wishes to preserve the traditional culture and to educate women within the context of women's traditional roles. Those who advance this view feel threatened by the influences of external forces (first Darwinism, then capitalism and Westernism). This fear, reiterated in Egypt today, is associated with a strain toward fundamentalism which may be seen as a response to the threat of invading Western culture. The traditionalists argue that female emancipation is in essence an imitation of Western values which would weaken the Islamic family unit. The traditionalist view was associated with the petit bourgeoisie who represented the small-scale productive sector of poor peasants, small land-owners and tenants, artisans and owners of small workshops, public service employees and military personnel. The view of the petit bourgeoisie was represented in the Muslim Brotherhood and the Free Officer's Movement of Nasser's time which demanded an end to foreign domination and continued to retain traditional views toward women.

The second perspective is rooted historically in the late nineteenth and early twentieth century when educational and social reform along Western lines was viewed by the nationalists as prerequisites for independence. This meant reform in marriage and family structure as well. Amin (1901) believed that the position of women could be improved only by education that was directed not solely to the proper management of the household, but also to increasing her opportunity to earn her own living. Economic self-sufficiency was the only sure guarantee of women's rights. Unless a woman could support herself, she would always be at the mercy of male tyranny, no matter what rights the law gave her. Education and economic independence would end the tyranny and with it also the veiling and seclusion of women.

The emancipationist view is usually associated with the ideas of Mohammad Abduh, Islamic religious reformer living at the turn of the century, who called for women's education, and who represented, by and large, the upper classes. It is in the upper middle-class that women have become professionally liberated. Among them, we find intellectuals, professionals working in the fields of science, medicine, and engineering, such as Dr. Nuwwal Saadawi, noted Egyptian physician and feminist as well as a leading figure in the Arab world. In her book, Women and Sex, Saadawi (1972) states:

> Work is a human necessity whereas conception is nothing but a biological function in which all living things engage from amoebae to apes. . . .

Unfortunately, Saadawi's views have been met with reserve and resentment.

Despite the teachings of Islam, women in Egypt, as in most of the world, are often regarded as subordinate citizens, and changes in their status are occurring at a slow pace. Inheritance, property, and family laws explicitly regard two women as equivalent to one man. Honor of the family depends on preserving the honor of its female members, but the responsibility for doing so resides in men, usually the women's brothers. Marriages are still customarily arranged by parents in the same social class, often tied by kinship. Children are the major source of women's emotional satisfaction, and sons, in particular, are their major source of power and prestige. At the same time, the high birth rate, encouraged by Islamic tradition, is a major source of Egypt's problems.

At the twentieth anniversary of the foundation of the Egyptian Women's Federation in 1944, Hoda Sharawi, Egypt's leading feminist, suggested that the Federation's goal is the betterment of women through raised standards of education and preparation for marital life so that she may "make her share in the promotion of the well-being of the country in general" (Olesen, 1977). The goals included the establishment of a free health unit for women and children.

Even social planners and change agents, who have a modern perspective concerning the goals of women's education, are wary of copying the Western experience. The following statement by a physician and development planner in the Ministry of Health (Hassouna, 1977: 49-53) reflects this apprehension:

I place the emphasis on educating women for responsible
motherhood because I believe that only through the education of mothers and fathers can we expect the behavioural
changes in the younger generation, who are, after all, the
beneficiaries of the development plans on the drawing boards
today. I would go so far as to suggest that because of the
importance of this role that women who choose this option
and participate fully in the education program would also
be given remunerative compensation for their services as
well as having social services channeled directly to them.
I would also say that a whole system of continuing education and refresher education should be provided for women
who wish to pursue a variety of career interests in their
life. I strongly urge us to benefit from the experiences of
other countries. Let us examine the statistics on the type
of jobs which women hold in countries in which they constitute a fairly large percentage of the labour force. If we
do this, we shall find that, all too often, the women have
been assigned the menial, crypto-servant jobs and that,
at the same time, their status has eroded because their
contribution as responsible mothers has not been accorded
at least as equal a status as a factory worker, in the sense
that they have not received compensations—both in money
and in kind—from society, commensurate with the importance of their role. When we talk about education in Egypt,
let us keep these points in mind. Let us seek together to
identify what types of contributions we really need in Egypt
to get ourselves moving in the right direction and then let
us structure our system of rewards, status and sanctions
so that those contributions which are most useful to the
nation will also be those which are appropriately awarded.

The speaker here observes that the women's labor market experience in industrialized societies has its problems. For example,
women enter the market in low paying jobs and at the same time, suffer a decrease in their status in their domestic roles. Such negative
outcomes should be avoided in Egypt or women will be double losers.

WOMEN AS HEALERS AND CONSUMERS
OF HEALTH SERVICES

The contradictions within Egyptian society are well illustrated
in the case of women as healers and consumers of health services.
It reveals the contradictions between Islamic law that provides for
female growth and freedom for self-actualization and cultural norms

that have developed over the centuries, which dictate female subordination.

How are the female healers in Middle Eastern society defined? For the woman physician, the concept of complementarity is valid here. According to Nelson and Olesen (1977), what is perhaps not appreciated by Western feminists is that the large extended family which they view as a source of women's oppression in the Islamic Middle East is that which has provided women with their traditional source of power as well as legitimate authority. When women enter the paid work force, they "generally find relatively little resistance with regard to employment from men. Instead of resistance and jealousy, women frequently meet encouragement from male colleagues." (Mohsen, 1977). A recent study (El-Mehairy, 1978) found that the woman physician does not view her role as in any way different from that of her male colleague. The data suggest that she views herself as an equal who is expected to perform her role in the same manner.

Who gets medical care? A hierarchy of status appears to exist within the family which determines who will go to the doctor and seek expensive treatment. Although the treatment in the rural health unit is free, the cost of a day's wages lost, medications that must be purchased if unavailable at the clinic, and the reluctance of Middle Eastern village women to be seen by a male doctor all contribute to their not receiving adequate care. Scarce resources are more frequently allocated to men, especially male household heads, than to women. It is explained that a man's illness is more detrimental to household welfare since resources may have to be diverted to hire wage hands to work on the family land in his place. One survey of village family expenditures for illness during a four-month period, revealed an average of 2.20 L. E. (Egyptian pounds) for men compared to 1.50 L. E. for women (Pillsbury, 1978).

Age is also a major factor in evaluating the severity of an illness and may interact with sex. A woman who has gained the high status of a mother of an adult son receives prompt and more costly treatment than a young childless daughter-in-law or a male infant in the same household, or maybe even more than the adult son's wife (Blackmann, 1968).

How do doctors perceive women's problems? In a study (El-Mahairy, 1981), Egyptian male and female physicians were asked to identify problems in the community that they found in the course of their work. Examples of possible problems presented to them that related to women's status are: "Women come in advanced stages of diseases due to the negligence of husband and father," and "the weak position of women." It is interesting that no male physician cited these as problems. Poverty and the lack of education were cited as major problems by 49 percent and 35 percent, respectively, of the doctors working in the rural areas of Menoufia and in Minia, and by only 16 percent of the doctors working in Cairo. These differences in the responses reflect those of the conditions in the three areas. The more rural and southern areas have higher rates of illiteracy, and the villager is generally poorer than his city cousin. In the physicians' analysis, the proportions who cited problems as arising from "primitive" traditional belief systems are: Cairo, 8 percent; Menoufia, 18 percent; and Minia, 21 percent. Considering the amount of concern often voiced about traditional healers, especially the traditional birth attendant, the daya, it is surprising that the proportion of physicians who cited traditional beliefs to be a problem was considerably low compared to the proportion citing "poverty/lack of education." Perhaps, this indicates that the overemphasis in modern medical programs on traditional culture as an obstacle to change may need rethinking. It is this overemphasis that reflects the elitist position that it is specifically the culture of the masses that constitutes the more crucial obstacles to the improvement of public health. However, it may be seriously misleading to focus solely on culture rather than on objective conditions of poverty and ignorance. Although the educated elite woman shares the same cultural traditions and primarily the same religion, she is highly advantaged compared to her poor sister.

The diverse views concerning the question of educating women for a suitable role represent a central issue in the public debate over the status of women in Egyptian society. Perhaps, rather than following Western models and educating women for work, we should consider seriously using the educational system to reach the illiterate woman, the young mother in particular, together with her daughter, and to educate her for her traditional role.

REFERENCES

Al-Azhar University. 1979. Population Studies Research, Appendix A., Research Activities, 1975-1979, Mimeograph, pp. 3-4.

Amin,Quasim, Tahir al-Mar'a, Cairo, 1899, cited by Hourani, A. 1970. Arabic Thought in the Liberal Age, 1798-1938, pp. 116-31. London: Oxford University Press.

Amin,Quasim, al-Mar'a al-jadida, Cairo, 1901, cited by Hourani, ibid.

Blackmann, W. S. 1968. The Fellahin of Upper Egypt: Their Religious, Social and Industrial Life Today with Special Reference to Survival from Ancient Times, Reprint. New York: Barnes and Noble.

El-Mehairy, T. M. 1978. "Medical Doctors: Managerial Abilities and Role Definitions." Middle East Management Review, Vol. II, No. 1., pp. 121-37.

El-Mehairy, T. M. 1981. Medical Doctors: A Study of Role Concept and Job Satisfaction: The Egyptian Case, Unpublished doctoral dissertation, Salford University, England.

Hassouna, W. 1977. "Education of Women—For What?" The Cairo Papers in Social Science—Women's Health and Development. Cairo: The American University in Cairo Press, Vol. I, Monograph 1., December, pp. 49-53.

Mohsen, S. 1977. Illness Concepts and Structural Constraints: Health Care in an Egyptian Village, Paper read at the Middle East Studies' Association Annual Meeting, New York City, November 9-12.

Nelson, C., and Olesen, V. 1977. "Preliminary Notes on Healing Systems, Social Control and Articulation of the Moral Order." The Cairo Papers in Social Science: Women's Health and Development. Cairo: The American University in Cairo Press, Vol. I, Monograph 1., December, p. 20.

Olesen, V. 1977. "Styles and Sources of Social Change: Women's Movements as Critiques of Health Care Systems." The Cairo Papers in Social Science: Women's Health and Development. Cairo: The American University in Cairo Press, Vol. I, Monograph 1., December, pp. 21-34.

Pillsbury, B. 1978. Traditional Health Care in the Near East. A report prepared for the U.S. Agency for International Development, Washington, D.C., Contract No. AID/NE-C-1395, March.

Saadawi, Nuwwal. 1972. Women and Sex. Dar ash-Shafab, Cairo.

26 THE IMPACT OF CROSS-CULTURAL CONTACT ON THE STATUS OF ARAB WOMEN IN ISRAEL

Khawla Abu-Baker

URBANIZATION AND LEGAL REFORM

Many of the Arab villagers whose villages were conquered or destroyed during the 1948 war, moved to cities that had become pre-dominantly Jewish. To preserve their cultural identity and because they were manipulated by the Israeli authorities, Arabs settled in separate and identifiable neighborhoods in the cities, to create what in Israeli jargon are called mixed cities such as Haifa, Acre, Lydda, and Ramle (Shanel, 1980). This process of urbanization had two important consequences: Achievement related criteria became more important and ascriptive attributions less important as the basis for social class differentiation. In addition, Arabs living in urban settings were more intensely exposed to cross-cultural interactions than were their rural counterparts. These interactions, furthermore, were not limited to work settings or to men only.

Another major transformation, which took place along with urbanization, was the subjugation of the Arab minority to Israeli jurisdiction. Especially relevant for the status of women was the law passed in the early 1950s that established universal compulsory education. For the first time not only all Arab boys, but also all girls had to attend school.

Another law, which had an even more immediate impact on the status of women, granted full autonomy to adults (18 years and over) in all matters of personal life. Thus, Arab women were legally protected from culturally determined punishment for exercising their rights to personal liberty. In addition, polygamy was outlawed and the minimum marital age for girls was raised to 17 years.

All these developments—the growth of urbanization, compulsory education, legal protection from traditional sanctions, and greater equality combined with cross-cultural interactions—prepared the way for the realization on the part of the Arabs of their aspiration to become more modern. The impact of the thrust toward modernization on the status of the Arab women was greater in the mixed cities than in the all-Arab rural settings or even than in the all-Arab towns. In the city, both the family and the individual are more anonymous; there are more jobs available for both men and women; laws are more strictly enforced, educational opportunities are more plentiful, the standard of living is higher, and traditional patterns of social control are considerably weaker than in the small towns or rural villages. Most important in the city, Arabs and Jews have many more opportunities for cross-cultural interactions.

A COMPARISON OF TWO LOCALES

To test the hypothesis that cross-cultural contact improved the status of Arab women, two sites were studied: Acre (Akko), a mixed city where Arabs (Muslims and Christians) comprise 31 percent of the population and, Shefar'am, an all Arab town some 15 miles from Haifa, inhabited by Muslims, Christians, and Druse.

Acre, a small seaport town and subdistrict of Israel (administratively within the Northern District) was a city of ancient Phoenicia and later of Palestine and a former Turkish fortress. It lies at the northern point of the Bay of Acre, on a tongue of land ending in a reef which forms a natural harbor. In the plans to partition Palestine into Arab and Jewish states, the town was allotted to the Jewish state by Britain but to a detached Arab district of Western Galilee by the U.N. Commission, whose report was accepted by the General Assembly (Nov. 29, 1947). It was occupied by Israeli forces on the expiration of the British mandate (May 1948). Shortly after 1948, a new quarter was built east of the Old City. The city later expanded further to the north and the northeast. It serves most of Western Galilee in trade and administrative matters, being the center of the Acre subdistrict as it had been during the British Mandate. Acre is an important Muslim center, its al-Jazzer Mosque is the largest within Israel's pre-1967 borders. Together with Haifa, it is also the world center of the Bahai faith. There are churches of several denominations (Roman Catholic, Maronite, Melkite) and a considerable number of synagogues. The population today includes Jews, Muslims, Christians, and Bahai.

Shefar'am is a town in Western Galilee. First mentioned in Talmudic sources, it was the headquarters of Saladin (1811), when it was renowned for the woods and vines growing in the vicinity. When the town was occupied by the Israel army in June 1948, a number of

Muslim inhabitants fled, while other Arab villagers from the vicinity moved in. The population, Christian, Druse, and Muslim, grew from 3,412 in 1948 to about 20,000 in 1980. Until modern times, Shefar'am developed within the confines of its narrow ancient nucleus. With the onset of expansion, the inner quarter remained inhabited by Christians, while Druse resided in a northwestern quarter and Muslims in a north-eastern section. After the establishment of the state, new suburbs with a mixed Arab population were built including a government sub-sidized housing development. Approximately 12 percent of the popu-lation works in agriculture, 44 percent in local commerce and ser-vices, and the remainder commute to work in Haifa's industrial zone.

Methodological procedures for this study included in-depth in-terviews with a total of 60 Arab women in both sites as well as par-ticipant observation which extended over two years.

FINDINGS

In Acre, even though the vast majority of the population had originated from rural areas, the status of women improved far more than it did in Shefar'am. This improvement is evident in the level of education achieved, the types of jobs held, in women's influence within and outside the family, and their sociopolitical involvements and achievements of leadership positions.

Within the mixed city, change occurred earlier among the Chris-tian Arab women than it did among the Muslims. This difference may be explained by the greater Western orientation that existed among the Christians than among the other Arab groups which predisposed the Christians to experience cultural contacts and to be influenced by them. In addition, at the early stage of Arab-Jewish contact, inter-action was perceived as threatening and dangerous. Modernity was identified with being Jewish and thus was rejected. The Christians were the first group to differentiate between modernity and being Jew-ish. The stance adopted was that one could learn from the Jews to become modern without assimilating, a distinction that greatly facili-tated the utilization of the cross-cultural experience as a modernizing one. The first Arab families to relocate in the Jewish neighborhood were of Christian origin. Altogether, however, more Arabs in Acre than in Shefar'am are bi-lingual and even bi-cultural.

In Shefar'am, the cross-cultural domain was initially not directly accessible to women. The results of interaction were transmitted to the women by their men. Consequently, at least at the early stages, Arab males, as the only ones who came into contact with Jews, were the initiators of change and controlled its pace and contours. The pro-cess of modernization among women was thus delayed and when it occurred, did so at a slower pace.

In Shefar'am, the rate of change was fastest among Christian women, followed by Muslims, and was slowest and least among the Druse. The fact that Druse women were the slowest to change as a result of cross-cultural contact is, at first, surprising considering that Druse males engage in the most intensive and deepest cultural interaction with Jews as the only Arab subgroup to serve in the Israeli army. It may be that overexposure to modern culture in too short a time led Druse males to lead two separate lives, with two parallel subidentities; one modern in the Jewish context, the other ultratraditional in their own cultural context.

In the all-Arab town, social stratification remains based on traditional cultural criteria. In the mixed city, however, one can differentiate between social classes with parallel ethnic and religious categories with respect to cross-cultural exposure. Thus, we find the following class differences among women in these cities.

(1) Women of the wealthy higher classes have generally remained passive while enjoying the security of the status ascribed to them by virtue of their males. Change in their roles and functions is a threat to these privileges.

(2) Women of the middle class are much more achievement-oriented, more geared toward self-realization using education as their basic instrument. Furthermore, their cross-cultural contacts are more meaningful in the sense that they are more personal and can thus serve as a learning source.

(3) Women of the working class developed in two directions which in many respects are mirror-opposites to each other. Those who did not go to work outside their home, continue to be suppressed by their men who are not themselves less suppressed by their employers. They remain strongly conforming, dependent, and with rather a minimum level of education. They are the objects of violence and abuse—sexual and social—by their husbands. Women who went into the labor market increased the centrality and power of the women in the household; they became less conforming, more independent, and assertive. They are active in encouraging their children to strive for upward mobility, girls as well as boys.

SUMMARY OF FINDINGS

One can summarize the findings by stating the most salient factors of the cross-cultural and cross-social interactions between Arabs and Jews in Israel as far as the status of women is concerned as follows.

(1) Following the radical social, political, economic, and demographic changes that took place as a consequence of the 1948 war,

social status had increasingly to be achieved rather than socially inherited. While this applied more to young Arab males, it was also significantly true for females.

(2) While legal undertakings of the newly created state of Israel were received by Arabs as an undesired form of interference, they nonetheless provided women with legally granted equal opportunity and protection of their freedom of choice.

(3) Initially, being modern was identified with being Jewish and was thus perceived as threatening and rejected. Later on, the two were differentiated, a fact that facilitated the utilization of the cross-cultural experience as a modernizing one.

(4) In general, at the early stage, Arab males, as the only ones who came into contact with Jews, were the initiators of change and its controllers. But later, especially in mixed cities, women became directly involved in the cross-cultural domain. This accelerated the improvement in their status which changed at a faster rate than in homogenous Arab settings.

(5) Christian Arabs, whose western orientation predisposed them to cultural influences, changed more rapidly than did Muslims. The Druse Arab group, although its males are more involved in cross-cultural contacts, remains the least influenced by that contact as far as the status of women is concerned.

(6) The impact of cross-cultural contact is also affected by socio-economic class: middle-class women are the most influenced, although lower-class women who enter the paid labor force primarily in the Jewish sector also gain greater autonomy and authority within their families.

REFERENCES

Shanel, Etshak. 1980. Tayba: Social Areas Undergoing Modernization and Urbanization (in Hebrew). Haifa.

27 THE ROLE OF WOMEN AS CHANGE AGENTS IN ARAB SOCIETY IN ISRAEL

Mariam M. Mar'i and Sami Kh. Mar'i

Arab women in Israel and elsewhere (Nath, 1978; Smock and Youssef, 1977; Prothro and Diab, 1974) are becoming divorced from their traditionally passive and marginal roles. Tuma (1981) suggests that in Israel Arab women have become more active participants not only in the sphere of family decision making, but also in all spheres of public life traditionally prohibited to them. While changes in the position of women in Arab society are easily observable (Ginat, 1981), the processes and dynamics underlying these changes are subtle and less evident.

Arab women in Israel, as part of the Palestinian Arab minority, are simultaneously and organically linked to the two conflicting forces—the Palestinians on the one hand and Israel on the other. Like other Arabs in Israel, they are thus vulnerable to the complex sociopolitical dynamics inside Israel as well as in the larger context of the Middle East. Consequently, while trying to understand the role of Arab women in sociocultural change of the last few decades, one must relate the dynamics of change to political developments, especially as these have their impact upon the sense of security of the Arab population in Israel.

One can relate much of men's need to control women to men's sense of insecurity. John Gulick (1976) suggests that the Arab male develops "ego vulnerability" with regard to aspects of his "significant" female's behaviors. This vulnerability, as a rule, increases his need to control the female as potential "stress producer." "Improper" female behavior endangers the male's ability to cope with other sources of stress such as the struggle for economic survival; the maintenance of cultural integrity in the face of invading cultural forces; and his relationship to the national conflict between his people, the Palestinians, and the state in which he lives, Israel.

The Palestinian Arab minority in Israel is manipulated and controlled through a sophisticated system of hegemony devised by Israeli
authorities (Lustick, 1980). Until recently men have been the major
target of such control. Women were not considered a political or economic threat, since they were rarely politically active, and traditionally were not employed outside the home. Thus, as males attempted
to cope with the various stresses in their lives, including the stress
inherent in their being a target of control and manipulation by the
authorities, female behavior became especially significant for their
sense of security. This constellation of factors greatly influenced the
extent to which Arab women in Israel could play an active part in
sociocultural change.

In 1948, when Israel was created, Palestinian Arab society
underwent abrupt discontinuity. The internal political institutions and
organizations collapsed, the social structure was shaken, vast economic transformations took place, and cultural traditions were challenged. In fact, total communities disintegrated and their members
became refugees either on their land inside Israel or dispersed in the
neighboring Arab countries. Under such traumatic conditions, cultural
traditions, although undermined by the great upheaval, remained the
major vehicle through which Arab identity could be nurtured and maintained. Threats to that identity were greatly felt by that segment of
Palestinian society that remained on its land and came under the
control of Israel, after 1948.

1948-56: CONTINUOUS STAGNATION

Few observable changes in women's status took place in the first
few years following the establishment of Israel. The situation of wom-
en in these years was essentially one of continuity with century old
traditions. In fact, traditionalism became stronger as a reaction to
the overwhelming threat to the identity of those who remained. As
both the present and future were uncertain, and as Israeli authorities
stepped in to control the lives of the Arabs inside its borders, the
heritage of the past became the most salient source from which Arabs
drew content and form as they sought to protect and preserve their
identity.

The heritage of the past, however, was organically associated
with an economic base and a larger system of social relations both of
which had been seriously shaken. After much of their cultivatable
lands had been confiscated by Israel (Jiryis, 1976), Arab males, for
the first time, had to search for external sources of income in the
Jewish economic sector. This changed not only the economic base of
the community, but also the lifestyle of the family. It meant that men

(fathers and brothers) remained outside the family circle all day and in many cases, all week. In addition, Arab men came into contact with a whole new realm of experience in a society and culture different from their own.

Under these conditions, the feelings of insecurity among men were overwhelming. Their continuous absence from home, their subordination to Israeli Jewish institutions and their observation of the behaviors of Jewish Westernized women all intensified the threat to both their identity and their status. While their political and economic subordination symbolized to them that they had been incorporated into Israel, their observation of Jewish women symbolized cultural invasion. Consequently, men in Arab society controlled their women even more intensely, not only as a vehicle of cultural continuity, but also as a response to men's deep sense of insecurity aroused by their new conditions.

However, as Arab men went to work on Jewish farms or in metropolitan areas, their absence created a vacuum. Thus, for the first time in centuries, Arab women were faced with the paradox of having increased discretionary power in areas traditionally defined as male domain. At the same time, they were expected to use that power to pass on traditions and values in which female status was inferior (Mar'i, 1978). This apparent paradox did not seem to have created a conflict at the time. The structural change was not transformed into a subjective consciousness. Women continued not only to be psychologically dependent on men, but also to reproduce the very conditions of their own subordination.

Thus, it becomes clear that women had drifted into change rather than having initiated it. The male-dominated Arab society could cope with such a change which was not stress producing. In fact, as women assumed the role of culture preservers, involved in the reproduction of the conditions of their own subordination, stress was greatly reduced. Yet, this change was not without its positive effects for women. They were jolted from their traditional passivity and became more influential actors in family life. They gained a sense of self-worth as well as a cultural and political relevance.

The introduction of universal compulsory education in the early 1950s was another development that had far reaching consequences. At first, it was met with resistance and was rejected for females. Most parents held traditional stands less favorable to the education of females than to that of males. In addition, they were apprehensive about the school culture and curriculum; it was not a Palestinian school, but rather an Israeli school for Palestinians. Parents who wanted their daughters to have an education enrolled them in all-female Christian boarding schools. These schools were not only exclusively for females, but until then, they were untouched by Israeli authorities.

Arab educators, assisted by the compulsory education law, made significant efforts to rehabilitate their educational system. They were very instrumental in increasing the number of school children, including females. To them, education was the means through which their society could be rebuilt and their culture reconstructed. In the process, women entered the teaching profession. The presence of female students provided legitimacy for women becoming teachers. The role models provided by female teachers, in turn, heightened the legitimacy of female education. This resulted in the massive enrollment of female students, a breakthrough which was probably the single most salient feature of this period as far as women and change in Arab society are concerned.

1956–67: RELATIVE OPENNESS

Until 1956, Arabs in Israel viewed themselves as living on what may be characterized as a "provisory" basis. Leaders and the media of Arab countries related to Israel as a rather unfortunate but temporary phenomenon. Arabs in Israel exposed to these messages, therefore, also viewed their existence under Israeli rule as temporary. This attitude heightened resistance to change. Among other things, change meant becoming "modern," and becoming modern was associated with becoming Jewish-like, hence with the loss of identity.

After the 1956 War of Israel, Britain, and France against Egypt, Arabs in Israel began to relate to their existence under Israeli rule as a relatively permanent condition or at least as less temporary than before. Their redefinition of the situation led to a coping strategy of greater openness to change for the benefits it could bring, at least in economic and educational spheres. Change was also associated with social and national development, especially in the eyes of the educated elites, and authentic political movements surfaced in the late 1950s such as the El-Ard movement and the Israeli Arab Front.

Furthermore, after ten years of interaction with Jewish society and institutions, Arabs had acquired a measure of competence and confidence in coping without sacrificing their cultural authenticity. The economic recession (1965–67) in which unemployment rates for Arab males were especially high, coupled with rising aspirations for a higher standard of living, produced economic pressures which pushed Arab women into the unskilled labor force.

Compulsory education increased the demand for Arab teachers and created opportunity for women. The education of females gained an economic value. It also became a source of status for the females themselves as well as for their families. Access to education, however, was premised on an implicit agreement still in effect, although to a less degree, that in return for the opportunity for education and employment, females would remain conforming to the cultural values and traditions. It was understood, for example, that a female student who "misbehaved" or did not conform to traditional norms of behavior, could and would be forced to drop out of school.

The period 1956-67 was one in which women's consciousness developed and was reinforced by male and female writers. Tradition was openly criticized as a perpetuator of backwardness and the inferior status of women. Education continued to bloom and in cities of mixed Arab and Jewish populations, the number of female students often exceeded that of males. Education gained popularity as instrumental for accelerating modernity and thus became central in the consciousness of Arabs in Israel. This set in motion the forces that propelled the development of future challenges.

1967+ : A PERIOD OF CHALLENGE

Israel's military victory in 1967 had far reaching implications for the Arabs in Israel. To begin with, more aggressively than at any time before, they demanded full national and civil rights as well as recognition as a national minority. They felt that the security claim, which the Jewish establishment had given as the major impediment to equality, could not now be as easily argued as before the war.

The occupation of the West Bank and Gaza Strip by Israel in the 1967 War created an opportunity for Arabs in Israel to interact with other segments of the Palestinian people. A process of re-Palestinization developed in which Arabs in Israel emerged with a clear sense of their distinct national identity. Through their interaction with other Palestinians, Arabs in Israel also discovered that women's emancipation was an issue of common concern to the larger Palestinian nation. They became aware that women's equality was not a Jewish induced problem, but rather an issue of indigenous concern to Palestinians. Thus, "becoming modern" no longer necessarily meant becoming "Jewish-like." These developments, reinforced by economic recovery from the painful recession, further enhanced the sense of security.

These changes were reflected in the entry of large numbers of women into the labor force, especially in low level occupations, as well as into the universities. The latter movement was especially significant, for example, in three years (1969-72) the number of female Arab students enrolled in Israeli Universities more than doubled (from 141 to 305), while that of male students increased by only 25 percent (from 450 to 565). For the first time, women became involved in Arab student unions, known for their high levels of political activism. They were elected representatives and executives in these unions. Women's associations and ad hoc groups became popular. These developments were the most salient and observable manifestations of women's new awareness in this period of challenge. The greatest transformation was that women's role had changed from that of culture preserver to that of culture transformer.

Our analysis thus far has focused on macrolevel dynamics of stability and change in the position of Arab women in Israel. We now shift to the microlevel study of the Arab community in the mixed city of Acre through which these macrodynamics and development were observed empirically.

THE CASE OF ACRE'S WOMEN

In 1981, Acre, a town in Galilee in the Northern part of Israel, had a population of nearly 36,000, 31 percent of which were Arabs. During the 1948 War, the majority of the Arab population of Acre left the town. Immediately after that war, Arab families whose towns elsewhere had been destroyed moved into Acre. Today these families compose most of Acre's Arab population. Lacking leadership, suffering from disrupted social order and organization, and with insufficient education, the Arabs of Acre had to face their new situation in the newly created Jewish state. They were concentrated, by Israeli authorities, in the ghetto-like Old City and denied the opportunity to move into the new city where more appropriate housing, advantageous employment opportunities, educational facilities, and interaction with the Jewish population were available (Cohen, 1973).

The abrupt discontinuity with their traditional way of life, coupled with the fact that most families were strangers to each other, reduced social pressures for conformity and permitted change to take place with relatively little resistance. Furthermore, as economic conditions were very difficult, males, including school age children, had to work. Consequently, formal education became and remained until recently, primarily the privilege of females. The availability of Christian schools for girls accelerated the spread of female education. The villagers who migrated to Acre in 1948 escaped the social pressures against female education present in their home village.

The existence of separate educational systems for Arabs and Jews in Acre, coupled with the urgent need for Arab teachers (most of the teachers had fled in 1948) made it easier for Arab women, even though not fully qualified, to penetrate an occupation traditionally filled by men. The benefits to be gained from the opportunity to work within their own cultural community and the status attained by entry into a prestigious position outweighed the potential costs in the form of threats of this development.

The entry of Arab women into the teaching profession as noted earlier, encouraged the spread of female education. These teachers became role models for other women to follow not only in their investment in education, but also in their leaving home to enter the labor force. Most teachers initially came from relatively highly prestigious families traditionally opposed to women's employment out of the home. This break with the traditional pattern made women's employment respectable for women of lower social classes as well.

These developments had two major consequences for Acre's Arab women. One was that many women, regardless of their educational achievement, became economically more independent. The other was that women dominated the educated elite of Acre's Arab community both in number and in level of activity or by what in Arabic is called their "social presence." In 1973, among every ten Arab university students from Acre, seven were women.

Acre's educated Arab women took the lead in the process of re-Palestinization of their community. In fact, the first Arab student on an Israeli campus to have the courage to declare in public that she was Palestinian, was a female. She was a student from Acre studying at the University of Haifa during the early 1970s. It seems that the fact that Acre's Arabs live among Jews magnified their identity needs and made them more urgent. The fact that women dominated the educated elite among Acre's Arabs meant that they took the lead in meeting those needs.

In 1974, the educated elite formed Acre's Arab University Student Association. Initiated and led mainly by female students and graduates, this association had many objectives. The most important objectives were: to improve housing conditions; to upgrade quality of education; to revive and further develop Palestinian folklore; and to enhance the sociopolitical awareness and commitment of youth. Being Arab, the Association had to cope with Israeli authorities on both local and national levels. Being largely female dominated, it had to struggle against internal forces mainly stemming from the male dominated larger society. However, quite unexpectedly, the local Arab community supported the Association both morally and financially. This paved the way for the association's success. It seems that the great relevance to the community of the objectives and activities was enough to prevent the expression of whatever objections may have existed.

In the beginning there was no explicit opposition by the Israeli authorities to the existence of the association. Only when the authorities witnessed the successful activities of the association and observed the growing Arab community's support for it did they step in. Such opposition was consistent with their policy against independent organization among Arabs in Israel (Lustick, 1980).

Two tactics were used for disintegrating the association. First, active measures to deprive members of work opportunities were taken by not permitting qualified teachers to obtain available teaching positions unless they dissociated themselves from the association. The other tactic seems to have been geared to exploiting a cultural dynamic. As the conflict with the authorities widened, rumors were spread to the effect that authorities were planning a crack-down on members of the association in order to crush it. The fact that the leaders of the association were predominantly women, put fathers, brothers, and husbands on the alert as the imprisonment of the "significant" females would be considered a strong violation of their cultural integrity. These two tactics lead to the virtual disintegration of the association in 1976.

However, immediately after the collapse of the association, a new initiative sprung up. The leading women in the association reorganized and formed Acre's Arab Women's Association. The formal objectives as well as activities of the association were best characterized by the notion that they were depoliticized at least in the immediate sense of political activism. They included: establishing a nursery school, raising women's consciousness, sponsoring cultural activities and training seminars (in preschool education) for women in the surrounding Arab villages, as well as helping women in these villages to organize and become active. These activities, while not directly political, were definitely relevant to society in general and to women in particular, and had important potential political consequences. Under tremendous pressure from the authorities and consequently from their own male dominated society, the women rechanneled their efforts and shifted the focus of their involvement, without, however relinquishing their self-image as change agents.

In conclusion, our study of Acre's Arab community points to a number of observations that pertain to women as change agents, which may be summarized as follows:

(1) Under conditions of insecurity over cultural identity due to external threats, women were the first to be controlled and guarded from foreign cultural "contamination," (the second group is youth). These conditions changed and women were allowed more freedom and equality in education and employment.

(2) Education had great relevance for women as change agents. Indeed, knowledge that enhances awareness is a generator of power. Furthermore, higher education coupled with economic independence had a radicalizing effect on women both socially and politically.

(3) Once highly educated and politicized, Arab women ceased to be only preservers of culture. They took charge and became active in the process of culture renewal.

(4) Israeli political authorities successfully manipulated Arab society partly through its value system in relation to women, consequently decreasing the level of political activism of the whole community.

(5) Finally and paradoxically, the tragedy that befell the Palestinian people in 1948 and which brought dispersion and disintegration to total communities created conditions for the development of women's consciousness, relevance, and relative power in the process of change. The demise of traditional structures and patterns created an opportunity for many women to move out of oppression and to find their way in the process of reconstruction and reestablishment.

REFERENCES

Cohen, Eric 1973. "Integration vs. Separation in the Planning of Mixed Jewish Arab City in Israel." The Levi Eshkol Institute for Economic, Social and Political Research. Jerusalem: Hebrew University (in Hebrew).

Ginat, Joseph. 1981. Women in Muslim Rural Society. Rutgers: Transactions Books.

Gulick, John. 1976. "The Ethos of Insecurity in Middle Eastern Culture." In Responses to Change, edited by G. A. DeVos. New York: Van Nostrand Reinhold.

Jiryis, Sabri 1976. "The Arabs in Israel." New York: Monthly Review.

Lustick, Ian. 1980. Arabs in the Jewish State. Austin: Texas-University Press.

Mar'i, Sami. 1978. Arab Education in Israel. Syracuse: Syracuse University Press.

Nath, Kamla. 1978. "Education and Employment Among Kuwaiti Women." In Women in the Muslim World, edited by L. Beck and L. Keddie. Cambridge: Harvard University Press.

Prothro, Edwin, and Diab, Lufy. 1974. Changing Family Patterns in the Arab East. Beirut: The American University.

Smock, Audrey Chapman, and Nadia Haggag Yousef. 1977. "Egypt: From Seclusion to Limited Participation." In Women: Roles and Status in Eight Countries, edited by J. C. Giele and A. C. Smick. New York: Wiley.

Tuma, Emile. 1981. "The Issue: Liberation of Arab Women not Sexual Crisis." Haifa, Al-Jadeed, no. 12, December (In Arabic).

28 ISRAELI WOMEN AND MILITARY SERVICE: A SOCIALIZATION EXPERIENCE

Anne R. Bloom and Rivka Bar-Yosef

From its early origins, it was recognized that although the primary function of the Israel Defense Forces (IDF) was that of guarding the State, this was not its only function. "The army," Ben Gurion wrote, "must also serve as an educational and pioneering center for Israeli youth—for both those born here and newcomers. It is the duty of the army to educate a pioneer generation, healthy in body and spirit, courageous and loyal" (Ben Gurion, cited in Perlmutter, 1969). This was a vision of the army as a citizen's academy and, therefore, as an agent of socialization.

The universal service requirement for Israeli youth, both male and female, makes the IDF unique among the armies of the countries of the Western world. Although not everyone serves, all must register, which allows the researcher to study the influence of the armed forces, on life-span development during a critical stage for identity formation of the total age cohort.

This chapter reports findings of a longitudinal study of women in the IDF. According to a before/after design, a cohort of young women were surveyed at the time of registration for service (age 17) and in a follow-up study four years later. The problem of inquiry focused on issues of development that derive from psychological theory about this particular stage of life.

---

*This research was supported by a grant from the Harry Frank Guggenheim Foundation.

BACKGROUND OF THE INQUIRY

Within the theoretical context of life-span development, the first period of postadolescence takes on new coloration. Kenniston (1960) talks of this period as a new stage, calling it "youth," a period between "self and society." For Kenniston, this period has an emergent quality, as indeed it would for Erikson (1963), in between identity and intimacy, for a person more developed than the adolescent, but not yet as secure as an adult.

Levinson (1978) in his formulation of a sociopsychological conception of the life course, calls this time "early adult transition." For the individual, the transition period is one of extraordinary growth and a crucial turning point in the life cycle.

How social institutions influence this developmental process has been a continuing subject of research. A major problem of such inquiry, however, is precisely that it is in this transitional age when the common institutional experiences of the individual in modern society are differentiated. In Israel, however, the IDF provide a common expectation for all persons for the next postadolescent years.

The sociopsychological implications of such a universal requirement for this age group have been recognized by Bar-On (1966) in his description of the meaning of army service for Israeli recruits. He challenges the popular belief that at 18 a person can be changed very little. The IDFs experience not only negates this belief, but shows that in the course of military service, many youngsters have an additional opportunity for reshaping their personality. Indeed, service in the Israeli army is considered by its citizens an integral part of growth and development for the individual, an intrinsic part of one's life, influencing attitudes and ideology.

Against this background, the IDF offer a unique setting for the study of the socialization of women. The Defense Law of 1959 declared that all men and women reaching the age of 18 must report for conscription into national service. Exemptions for men were limited to yeshiva (religious school) students and those with severe mental or physical handicaps, and result in about 90 percent of males serving in each age cohort. For women, on the other hand, deferments were extended to include domestic, religious, and educational criteria, so that only 50 to 60 percent of each cohort actually serve (Prime Minister's Commission, 1978).

For those women who serve in the IDF, there are three levels of participation: Kevah: the small professional career nucleus; Khova: male and women recruits in compulsory military service, and Miluim: the reserves, who annually return for a limited period of active duty. Every member of the IDF must enter by the same door, in the universal national service; there is no separate enlistment of professionals or officers. For both men and women, therefore, rising in the military requires that all recruits begin at the same level and presumably through successful achievement attain promotion to higher ranks.

METHOD OF STUDY

This project was begun in 1974. At that time data were collected from a sample of 1,530 17-year-old women who came to register at the five major recruitment centers. In 1977, with the assistance of the Social Science Research Unit of the IDF, questionnaires were sent to those subjects of the 1974 sample who had been inducted into the army. Anybody who did not appear on the army list was presumed not to have been inducted. We were thereby able to ascertain the military status of all the original subjects' groups. Subjects were designated according to three categories:

(1) Those who served as officers;
(2) Those who served as regular recruits for their entire period of service;
(3) Those who were exempt from service.

From the cohort of 1,530, 42 women had served as officers, 37 of whom became our interview sample. In addition, data were acquired from 124 women who served and from 85 who did not. The subjects for both these categories were chosen at random. Each participant thus selected was contacted either by telephone or on a home visit to set up an appointment. The interviewers were students, recommended by the faculty of the Social Science departments at the various universities in Israel. The interviewers were trained by the senior author.

Data collection was based on a paper and pencil questionnaire, individually administered. The questionnaire contained both open and closed questions and required more than an hour to complete. To the preservice questionnaire, questions appropriate for postservice inquiry were added. Both administrations included a personality scale, the Stein Self Description Questionnaire (SSDQ).

The SSDQ consists of 20 paragraphs, each of which describes a manifest need or motivational factor in Murray's (1938) system of personality (Stein, 1966). Specifically, the subject is being asked to describe herself in terms of how she perceives her own behavior.

RESULTS

Because this chapter focuses on socialization, we will be concerned mainly with the results of the follow-up, analyzing the patterns

TABLE 28.1: Background factors and military status (percentages)

	Officers n = 37	Servers n = 124	Non- servers n = 85	Significance level
Mother's place of birth				
Israel	39	21	15	$\chi^2 = 22.13$
Europe/United States	50	51	36	$p < .00$
Asia/Africa	11	28	49	
Father's place of birth				
Israel	22	13	11	$\chi^2 = 18.84$
Europe/United States	64	58	39	$p < .00$
Asia/Africa	14	29	50	
Mother's education				
Elementary	17	43	63	$\chi^2 = 39.85$
High school	47	42	33	$p < .00$
Posthigh school	22	11	4	
University graduate	14	4	0	
Father's education				
Elementary	14	36	69	$\chi^2 = 50.64$
High school	39	44	23	$p < .00$
Posthigh school	22	11	3	
University graduate	25	9	5	
Prestige of father's occupation				
High	25	17	10	$\chi^2 = 8.46$
Medium	34	27	21	$p < .08$
Low	41	56	69	
Mother works outside home				
Yes	56	40	24	$\chi^2 = 12.40$
No	44	60	76	$p < .00$
Religion in family of orientation				
Very important	0	12	32	$\chi^2 = 30.98$
Somewhat important	51	44	44	$p < .00$
Not at all important	49	44	24	

of development, especially with reference to the service status (i.e., as officer, regular service, and exemption or nonservice).

BACKGROUND FACTORS AND MILITARY STATUS

In some respects our data document the expected. There is a significant relationship between service status and parental place of birth, education, occupation, and religious orientation (Table 28.1).

The majority among the parents of the officers were born in Europe, United States, or Israel. They are well educated (high school and post high school). They are secular or moderately religious. More than 50 percent of the mothers are employed, the majority in medium and high prestige occupations (Treiman, 1977). While the occupations of the officers' fathers are a less significant differentiating variable, they also tend to be of higher prestige than that of the fathers of the others.

TABLE 28.2: Mothers' occupation and military status (percentages)

Prestige of mother's occupation	Officers $n = 21$	Servers $n = 50$	Nonservers $n = 20$
High	22	14	0
Medium	65	23	33
Low	13	63	67

$\chi^2 = 20.73$, $p < .00$.

The nonservers' families have a different profile. About half of their parents were born in North Africa or Asian Middle East. The majority have only elementary education, the fathers are mostly in low prestige occupations, the mothers tend not to work outside their homes, and among the 25 percent employed, nearly 70 percent held low prestige jobs. This group is also more religious than the other two, which was predictable as Jewish families with Asian and African origin tend to be more religious than those from other regions, and religious orthodoxy is one of the legal criteria for female exemption from service. Among the nonservers, fully half are of Asian/African family origin, compared with one-fourth of the women who serve.

The regular servers are more heterogeneous in the above attributes than either the officers or the nonservers.

This research corroborates the general impression that the attitudes, certain personality traits, and the military status of the young women are partially predicted by the background variables.

However, background is not totally predictive. Certain findings indicate that the military experience affects the developmental process of the young women, changing their aspirations, attitudes, and self-perception.

LEVELS OF ASPIRATION AND MILITARY STATUS

Table 28.3 reports answers to the questions, "If you are working now or planning to work, which level in your occupation do you aspire to?" Both in 1974 and in 1978, there were four possibilities: aspiration to the top, to a high position, desiring a reasonable success, and no desire for success.

TABLE 28.3: Question: If you are working now, or planning to work, which level do you aspire to (percentages)

| | 1974 | | | 1978 | | |
	Officers	Servers	Non-servers	Officers	Servers	Non-servers
Top	14	10	4	22	11	7
High position	40	31	27	67	46	23
Reasonable success	32	52	56	11	38	61
No desire for success	14	7	13	0	5	9
	100	100	100	100	100	100

$x^2 = 10.56$, $p < 10$.
$x^2 = 35.38$, $p < .000$.

Although the differences between the groups were evident in 1974, these were not significant. A dramatic change occurred during the four-year period that included the service. After service, nearly 90 percent of the officers aspire to the two top levels, compared to slightly more than half in 1974. The change is less dramatic but in the same direction among the regular servers (41 versus 57 percent). In con-

trast to the army women, there was no change among the nonservers.
In both periods, about one-third expressed the desire to reach this
goal.

NEED HIERARCHY AND MILITARY STATUS

Need hierarchy was measured by the SSDQ. The subject was
presented with 20 paragraphs and asked to describe herself by ranking
all the paragraphs: rank 1 for the paragraph that described her best
through rank 20 for the paragraph least descriptive. The ranks are
used as scores that yield a hierarchy of needs for each of the groups
we are studying. The mean rank of each need allows comparison of
this hierarchy among our three groups. The higher the score the lower
the rank of the need.
The SSDQ presents us with three different types of findings.
Fifteen items on the personality scale did not show a systematic relationship with military status, and will therefore not be discussed
in this article. One item—abasement—differentiated among the three
categories in both periods (Table 28.4).

TABLE 28.4: Differences in SSDQ need "self-abasement"[a]
according to military status in 1974 and 1978

Need in "self-abasement"	1974	1978
Officers	19.02	18.72
Servers	16.08	17.45
Nonservers	12.94	14.11
	F = 16.34	F = 17.67
	p < .001	p < .001

[a]The lower the score, the greater the need.

Four needs appear only in 1978 as differentiating among the
three statuses. Table 28.5 shows that the officers are more involved
in achievement as mastery and control of their environment. They
express greater self-assurance than the other two groups.
The nonservers, in addition to remaining more abasive than
the women who serve, are more defensive, more dutiful (blame avoid-
ant), more deferent, and more compliant.

TABLE 28.5: SSDQ needs by military status in 1978[a]

Needs	Military status	SSDQ scores	F Value
Achievement	Officers	7.48	4.62^b
	Servers	8.37	
	Nonservers	10.29	
Blame avoidance	Officers	13.62	4.80^b
	Servers	12.22	
	Nonservers	10.71	
Deference	Officers	13.48	8.73^b
	Servers	10.62	
	Nonservers	9.25	
Dominance	Officers	10.29	3.94^c
	Servers	12.02	
	Nonservers	13.02	

[a]The lower the score the greater the need.
[b]$p < 0.01$.
[c]$p < 0.05$.

SENSE OF PERSONAL CONTROL

Respondents were asked about being in control of their life as opposed to often feeling helpless in dealing with events (Table 28.6). The proportion of women expressing a sense of control is greater for those who serve, 80 percent of the regular servers, and 95 percent of the officers.

TABLE 28.6: Sense of control by military status (percentage)

Military status	Feel in control n = 189	Feel helpless n = 57
Officers	95	5
Servers	80	20
Nonservers	65	35

$\chi^2 = 14.20$.
$p < 0.00$.

DISCUSSION

It is the formally stated purpose of the IDF that "the Women's Corps is a unique educational and social institution where girls from different countries and backgrounds learn to live and function together and contribute to the nation's advancement" (Khen, 1980).

Ben Gurion's vision of an army that would educate the nation's youth appears to have been realized for men. That vision, however, is only partially valid for women when a considerable proportion is allowed not to serve.

Not to be inducted, in a country where military service is so important, clearly has effects. Service in the IDF appears to have both social and intrapsychic consequences for its women. Serving appears to increase feelings of confidence and expressions of greater ambition. Being an officer has an additional advantageous effect of self-image, aspiration level, and feelings of personal control. Not serving appears to reinforce the traditional role and self-concept of the young women.

The often quoted comment by Binkin and Bach (1977), that "the character and composition of a nation's military system mirror the society, that it is established to protect and defend," needs an addendum. The military system once established feeds back images into the society, making it a force in itself rather than a mere reflection.

REFERENCES

Bar-On, Mordechai. 1966. Education Processes in the Israel Defence Forces. Tel-Aviv: Israel Press Ltd.

Binkin, Martin and Shirly J. Bach. 1977. Women and the Military. Washington, D.C.: Brookings Institute.

Erikson, Erik. 1963. Childhood and Society. New York: Norton.

Kenniston, Kenneth. 1960. Youth and Dissent: The Rise of a New Opposition. New York: Harcourt Brace Jovanovich.

Levinson, D. et al. 1978. Seasons in a Man's Life. New York: Knopf.

Murray, H. A. 1938. Explorations in Personality. New York: Oxford University Press.

Perlmutter, Amos. 1969. Military and Politics in Israel—Nation Building and Role Expansion. London: Frank Case and Co., Ltd.

Prime Minister's Commission on the Status of Women. 1978. Report on the Status of Women. Jerusalem: Prime Minister's Office.

Stein, Morris I. 1966. Volunteers for Peace: First Group of Peace Corps Volunteers. New York: John Wiley.

The Israel Defense Forces Spokesman. KHEN, the Women's Corps. 1980.

Treiman, Donald J. 1977. Occupational Prestige in Comparative Perspective. New York: Academic.

29 REVIEWING THE AUSTRALIAN SUBURBAN DREAM: A UNIQUE APPROACH TO NEIGHBORHOOD CHANGE WITH THE FAMILY SUPPORT SCHEME

Ruth Egar, Wendy Sarkissian, Dorothy Brady, and Leslie Hartmann

This chapter examines the Family Support Scheme, an innovative federally funded neighborhood development program in an isolated suburb of Adelaide, Australia. Aimed particularly at women and their families, the program follows an explicit "review and reflection" model of personal and group development. In the first three years of operation the program helped to encourage local initiatives by fostering a renewed sense of individual and family authenticity and competence. Preventative work on a personal level was used to maximize use of community services and facilities.

SUBURBAN LIFE AS A WOMEN'S ISSUE

Studies of the lack of participation and more wide-ranging equity issues in suburban life have developed a perspective that acknowledges that women as a user group bear most heavily the penalties of suburban development (Anderson, 1975; Keys Young Planners, 1975; Saegert, 1980; Wekerle, 1980; Wekerle, et al., 1980; Summers, 1975). Women's opinions of suburbia differ substantially from men's opinions: "Women moving from city to suburban houses are least satisfied with this choice and view their isolation from downtown and commercial locations as a major compromise. . . . " (Wekerle, 1979, p. 3).

This chapter is based on "Changes in the Australian Dream; Developing Community Support for Women." Sociological Focus, Vol. 18, No. 2 (April 1985). Reprinted with permission of publisher.

Saegert's (1977, p. 140) research in New York City and surrounding suburbs highlights the differences between male and female evaluations of suburbia:

> Many of the wives who actually moved experienced seri-
> ous emotional difficulty in adjusting and expressed a lack
> of personal fulfillment in the situation. . . . Almost all
> wives . . . felt they had more options and were person-
> ally happier in the city; most husbands preferred the
> suburbs for reasons of economic investment, status and
> increased activity options.

Hostile Neighborhoods

Many of the women in the isolated suburban areas were suffering from and struggling with anomie, of real loss of heart and spirit.
This was reflected in depression, lack of self-esteem, devotion to
TV soap operas, and characterized by an inability to take steps toward making themselves known in the neighborhood or welcoming
newcomers. Indeed, the neighborhood itself was perceived as a very
threatening and hostile environment. Young mothers were isolated
from family and friends; neighborhoods were devoid of friendly services. Few opportunities and no facilities existed for women at home
to share their experiences and support each other throughout some of
the most demanding years of their lives. Women who had previously
held challenging, exacting jobs, who were independent and reasonably
secure, lacked the support of companionable women with whom they
could learn and share the skills of motherhood. Lack of encouragement had lowered their self-esteem and confidence—thereby con-
tributing to their passivity.

Work Life and Family Life: A Competition

The demands of work life, the pressure to perform and conform, and the demands of two or more jobs placed extraordinary
pressure on relationships within marriage and family life. Conflict
was created by a "switch-off" after a day's work, and a "switch-on"
to interest in the family. Many men felt they could survive only by
ignoring most family needs and by leaving child care to their wives.
This continuing individualism and isolation denied people opportunities to understand their world. But only a simple process was
required to link the experiences of suburban living, and to identify
the most influential forces, pressures, and systems which families
experience but do not entirely comprehend.

A Tried Response: "See-Evaluate-Act"

A model was found in the work approach of Joseph Cardijn, a Belgian priest, whose work with young factory workers in the 1920s formed a movement based on a belief in the uniqueness of every person, and in workers' abilities to act with dignity in all parts of their lives. Cardijn emphasized each person's capacity to respond creatively and freely when aware of the forces at work in his or her life (Cardijn, 1974). His movement was based on small groups of young workers taking responsibility for their own lives and actions by a continuous process he called "see-evaluate-act." They discussed problems and examined causes and effects; under Cardijn's guidance they evaluated priorities, and were expected to undertake practical action to alter the situation, either individually or collectively.

Meeting in Small Groups

The suburban women demonstrated great capacities to explore each others' thinking and act from that shared strength. With encouragement, groups could easily be created. The next step was relatively simple: to encourage one woman to talk to another, to invite neighbors and friends to join small groups to review in more depth some of the causes and effects of life situations. Thus emerged the only method that appeared to do justice to their particular needs. The backing of the Christian Life Movement provided support to explore many structures, processes, and beliefs. In leadership training sessions, committed and enthusiastic men and women emerged, eager to assume more responsibility. Love, understanding, resourcefulness, and creativity began to be shared in ways that led to action to alleviate some community problems.

Within three months groups of young mothers and couples were meeting fortnightly to examine their lives, to work out strategies, and to support each other through the actions needed for change. The process the groups employed became known as "action-reflection-action."

Discovering Together

Knowing that others were experiencing similar situations immediately raised awareness and provided new motivation, not simply for "coping" better, but for changing responses. The first group of mothers bemoaned their lack of private time to think, shop, or have their hair done. Demands of small children always took precedence.

These women moved easily to the next stage of seeing that if they all felt alike, so must hundreds of other women. Together they began a phase of well-coordinated thinking, planning, and acting to organize a voluntary crèche, but were hampered by lack of a facility. Undaunted, they enlisted the aid of women from other local churches and in 1972 successfully established an "Emergency Home Help" support scheme for families under stress.

This experience led to the development of the method used in Salisbury. To meet the needs of families in a modern suburban setting, structures, processes, and the concepts were developed. The most effective structure, emerged as a network of small groups. The appropriate process was a pattern of action-reflection-action on the residents' expressed needs, developing toward more realistic social analysis of their causes. The concept was of the dignity of every person and fostering new ways to experience that dignity.

HOW THE VISION WAS TRANSLATED INTO REALITY IN SALISBURY NORTH

Selection of Workers

With federal funding in 1978 for the Family Support Scheme, Salisbury Council employed three Home Visitors, one full-time and two part-time for a three-year period. All were local women with potential as "models" for developmental growth; they had responded positively and creatively to challenges in their neighborhoods and work lives. Characterized by a sense of common struggle with the people, rather than by professional superiority, they were well aware of the frustrations (but also of the opportunities) inherent in encouraging and supporting the changing lives of "women at home." They were selected for qualities of openness, understanding, sympathy, and alertness and readiness to pick up the smallest action to encourage and help development.

Listening with the People to the Sounds of the District

The methodology had to be in each of its steps consistent with those values. The Home Visitors began by door knocking, a fairly daunting experience. Many residents expressed surprise. A usual opening introduction is followed by a question such as: "What has it been like for you living in this area?" That permits the person to "give back" something to the Home Visitor. Immediately a sense of equality develops—a "give and take." If there are questions, a need to listen to confusion or sadness or to know of some service, there is every possibility of being heard. In one of the first visits, for example, the Home Visitor had barely introduced herself before the young woman said: "Please come in. I really need someone to talk to. I've just come back from my step-brother's funeral. He killed himself."

In the Salisbury model, the Home Visitors try to reinforce people's strengths; to help them examine and question their present involvements; extend their thinking about themselves and their interests; develop their own themes; look again and establish their priorities (for example, isolation in the street previously accepted as "inevitable" can be looked at anew). Small steps can be taken to break down apparent barriers and identify alternative options and choices already being made.

Follow-Up Actions

The team tries to leave people with a challenge for action: calling a friend when there had been a misunderstanding, or some other "challenge": finding out about availability of child-care arrangements, or the location of the local rubbish dump; following up opportunities for marriage counseling, inviting a neighbor for a cup of coffee; or investigating Council regulations on some matter. No action is too small or insignificant; follow-up continues until the person has taken a more independent stance or is being supported within a neighborhood group. Seemingly insurmountable problems assume "everyday" qualities when a person has been supported in doing it for the first time.

Working with others means working at their pace. This necessitates "gradualness" and self-control in the face of the perennial question, "Are we getting anywhere?":

The "Everyday"

Far from being crisis-oriented, the Scheme focuses on "everyday" lives. Crises and "the spectacular" are too rare for sustained community growth. When required to meet crises the team attempts to place persons and needs in the perspective of a total community. Interests that are followed through usually involve the "workaday"; lessons learned can be fed back, hopefully to prevent or lessen future crisis situations. This approach demands respectful listening to the residents to discover together the potential in their lives for a better quality of community life.

The Review Method

The common link in the team formation and community work is the review method, which involves the process of discovery through seeing more of the issues surrounding an event; evaluating priorities in a situation; and acting (finding the next action to take which will be consistent with our knowledge and evaluation). A simple example is the case of Pat, a woman of 30, frustrated and depressed by past life tragedies, who felt free to "off-load" onto the Home Visitor much of her pent-up energy. After talking about other women who might be in the same situation, they examined what they could do about it. Pat was encouraged to speak to her friend and together she and the Home Visitor invited a few others to her home for coffee. They worked together through a series of six meetings and have now established a support group. The relatively simple review process, if truly integrated, provides a holistic framework for decision making which can be universally applied. From a "personal" review a "social" review can emerge.

The First Structures of Common Purpose

The first signs of the Scheme's vitality appeared when neighbor groups began to meet in the street; new play groups were formed; a meeting was held to examine public transport issues; and the Grandmas' (and other) groups were founded. Each new group had a unique character and experienced the growing demands of friendship, caring, understanding, and trust. For many it was a major breakthrough to discover that those "common" values were as essential to focus on as the actions that resulted. For some it meant rediscovering the courage to walk down the street with head up or calling on new courage to invite another previously "strange" neighbor to participate in a group.

One group of women, invited by a Home Visitor to a Department of Further Education women's group, found that they had lived in the same street—two living directly opposite each other—for four and a half years, but had rarely seen each other and had never introduced themselves. Through a highly successful home play-group they increased their knowledge of other neighborhood services and facilities. One of the greatest signs of shared concern was a street group formed where the most common behavior was overt hostility, fear, and resentment about being "dobbed in" to government welfare agencies. The growth of these small groups reaffirmed the old adage that the best information system still operates over the back fence.

During the first three years of the Scheme these people's actions succeeded in altering the face of the district. Some changes were structural, i.e., the reorganization of arrangements for hire and control of ovals and change-rooms, and increased preschool facilities. As important, however, were changed relationships and friendships that makes the neighborhood a much more stimulating and enriching place.

Some Examples of Group Actions

One group petitioned school and government officials and obtained another preschool room and teacher. Thus emerged the "Direk Action Group," a creative community-oriented group, which, within a year of its formation, was informing the community and taking action on local issues. The Group's public meetings urge people to identify issues of concern, and then to work with the group for change. Members remain aware of their own growth through periodically reviewing their own involvement.

In another example, the Direk Sporting and Recreation Association used a well-ordered (and documented) process, to form a "parent body" liaison with many other sporting bodies, and encourage the Council to alter the district's only oval, and obtained the club rooms lease. The "Neighbour Aide" program, formed by women gradually becoming aware of others' needs, attempted to match the needs of the district with "neighborly" responses, including home help, cooking meals, light housework, minding children, and the need for more community participation within the Neighborhood House.

Social Analysis

The leaders of a Family Support Scheme-styled project need to be able to interpret the lives of those they work for, by progressively discovering with the people what they are feeling, what expectations they are under, and what dynamics are at work. This is not something to be done as an academic exercise. A community leader cannot arrive with his or her answers, but has to discover the questions and answers with each person, small group, and population subgroup. In practice that means the leaders will need to listen for cues about the dynamics of each family, and family life in general. They will need to listen, reflect, and engage in dialogue about what is going on with a neighbor and the trend of a street or neighborhood. To have a set of high social ideals is one thing, but they will only be furthered if leaders can progress with the people to a useful grasp of what individuals, and groups, are experiencing. Leaders need to have the creative listening ability to construct some useful form of social analysis in their district.

At some stages that may extend to such things as talks, courses, various inputs from experts. For the most part, however, this social analysis scarcely warrants such a high-flown name. It is something everyday, piecemeal, gradual (to an exhausting degree), in the course of discussions and exchanges over cups of tea, at meetings, going back to previous discussions, gently reinforcing individual and small-group discoveries, values, and plans. Its stock-in-trade is not books or lectures (for the most part), but questions such as "What has been happening?", "How did you feel?", "How did this come about?", "Are you the only one in this situation?", "What did you do then?", "What can you do together?", and all those at a pace and in a style that is not oppressive. Despite the need to "keep pace" with the people, a good community leader needs to be ahead of the people with his or her own advanced social hypotheses about what is and should be established in homes, work-places, and in the community.

CONCLUSIONS

The Scheme described in this paper provides the link between suburban women—who are often isolated—and the wider community. It encourages more extensive use of services and facilities and promotes self-help initiatives, whereby, at little cost, social development can begin. Working within a supportive municipal government, the scheme has encouraged residents to help that level of government become more responsive and accountable. After three years, residents, elected members, and Council staff in Salisbury were remarking on the changes in Salisbury North: "What's going on there? We seem to get so many letters from that area. Who are those people, anyway?" When an established residents' group politely invites a senior Council Manager to attend its meeting to speak on rate increases, rebates, and possibilities of deferred payment, he or she can hardly refuse to attend. When formerly depressed house-bound women hold a rally for better child care, undertake a census of 1,100 homes, and succeed in lobbying State government for preschool facilities and staff, something is happening. When women begin to work together to learn leadership skills, form neighborhood support groups, take more interest in the way municipal facilities are leased and operated, and establish a highly efficient "Neighbour Aide" program, it is clear that the community is changing—and for the better.

Until planning processes "at the top" create environments that are more appropriate for women, that is, created to meet women's needs and concerns, grass-roots "preventative" measures such as the Family Support Scheme are recommended.

NOTE

1. Leonie Sandercock, Barbara Adams, Don Perlgut and David Wilmoth provided valuable comments on an earlier version. Bob Wilkinson contributed greatly to the final sections of this paper and provided guidance throughout. Vicki Bevan and Beverly Waters typed many drafts and the final report.

REFERENCES

Anderson, Robin. 1975. Leisure—an Inappropriate Concept for Women? Canberra Australian Government Publishing Service.

Cardijn, J. 1974. Laics En Premieres Lignes. Brussels: Les Editions Vie Ouvriere.

M. S. J. Keys Young Planners. 1975. Women and Planning: Women's Attitudes. Report for the Cities Commission. Surry Hills, N.S.W.: M. S. J. Keys, Young Planners.

Saegert, Susan. 1977. "Towards Better Person-Environment Relations." In The Behavioral Basis of Design, Volume 2, edited by P. Suedfeld, J. R. Russell, L. Ward, et al., pp. 139-43. Stroudsburg, Pa.: D. H. and R.

Saegert, Susan. 1980. "Masculine Cities and Feminine Suburbs: Polarized Ideas, Contradictory Realities." Signs Vol. 5, No. 3, Supplement (Spring): S96-111.

Summers, Anne. 1975. Damned Whores and God's Police: the Colonization of Women in Australia. Ringwood, Victoria: Penguin.

Wekerle, Gerda. 1980. "Women in the Urban Environment." Signs Vol. 5, No. 3, Supplement (Spring): S188-214.

Wekerle, Gerda, Peterson R., and Morley D. 1980. New Space for Women. Boulder, Colo.: Westview.

ADDENDUM

The Family Support Scheme continues to operate in Parafield Gardens, Salisbury, South Australia, with two full-time field workers and funding provided largely by the Federal Government.

30 FUTURE VISIONS OF WOMEN AND WORK

Ellen Boneparth and Emily Stoper

INTRODUCTION

Women's present disadvantage in the labor market stems in part from the fact that, unlike men, most women in the work force are also doing a second major job during many of their prime working years, namely, raising children and maintaining a home for their families. The demands of family work and paid work, as currently organized, are in competition with each other. While the twentieth-century trend is toward fewer children and more paid work for women, we would argue that the majority of women will not give up either family or paid work. Yet since women combine both kinds of work and men do not, and since paid work is organized on the assumption that all workers are men or can adapt to male work patterns, most women are at a perpetual disadvantage in both the labor market and the home.

The government policies initiated in the United States in the 1960s and 1970s relating to women's employment do not address this conflict between family roles and work roles. They focus, rather, on providing equity for women in work roles by eliminating sex discrimination and expanding employment opportunity (Boneparth, 1982; Freeman, 1982).

The failure of these policies to reduce the income gap between male and female workers or to reverse the continuing trend of increasing occupational segregation based on sex have given rise to new policy demands in recent years such as equal pay for work of comparable worth and flexible work patterns (Kahn and Grune, 1982; Stoper, 1982). While these represent important goals, the position of women workers as a secondary labor force will not be changed without a major restructuring of work.

Several aspects of work must be restructured. First, the deep split between home and work must be healed. That split is not only spatial but is also one of values (home focuses on personal relationships, work on the expansion of wealth) and structure (home is a small group, work is likely to be a giant bureaucracy).

Second, the rigidity of work-time requirements over a day, a year, a lifetime must be eased, not only to accommodate family responsibilities but also to make room for flexible patterns of education and leisure and to facilitate work itself.

Third, work needs to be organized less hierarchically so that it is possible for people to have some autonomy and influence in the work setting without making the major commitments of time and education currently necessary for the assumption of management positions.

It is crucial that these changes occur not only in the work of women but in men's work as well, for a transformation that is limited to women's work would merely reinforce the sex segregation of the work force. And it is sex segregation rather than direct discrimination on an individual basis that has been the chief factor in keeping most women in the lowest-paid, least interesting, least influential jobs.

There is reason to believe that the kinds of changes necessary for the transformation of gender stratification could occur. Alvin Toffler (1981) a noted futurist, predicts imminent changes in work because of the needs of a transformed Third Wave economy. According to Toffler, this is the new kind of economy that is emerging as the Second Wave (mass-production industry) recedes. (The First Wave, which was preindustrial agriculture, receded earlier when the Second Wave emerged.) Whereas the Second Wave was characterized by mass production and rigid work discipline necessitated by the rhythm of the machine, the Third Wave is typified by computerized production tailored to individual preferences. Handling the Third Wave's vast flow of information requires a more flexible style of work and involves more creative problem solving and less repetitive drudgery.

E. F. Schumacher, (1973) a less optimistic futurist, has warned that if we fail to alter radically the scale of our organizations and technology, as well as the values underlying them, we risk ecological and spiritual disaster. Yet the changes he calls for, involving decentralization and a renewed emphasis on the quality of human relationships rather than merely the standard of living, are in many ways consistent with the needs of the Third Wave economy as described by Toffler.

We will discuss four possible transformations of the organization of work: the content, styles, and values of work; the organization of work time; the split between home and work; and the exercise of power in the economy.

FOUR INTERLOCKING TRANSFORMATIONS

New Content, New Work Styles, New Values

During the industrial Second Wave, men typically worked in manufacturing and women preferred support services for them in the home while raising future workers. There was a vast difference in the personal qualities considered desirable for each sphere. For the manufacturing sphere, emphasis was placed on "masculine" qualities such as physical strength and stamina, emotional self-control, (for bosses) logical and objective thought, initiative and aggressiveness, technological ability, and willingness to focus on efficiency of physical production for a profit, if necessary at the expense of the quality of human relationships.

In the home sphere, emphasis was placed on "feminine" qualities like patience, nurturance, skill in smoothing interpersonal relations, esthetic appreciation, attention to detail, and willingness to subordinate one's own interests to those of the family group.

These character differences fit the needs of Second Wave work. The manufacture and marketing of "long runs" of identical products can be performed adequately with mostly masculine qualities. But as the economy shifts toward customized services and the manufacture of individualized items, (Toffler, pp. 179-93) work consists increasingly of dealing with other people and of the coordination of vast amounts of data about individual needs and preferences. Some traditional "masculine" qualities, such as technological ability, are more important than ever; others, like physical strength, become increasingly irrelevant. At the same time, many of the qualities needed to work effectively during the Third Wave are those traditionally considered feminine, most notably the ability to identify and respond to the needs of other persons. Because the qualities traditionally called "feminine" are central to Third Wave work, some of the rationale for discriminating against women (they are "emotional," parochial, and so on) may disappear.

The need for feminine qualities is already felt in services traditionally staffed by men. The masculine-dominated medical profession, for example, is notorious for its impersonality. Thus, its consequent inability to utilize the connection between the body and the mind, in understanding patients' emotional motives to be ill. This results in problems with patients about the reasons for the treatment and the need to alter their personal habits, and in preventing illnesses resulting from emotional factors like stress.

The delivery of services, as well as the management of personnel, has been affected by a shortage of feminine values in the workplace. Workers increasingly are unwilling to accept a lack of autonomy and variety on the job. Management is beginning to respond to those expectations. Some business schools, for example, now focus on inculcating "people-oriented" even more than "task-oriented" management skills. Today, for many workers, "human factors" means not merely one of the determinants of the amount of profit but one of the central purposes of work:to nurture the human being who does it.

Time Flexibility: Breaking Out of Lockstep

Because most women need more flexibility in order to meet the needs of their families, they are often unable to take full-time jobs with rigid hours. An increase in time flexibility in all work could make an enormous difference in diminishing the disadvantage in paid work of women (or men) who have major home responsibilities. If time flexibility at work were the norm for all workers, women's disadvantage in the job market would be greatly reduced.

In the 1970s a great deal of attention was given to two innovations in work-time schedules, flexitime, and job sharing. Under flexitime, which originated in West Germany, each employee has the right to choose, on a day-to-day basis, when his or her hours of work will begin and end, within certain limits. Some 12 percent of all U.S. employees were on flexitime in 1981, up from 6 percent in 1977 (Nollen and Martin, 1978, p. 6; Friedan, 1981, pp. 271-72).

Flexitime is enormously popular with both employers and employees since it increases productivity and at the same time makes it somewhat easier for employees to adjust their work schedules to their personal needs, including being somewhat more available when their children need them (Silverstein and Srb, 1979). Studies of the impact of flexitime on daily life, however, have yielded mixed results (Bohen and Viveros-Long, 1981). In its most limited form, flexitime does not always increase the amount of time parents spend with children (Stoper, 1982). However, more advanced forms of flexitime, accompanied by changing values, have the potential to do so.

In job sharing, the newest version of part-time work, two people hold a job that was formerly a single full-time job. True job sharing must be voluntary and must involve fringe benefits for both workers. Job sharing has the great virtue of opening up managerial and professional jobs that would otherwise be closed to people who only want to work part-time, such as many mothers of young children.

Although both flexitime and job sharing are desirable innovations, neither will make much impact in lessening the disadvantage of women in the job market. Flexitime, because it is limited and does not reduce the number of hours worked, does not go far enough in easing the burden of dual roles; job sharing, because it is done almost entirely by women, could even reinforce the sex segregation of the work force.

There are, however, several emerging trends in work-time flexibility that could make an enormous difference to women. Flexitime may some day be expanded around the clock, throughout the year, and even over the life span. The expansion of flexitime around the clock becomes possible when many more people can work independently in their homes at computer terminals, as Alvin Toffler (p. 198) predicts, or in neighborhood-based firms, as E. F. Schumacher (p. 289) would like to see. If flexitime were expanded around the clock, one could clock in on one's computer. Work could be done whenever the baby was sleeping or playing quietly, the spouse was available for child care, or the supermarkets were crowded. If the job involved teamwork with other people, core hours when everyone was working would be necessary, but the timing of the flexible hours could vary; they might, for example, be late at night or very early in the morning.

An even more meaningful increase in work-time flexibility would come from the introduction of "flexiyear," which is now being tried in a few West German firms. Under flexiyear, every employee contracts annually with management for a certain amount of work time (hours per day, days per week, months per year, or however they want to break it down). Management can then plan to have a work force of appropriate size for slack and busy times, while workers can maintain a continually changing balance between work time and time for family, education, travel, leisure, or starting small businesses. The distinction between part-time and full-time workers, which has been so damaging to women, then breaks down into a series of gradations. Workers need no longer forfeit any claim to "seriousness" if they want to work less than every day or even every month (Haller, 1977; Teriet, 1977, pp. 62-65).

An even more radical idea along these lines, the "full cyclic plan," has been developed by Fred Best (Silverstein and Srb, p. 43). Under this plan, education, work, and leisure would be much more evenly distributed over the life span, instead of being concentrated in youth, the middle years, and old age, respectively. Work flexibility during the life cycle, could turn taking off a few years for childrearing into a routine and easily accommodated work pattern, rather than the troublesome violation of work norms it is today. There is no solid reason to have prime career-building years, the prime childrearing years coincide, as they usually do today. Individuals could be freer to set their own timetables for childbearing, education, and intensive work. Women could set timetables that eliminated much of their disadvantage as childbearers. And men could arrange to take time out for participation in childrearing with much less damage to their education and work. The introduction of a plan such as Best's would also facilitate current trends toward lifelong education, early retirement, and childbearing over an increasingly wide age span, from 15 to 45.

In the more highly technological economy of the future, possibilities may increase enormously for changes in both when we work and where we work.

The Home-Work Split

In the traditional view, women work in the home and men work in the factory, fields, or office, a split brought about by the industrial revolution and the resulting trends toward urbanization, suburbanization, and consumerism. Yet the contemporary realities of work and family in the Western world clearly belie the traditional view. In the United States, over half of all women work outside the home and there is a growing conflict in women's lives between home and work (Safilios-Rothschild, 1974, pp. 18-73). In an ideal world of the future, work and family roles would be integrated for both sexes, preferably by bringing work into the home or neighborhood.

Paid work in the home is a reality for a small number of professionals (writers, academics, and therapists, for example) and a few sales workers who conduct their business by telephone. Couples who are able to take advantage of such arrangements find that working at home allows them to share child care and housework more equitably (Rapoport and Rapoport, 1977). They have more time for domestic responsibilities and for leisure when freed from the demands of travel to and from work and from the time constraints of a nine-to-five job. Single parents are in even greater need of such arrangements. If technology of tomorrow changes the way we work, that change can be used not only to increase productivity and efficiency but also to create better integrated human beings by reintegrating home and work and thus laying the basis for easing the sexual division of labor.

Control in the Organization: Democratic Structuring

The rebirth of feminism in the 1960s brought with it an interest, derived in part from the New Left, in the restructuring of power relations to expand responsibility, participation, and accountability. In the early movement years, most of this discussion focused on feminist organizations rather than government bureaucracies, factories, and corporations (Freeman, 1974, pp. 202-14; MacDonald, 1981; Freeman and MacMillan, 1981). Yet the workplace may now be a possible locus for transformation. And without changes in the control of work, women workers, despite their increasing numbers, will continue to constitute a secondary labor force.

How can workers exercise more power over their work lives?

One approach followed in numerous European countries has been to pass legislation that brings workers into management, either by having workers' representatives on boards of directors or by creating workers' councils to participate at the level of a particular firm and/or shop floor. In Europe, unions are usually deeply involved in worker control. As women become an ever-larger sector of the work force, they may pressure both unions and worker representatives to help in alleviating the home-work split by pressing demands for benefits such as child care, flexible work schedules, and more work autonomy (Stoper, 1982, pp. 104-6).

Even without strong unions or worker control, greater work-time flexibility could have an impact on worker autonomy. To the degree that workers decide when to work they may have more freedom to decide how to organize the work, in what order to do different tasks, and what aspects of the work to devote more time to. Petty supervision is far more difficult if the supervisor simply cannot be there during all of the workers' hours. This expansion of job autonomy for ordinary workers is especially significant for women because under present conditions they are often unwilling or unable to make the commitment in education or time to become managers or even worker representatives.

INTERCONNECTIONS

These aspects of work, (content, work styles, values, time flexibility, location, and control) are clearly interconnected, for a change in one will affect the others. Changes in the content of work, for example, could lead to a demand for changes in the schedule and location of work, each of these changes both reflecting and stimulating the desire of workers to have more control over their work lives. Likewise, new management styles and increasing worker participation in management could lead to new ways of structuring the times and places that work is performed, and the other way around.

These possibilities are suggested by changes in the underlying economy. Toffler and Schumacher, on whose work this study is largely based, have contrasting views of the relationship between the underlying economy and the changes in work. Toffler sees them as the nearly inevitable result of the new possibilities created by the explosion in high technology; Schumacher, in contrast, sees them as the probable, but by no means inevitable, outcome of the moral confusion that has led to inappropriate technology, excessively large-scale institutions and environmental destruction. Perhaps there are elements of truth in both; changes may occur because of both past failures and future possibilities. Neither theorist, however, pays much attention to the barriers impeding these changes, except insofar as Schumacher implies that the moral blindness that led us into our present predicament will keep us from making the changes necessary to extricate ourselves. The next two sections examine the barriers to change and suggest ways to overcome them.

Barriers to Change

In order to travel from here to there, we must realistically examine the barriers. A major barrier is that many persons do not subscribe to the values expressed or implied in the future world described above. We need to recognize that social arrangements have shaped, and continue to shape, our values. For those who lack the desire to organize their own time, major increases in time flexibility will be unwelcome. Both for people who like to be supervised and for those who like to supervise others, more work autonomy would be difficult to accept. For others, the advantages of eliminating rush hour or the weekend rush to the beach will be offset by the lack of a sense of social rhythms and by the fact that family and friends may not be free from work at the same time they are.

Some people might respond to the new time flexibility by working longer and harder, thus putting at a disadvantage those who seek a balance between education, work, leisure, and childrearing. However, in a period of change the absence of fixed norms may encourage the tendency to postpone work and thus get very little done. For many workers, the home-work split may be valued. Going to work may be an opportunity to escape for many hours every day from the demands of family life.

Fortunately, people whose values or character structures make them feel uncomfortable with the more modern organization of work need not be forced into the mold. There will always be numerous tasks for which the older style of work organization is appropriate, just as small farms left over from the First (agricultural) Wave have continued to survive throughout the Second Wave in many places where they are most appropriate both socially and ecologically. Even Toffler (pp. 248-50) points out that only a minority of workers in the next 20 to 30 years will have distinctively Third Wave work patterns.

POLICIES TO START US ON THE ROAD

What is needed, then, is public policy that addresses the sexual division of labor as a future transformation of work that cuts across all other changes discussed above. Women workers must participate as equals in the technological revolution. Women must be reeducated on an equal basis with men in the new technologies.

Women workers have already taken on new responsibilities in word processing, computerized accounting, and a wide range of information-management tasks (Johnson, 1981, p. 30) that have been revolutionized by the new technology. Far more effort is needed to recognize and compensate women workers for their new skills and expertise. Women's work must be upgraded through comparable worth policies that remunerate office workers fairly for the increasingly complex tasks they perform.

A second need is for government policies that assist organizations in adapting to new modes of work that benefit both male and female workers. Incentives must be provided to organizations to develop alternative work patterns. For example, governments could provide subsidies and tax benefits for introducing flexible work schedules over the week, year, and life span, and for relocating workers in the home and neighborhood. "Sabbaticals" could be extended by allowing workers time off with government benefits in exchange for later retirement.

Finally, a new set of professionals is needed to organize and lobby for transformations in the world of work. Labor organizers are needed whose perspectives extend beyond those of contemporary union leaders. The organizational development experts of the future must understand how the new technology can be used to heal the home-work split caused by the present organization of work.

These new professionals, many of them women, have already made an appearance in the environmental, women's, and alternative work patterns movements, as well as in some of the more progressive labor unions. The socialization of women as nurturers, their experience with the dual burden of work and family roles, and their subordinate positions in the work force, all make them especially suited to roles as advocates for humane changes in the world of work.

Perhaps most important, women must persuade policy makers and business leaders that the elimination of the sexual division of labor will foster rather than hinder economic well-being. Democratic control of the new technology helps make that promise possible. A new political coalition built around the issue of work must be organized in order that women, men, and children may successfully navigate rather than drift on the waves of change.

REFERENCES

Bohen, H., and Viveros-Long, A. 1981. Balancing Jobs and Family Life: Do Flexible Work Schedules Help? Temple University Press

Boneparth, E., editor. 1982. Women, Power and Policy, pp. 48–67. Elmsford, New York: Pergamon Press.

Freeman, A., and MacMillan, J. 1981. "Building Feminist Organizations." In Building Feminist Theory: Essays from Quest, pp. 251–67. New York: Longman.

Freeman, J. 1974. "The Tyranny of Structurelessness." In Women in Politics, edited by J. Jaquette, pp. 202–14. New York: Wiley.

Freeman, J. 1982. "Women and Public Policy: An Overview." In Women, Power and Policy, edited by E. Boneparth, pp. 48–67. Elmsford, New York: Pergamon Press.

Friedan, B. 1981. The Second Stage, pp. 271–72. New York: Summit Books.

Haller, W. 1977. Flexyear: The Ultimate Work Hour Concept. New York: Interflex.

Johnson, S. 1981. "Word-Processors Spell Out New Role for Clerical Staff." New York Times. October 11, 1981, Sec. 12, p. 30.

MacDonald, N. 1981. The Feminist Workplace, pp. 251–67. New York: Longman.

Nollen, S., and Martin, H. 1978. Alternative Work Schedules, Part 1, p. 6. New York: AMACOM.

Rapoport, R., and Rapoport, N. 1977. Dual-Career Families Reexamined: New Integrations of Work and Family, pp. 111–25. New York: Harper & Row.

Safilios-Rothschild, C. 1974. Women and Social Policy, pp. 18–73. Englewood Cliffs, N.J.: Prentice-Hall.

Schumacher, E. 1973. Small is Beautiful. New York: Harper & Row.

Silverstein, P., and Srb, J. 1979. Flexitime: Where, When and How? Ithaca, N.Y.: Cornell University Press.

Stoper, E. 1982. "Alternative Work Patterns and the Double Life." In Women, Power and Policy, edited by E. Boneparth, pp. 75–108. New York: Pergamon.

Teriet, B. 1977. "Flexiyear Schedules—Only a Matter-of Time?" Monthly Labor Review, December, pp. 62-65.

Toffler, A. 1981. The Third Wave. New York: Bantam.

CONCLUSIONS

For a decade and a half feminist scholars have lived with discovery. As we sit down to write these concluding remarks, we are
being assailed, in the summer of 1984, with new "firsts." The gender
gap may be only a U.S. phenomenon, but its culmination, in the nomi-
nation for the first time in U.S. history, of a woman as vice-presidential candidate, has more than local significance. "The timing . . . is
exhilarating. Women are storming national politics this summer; long
delayed bills addressing pension disparities are passing without opposition. . . " (Washington Post, Aug. 11, 1984). Women's vote is being
courted but more important, "just the sight (emphasis added) of the
new Democratic vice-presidential nominee is stirring crowds across
the country. . . " (Washington Post, 1984). And too there are the
Olympics, an event made stirring even for those lukewarm about
sports competitions, by the degree and quality of involvement of wom-
en. "My reaction was very similar to what I felt when Geraldine
Ferraro was nominated"—that comment was about the drama of the
running of the first women's marathon at an Olympic. "It was really
not a patriotic feeling. That was not it at all. It was just this sense
of—we can do anything (emphasis added)" (Washington Post, 1984).

Can a selection of articles written in 1982 after such events still
have merit, and, more important, provide an impetus for new research and ideas? We think yes. As another observer commented
about the Olympic firsts,

When you are in the Olympic games, you're still dealing
with all those years of people who thought women couldn't
run, or they'd get big legs . . . (or) couldn't have babies.
. . . [This marathon is] going to be watched by 2.5 billion

people. And I mean, there are women in Saudi Arabia
wearing veils, watching this marathon, and making connections (emphasis added) (Washington Post, 1984).

The themes of these public events are about change in how wom-
en are perceived in relation to power and status, to traditional roles,
and to their own bodies, and these are also the themes of the book.
This book is also about connections—the connections that are international, and the connections that are interdisciplinary, important for
a female world that has been unknown for so long. Because of the ingrained masculine bias in all knowledge, we have learned that each
reality may hide a new one, that current models contain biases which
must be confronted and changed or revised and that social change is
the result of many, often unexplicated forces. We have learned of the
unintended consequences that may flow from such social change. These
chapters also reveal and discuss the tensions inherent in this uncover-
ing scholarship. There is, for example, the tension between the push
to integration into a male world and the push to separation. Clearly,
as the public events show, women want to be part of man's world with
its rewards and costs. But they are now still in the process of learning what women's world is and as these studies have illustrated, this
scholarship must be only about that world. The chapters in this book
peel away layer after layer of old knowing as the writers looked at the
worlds of different women in different times, places, and eras. The
male world is known but the female world is not and until its character
has been more fully revealed, questions about separation versus integration cannot be fully answered. The search is made even more
imperative by the apparent public victories of women. As noted in the
last chapter of the book, many radical feminist demands about the
structure and relations of work and family will be socially normative
with further technological advance. Unisex and androgyny, once associated with "women's lib" and considered outrageous, are part of the
popular culture, typified by Michael Jackson and punk rockers. And
serious futurists are predicting a merging and transcending of roles.
　　Are these truly women's victories? Does it tell us we have ar-
rived? Certainly in the view of the scholarship presented herein and
of that presented at the Second International Interdisciplinary Congress
held in Groningen, The Netherlands in 1984, the answer is no. How
can two worlds merge when one is only now being discovered? These
chapters have moved us toward knowing the world for which we search,
but there is still much to be done. Merging too soon will leave unan-
swered central questions such as self-definition and female empowerment.
　　Events like those of the summer of 1984 can encourage the
feminist scholar as much as the activist—perhaps there will be added

strength emerging from such public approbation. This is important, but the book also tells us that real change is elusive, that it is built on a very complex set of prior events. Finally, an understanding of women in relation to the total world can only be built upon an understanding of their own world.

APPENDIX

Dina Goren
Judith Hill
Noah Milgram
Michal Palgi
Phyllis Palgi

Ilsa Schuster
Alice Shalvi
Ruth Sharabany
Joseph Shepher
Anita Wiener

ORGANIZATIONAL SPONSORS

Division of the Psychology of Women, American Psychological
  Association, U.S.A.
Federation of Organizations for Professional Women, U.S.A.
Association for Women in Science (International)
Canadian Psychological Association, Section on Women and Psychology
Center for Study of Women and Sex Roles, City University of New
  York, U.S.A.
Council for the Status of Women (Ireland)
Population Association of America, Women's Caucus
Sex and Gender Section—American Sociological Association, U.S.A.
MAFERR Foundation Inc.—Male Female Role Research U.S.A.
Centro de Estudios de la Mujer (Argentina)
Dutch Association of University Women (Holland)

INDEX

ABOUT THE EDITORS AND CONTRIBUTORS

Khawla Abu-Baker is a graduate student of Counseling at the University of Haifa and a counselor at the Arab Comprehensive School in Acre. Her major concerns are the areas of Arab-Jewish relations and the status of women and children in Arab society.

Ikuko Atsumi, a business consultant, formerly of Aoyama Gakuim University in Japan, is president of the New England Japanese Center in Stow, Mass. Her interests include women's issues and Japanese feminism and cultural movements.

Rivka Bar-Yosef is in the Department of Sociology and director of the Work and Welfare Research Institute at the Hebrew University in Jerusalem, Israel. Her research and teaching interests are in the relationships between work, family and social welfare with emphasis on the problems of women.

Jessie Bernard is Professor Emerita of sociology at Pennsylvania State University. Her more than fifteen books include such influential books about women as <u>Academic Women</u>, <u>The Sex Game</u>, <u>The Future of Marriage</u>, <u>The Future of Motherhood</u>, <u>Self-Portrait of a Family</u>, and <u>The Female World</u>.

Anne Bloom is a senior research associate in the Center for Advanced Studies in education at the Graduate Center of the City University of New York. Her research is in studies of personality and social structure including family, school, and military institutions, with a particular emphasis on the psychology of women.

Ellen Boneparth, formerly professor of political science and an associate dean of social science at San Jose State University (California, U.S.A.), is now in the U.S. Foreign Service. She is the founder of the International Institute of Women's Studies.

Dorothy Brady works with the Family Support Scheme in Salisbury, Australia.

Martha R. Burt is Director of Social Services Research at the Urban Institute in Washington, D.C. Her research interests include adolescent pregnancy, recovery processes among rape victims, and evaluations of social service programs.

Arza Churchman is an environmental psychologist in the Faculty of Architecture and Town Planning of the Technion—Israel Institute of Technology. Her research interests include issues of housing, children's play spaces, and women's environmental needs.

John Court formerly associate professor of psychology at Flinders University of South Australia is now director of Spectrum Center, Adelaide, South Australia.

Florence Denmark is the Thomas Hunter professor of social science at Hunter College of the City University of New York. She has published extensively on the psychology of women and is a past president of the American Psychological Association.

Alice Hendrickson Eagly is a social psychologist whose research concerns attitudes and social influence as well as sex differences in social behavior. She is a professor at Purdue University in West Lafayette, Indiana.

Ruth Egar, is co-ordinator of the Christian Life Movement in Adelaide, South Australia.

Theresa El-Mahairy is a sociologist at the American University of Cairo. She has studied various aspects of medical care in Egypt.

Eleanor R. Fapohunda, a specialist in Labor Economics and Industrial Relations, is a Senior Lecturer at the University of Lagos in Nigeria. Her research interest is in women and employment in Nigeria.

Dr. Margret Fine-Davis, a social psychologist, is Senior Research Fellow in the Department of Psychology at Trinity College at the University of Dublin. Her research interests include: attitudes toward the role and status of women and social-psychological factors associated with employment of married women.

Leslie Hartman is an associate of Wendy Sarkissian in the Family Support Scheme, Salisbury, Australia.

Nancy M. Henley is professor of psychology and director of Women's Studies at UCLA. She is the author of Body Politics (1977), and co-editor of Language, Gender and Society (1983).

Dafne Israeli is a senior lecturer in sociology at Bar-Ilan University in Israel. Her research is in the fields of sex roles and work, organizations, and power, and she is currently studying women in Israeli management.

Leanor B. Johnson is Senior Research Associate at Westat, Inc. Her present interests are work-family issues and women in non-traditional occupations, gender role attitudes and behavior, and human sexuality. She is editing a book on minority families.

Anne Jones writes for The Nation, the New York Times, and many other national publications. Her most recent book is <u>Everyday Death:</u> <u>The Case of Bernadette Powell.</u>

Bennetta Jules-Rosette is professor and chair of sociology at the University of California, San Diego. Her major research focuses on the new African religions, religion and state control, the sociology of art, urban migration in Africa, and women in development.

Eleanor Lerner is an associate professor of sociology at Stockton State College in New Jersey. She has done research and published on women's political history and anti-semitism.

Amia Lieblich is in the department of Psychology and the Program of Gender Studies at the Hebrew University in Jerusalem, Israel. Current interests include transitions in adulthood for women and men in the context of the Israeli culture.

Sami Kh. Mar'i is head of the counseling division at the University of Haifa. He has extensively studied Arab society and education in Israel. He is the author of <u>Arab Education in Israel</u>; Syracuse University Press, 1978.

Mariam M. Mar'i is a counselor at the Arab Orthodox College in Haifa. Her doctoral dissertation dealt with sex role perceptions among Palestinian Arab men and women in Israel.

Martha T. Mednick is professor of psychology at Howard University, Washington, D.C. She has published on the psychology of women, especially in the area of achievement and is a past-president of the Division of the Psychology of Women of the American Psychological Association.

Martin Meissner is in the sociology department at the University of British Columbia in Vancouver, Canada. His interests include dimensions of task and skills in women's work. A current publication is "The reproduction of women's domination in organizational communication."

Aili Nenola-Kallio is acting professor of Folklore and Comparative Religion at the University of Turku. Current interests are in women's folklore and the anthropology of death. She has published Studies in Ingrian Laments.

Måria Nordström is a psychologist at the National Institute for Building research in Lund, Sweden who studies housing and environment from a psychological perspective.

Naomi Nevo is a social anthropologist coordinating a team of rural sociologists in the Jewish Agency in Israel. Her current research interests include rural women, the sociology of new communities, and voting patterns.

Ofra Nevo is a student of psychology at the University of Haifa, Israel. She studies racism and sexism in humor.

Jan Pahl is a Research Fellow at the University of Kent at Canterbury, England. Her publications include Managers and their Wives (1971), A Refuge for Battered Women (1978), and Private Violence and Public Policy (1984).

Marilyn P. Safir is a Senior Lecturer in the Department of Psychology and directs the Women's Studies Program at the University of Haifa. She has co-edited Sexual Equality: The Israeli Kibbutz Tests The Theories, with Michal Palgi, Joseph Blasi and Menacham Rosner.

Wendy Sarkissian is Lecturer in Planning, University of New England, Armidale, New South Wales and Principal of Sarkissian and Associates Planners, a social planning consulting firm.

Ilsa Schuster is a Research Fellow of the Faculty of Social Sciences at the University of Haifa. Author of The New Women of Lusaka, she has published numerous articles on the participation of women in development.

Rachel Sebba is an architect in the Faculty of Architecture and Town Planning of the Technion—Israel Institute of Technology. Her interests include designing for children, territoriality, home environments and perception.

Emily Stoper is professor of political science and co-director of the Women's Studies Program at California State University at Hayward U.S.A. She teaches and writes about public policy and the family.

Professor Gillian Straker is the Head of the Division of Applied Psychology at the University of Witwatersrand, Johannesburg, South Africa. Her areas of special interest where she has published extensively are the treatment of violence in the family, and the study of liberation movements.

Sandra Schwartz Tangri is professor of psychology at Howard University. Her research interests include women and work, ethical issues in population programs, sexual harassment, and work–family conflicts.

Rhoda Kesler Unger is professor of psychology at Montclair State College. She has written and done extensive research on gender and social psychology. She is the first recipient of the Carolyn Wood Sherif Memorial Lectureship.

Barbara Strudler Wallston is professor of psychology at the George Peabody College of Vanderbilt University in Nashville, Tennessee. She has studied feminism and methodology, professional women, and health.